TO PLEASE
A CHILD

Merry Christmas, Carol
1968
from Dad

TO PLEASE A CHILD

A BIOGRAPHY OF

L. FRANK BAUM
Royal Historian of Oz

"To please a child is a sweet and lovely thing that warms one's heart and brings its own reward."
—BAUM

Frank Joslyn Baum
and
Russell P. MacFall

Reilly & Lee Co.
Chicago   1961

TABLE OF CONTENTS

ACKNOWLEDGMENTS

A BIOGRAPHY such as this grows up almost like a child; so many elements make up its environment that the precise influence of each is often impossible to evaluate. For this reason it is possible to give credit to many who helped make this book, but the names of many others should properly be included among them. To these silent partners the authors of this book give thanks.

More particularly, however, they wish to thank Dr. Edward Wagenknecht of Boston University for encouragement, advice and many suggestions; to Dick Martin, who owns a notable collection of L. Frank Baum books, for constant help, especially with bibliographical facts; to Fred M. Meyer of Kinderhook, Illinois, for the enthusiasm that first brought the co-authors together; to Harry Neal Baum, of Bass Lake, Indiana, for his friendship and recollections of his father; to Mrs. Robert S. Baum, of Claremont, California, for use of pictures and other family treasures; and to Robert Pattrick of Glendale, California, for invaluable information about the Baum family.

Among many others: Justin Schiller of Brooklyn, editor of the *Baum Bugle;* Frank O'Donnell of the Reilly and Lee Company; the late Mrs. Eleanor Hall Wilson, for mementoes of W. W. Denslow; Mrs. Mark Ratliff, formerly of Syracuse University, for research into Baum family history; D. Laurance Chambers of the Bobbs-Merrill Company, for invaluable information about the early history and sales of *The Wizard of Oz;* Mrs. Olga Dammert of St. Louis, sister of Paul Tietjens, and his daughter, Mrs. Chester Hart of Oak Park, Illinois; Mrs. Chauncey L. Williams of Colorado Springs, for information about the Williams family; Ralph Fletcher Seymour for recollections of Baum and Denslow; Charles Collins of Chicago, for theatrical recollections; J. Duncan Williams of Cocoa Beach, Florida, for the later history of the *Show Window;* Elbert Hubbard H of East Aurora, New York, for facts about his father and Denslow; Mrs. Robert Ford of Lake Worth, Florida, specialist in Baum books, and the staffs of the Newberry Library and the library of the Chicago Historical Society.

For errors, misjudgments, and misinterpretations, the authors must take exclusive credit.

FOREWORD

THE FIRST recollection I have of my father is when I was about three years old.

I awoke in the middle of the night screaming with fright at some childish nightmare. By the light of a small kerosene lamp placed in the hall just outside the door to my room I saw him come striding into view. As he hurried to my crib I could hear the skirts of his long white nightshirt flapping around the calves of his legs.

He picked me up in his arms and snuggled my head against his shoulder. As he walked back and forth I was conscious of the sound of his bare feet pacing the cold board floor. Murmuring soothing words, he soon reassured me, and I stopped crying and in a few moments was asleep. Nor did I awaken when he put me gently back in my bed and quietly left the room.

The last time I saw him was after he had returned to Ozcot from the hospital where he had undergone a serious operation. He was in bed, and he was still wearing one of the long, characteristic, white nightshirts I remembered from my childhood.

"I won't wear those danged, new fangled pajamas!" he protested. "Never did! Never will! No man should wear pants to bed!"

Much of the material in this book is the result of my association with him during years of intimate relationship, discussing frankly our joys and sorrows, accomplishments and failures.

I spent many hours with my father. At Coronado, California, I worked with him daily—typing his plays and making extra copies of his stories for children. We frequently played golf together, and I was on the road with him in 1908 during his lecture tour with the *Radio Plays*. On many evenings we played chess, a game he especially enjoyed. We were closely associated in the Oz Film Manufacturing Company, of which I eventually became general manager. During years of such intimate contact, he often confided his recollections to me. Some of these will be found in this book.

FRANK JOSLYN BAUM

Westwood Village, Los Angeles, California

TO PLEASE
A CHILD

I

THE WIZARD OF OZ

DEAFENING APPLAUSE and calls of "author, author" rang through the Grand Opera House in Chicago as the curtain fell on the second act of *The Wizard of Oz*. The young author, slim and elegant in a dark suit, left his box to go down into the wings and walked out on the stage, smiling as he faced the opening night's audience. Silencing the applause with a gesture, he said:

"Kind friends, thank you for your enthusiasm. It is heart-warming. You have been generous enough to call for the author, but I do not need to remind you that he is only one of many whose efforts you are enjoying tonight. If you will pardon a homely comparison, our play is like a plum pudding, which combines the flavor of many ingredients. The author contributes only the flour—necessary, of course, but only to hold the other good things together.

"What would *The Wizard of Oz* be without the spice of Paul Tietjens' music or the brilliant scenery of Walter Burridge; the skill of that master stage chef Julian Mitchell; the golden touch of Manager Fred Hamlin, and above all, our agile comedians Dave Montgomery and

1

Fred Stone, and the plums and peaches of our talented
stage company? All of us are happy that you have enjoyed
the show, and we hope that you and your friends will be
back for a second helping."

Baum left the stage, but again and again he was recalled
by the applause. The third time he brought Montgomery
and Stone with him in front of the curtain. When he returned to his wife's side in the box, he was enjoying one
of the proudest moments life would ever bring him. After
forty-six years which had often been difficult, he was at last
firmly on the way to success. For it was plain that *The
Wizard of Oz,* inspired by his children's story published
two years before, was a winner.

This auspicious night of the first performance in Chicago was June 16, 1902, and the theater on Clark Street
was filled to the last seat with first nighters who had come
in for the occasion from their summer homes, and with
Chicagoans lured out on the warm summer evening by
adroit advance publicity and by two postponements of the
opening caused by late delivery of the costumes from
New York.

The curtain rose on Dorothy Gale and her pet cow, Imogene, in a peaceful Kansas farm setting. Then the stage
lights dimmed and a deafening roar almost drowned out
the cry of "cyclone." While the wind machine shrieked
in the darkness, a gauze screen was lowered. On it the
startled audience saw scudding clouds that gave the illusion of a violent storm. Barns, houses, cattle and people
seemed to hurtle across the stage. Then suddenly the storm
was over. Dorothy and her cottage reappeared, but this
time in the peaceful and sunny country of the Munchkins
in the Land of Oz. Blown there with Dorothy and Imogene

were a waitress, Tryxie Tryfle, and a Topeka streetcar conductor named Pastoria, whose adventures formed a thread of the diaphanous plot that held together the songs and comedy.

Setting off for the Emerald City in search of the Wizard, whose powers she hoped would be great enough to get her back to Kansas, Dorothy picked up a motley company, including the Scarecrow and the Tin Woodman. These were the parts, of course, in which Montgomery and Stone literally leaped to fame in a single night. At the end of the first act, the darkened stage was suffused with golden light, disclosing the pretty faces of chorus girls dressed as brilliantly hued poppies. Dorothy and the Cowardly Lion, being breathing creatures, began to nod as the narcotic perfume of the flowers overpowered them. The Scarecrow and Tin Woodman vainly tried to waken Dorothy. But just as she was dozing off she called "Oh, Locasta, Locasta," and the good Witch of the North flew to her assistance. Seeing the girl to whom she had promised protection in the "deadly grasp of these treacherous blossoms," the good Witch exclaimed:

"Heartless and poisonous flowers, dare you defy the power of the Witch of the North? Defy me, who rules the North Wind and holds the Frost King as a willing subject? For this you shall die. For this shall I cloud the sunshine which is your breath, and chill the warmth which gives you life. Hail! Winds of the Frozen North! Come to my aid! Embrace these false blossoms and wither them with your cold caresses! King of the Frost, you do I invoke in this, my hour of vengeance! Hurl your glittering atoms upon these cruel flowers."

As the poppies knelt, she continued: "Congeal their sap

of life and set upon them the icy seal of your freezing kiss, which kills as surely as does their own treacherous breath. Thus shall my enemies perish! Thus shall I restore to life these mortals who now sleep, and rescue the maiden I have sworn to protect."

Shadows fell across the stage; on the gauze screen was projected the illusion of a snowstorm; the poppies shrank away, drooping, and fell to the ground. As the Poppy Queen fled from the cold and dreary scene, the Storm Queen appeared, drawn on the stage by reindeer hitched to a sleigh. Dorothy and the Lion were duly aroused from their deadly sleep by the cold, clear air, and they and their retinue resumed their colorful march toward the Emerald City.

Baum from his box could not help but deeply enjoy the furor which his poppy scene aroused in the opening night audience. It was the first of the memorable spectacles of the play, and it never failed to win volleys of applause.

Act Two, in the courtyard of the Wizard's Palace, opened on a dimly lighted stage. The Phantom Patrol of girls in glittering military dress displayed well-turned ankles and calves as they marched from high in the rear of the stage down a winding path until they disappeared in the dusk of the background. Again the sheer brilliance and perfection of the chorus, the lighting and the setting, won a clamorous tribute from the audience. The third act wound up the threads of the plot by rescuing Dorothy and her cohorts, the Scarecrow and Tin Woodman, while the other principals, surely as varied a crew as was ever seen on any stage, came to a comic opera end in a potpourri of topical songs and banter.

The final curtain was not allowed to fall until one A.M.,

so many were the encores and curtain calls. Even then the
audience filed out slowly. The magic effect of *The Wizard
of Oz* on its contemporary audiences has seldom been
equalled by any musical before or since. One spectator recalled that as he walked home, he saw groups still standing
on downtown street corners, whistling tunes, comparing
impressions, and generally reliving parts of that first performance.

Next day's newspapers were generous in their critical
comments. "The most superbly arrayed, beautifully set
and humorously played spectacular burlesque ever given
at any time in this summer show town," wrote Amy Leslie
of the *News*. "Money fairly drips from the gorgeous walls
and skies of the Emerald City and the Land of the Munchkins, and from the costly robes of the pretty girls and amazing atmospheres of silver mists and golden lights."

"Unhackneyed and fascinating," commented another
critic, while a third described *The Wizard of Oz* as the
"handsomest show of its kind ever put on here." From the
score of songs, they distinguished two with lyrics by Baum
—"When You Love, Love, Love" and "The Traveler and
the Pie," both set to Tietjens' music. The former, which
critics guessed correctly would prove to be the "hit" song
of the show, was sung by Anna Laughlin as Dorothy with
Montgomery and Stone in front of the curtain while the
stage was being set for the Poppy Scene. Montgomery, as
the Tin Woodman who lacked a heart, sang:

>   Oh, love's the thing that poets sing
>   Their sweetest lays regarding
>   And none say nay to love's gay sway
>   Which wounds when not rewarding.

> Naught can allure the heart so sure
>   As one swift dart from Cupid.
> And none I know would dodge his blow,
>   Unless exceeding stupid.
> For love's the thing that poets sing
>   Their sweetest lays regarding,
> And all are gay 'neath Cupid's sway,
>   All worldly cares discarding.

And then the chorus, first by Montgomery alone, and then with Dorothy and the Scarecrow:

> When you love, love, love
>   In mad delirium;
> When to love, love, love
>   That's quite sincere you come,
> There is nothing so divine,
> There is nothing half so fine
>   As the gladness of your madness
> When you love, love, love.

"It is possibly the most whistleable song and dance article in the new musical piece," one reviewer reported.

Another song which kept its place in *The Wizard of Oz* until the play left the boards nearly a decade later was Baum's "The Traveler and the Pie," also to Tietjens' music. With its intricate rhyming and verbal dexterity, "When You Love, Love, Love" is in the tradition of W. S. Gilbert, but the robust, anecdotal humor of "The Traveler and the Pie" is as purely American as James Whitcomb Riley. It was sung in the third act by the Scarecrow and the chorus:

> One day a weary traveler walked down the dusty street
>   Did he? I think he did.
> He thought he'd stop and ask a lady for a bite to eat.
>   Did he? I think he did.

He knocked upon the door and said
    In accents most polite:
"Dear Lady would you kindly let
    Me have a little bite?'
"Oh you shall have my pie," the young wife answered
    In delight.
Did she? I think she did.

CHORUS

Oh, the weary, weary traveler,
    The weary, weary traveler.
He took one little bite, next minute took to flight
    Did the weary, weary traveler.

Like the first verse, the second is nothing but an expert elaboration of a situation as old as the comic strips:

He went into a restaurant and ordered quite a spread,
    Did he? I think he did.
The waiter brought the bill to him before the man was fed,
    Did he? I think he did.
He rapped upon the table and
    Exclaimed: "See here, mine host,
I'm hungry and of course I'd like
    A course of quail on toast."
The landlord didn't quail but yet he gave his guest
    A roast.
    Did he? I think he did.

Slapstick and sentiment in the mood of the time, agile dancing and pretty girls, golden lights and spectaculars—to all this favorite fare of the turn of the century the critics and first nighters gave themselves over almost without reservation under the enchantment of the Land of Oz. Baum and his company had built on the stage a utopia where problems were evanescent and tears were shed only in joy. Then, as now, people had need of refuge from reality. Decades after this first night, Walt Disney created something like the world of *The Wizard of Oz* in his film fantasies, with their humor and splendid color and their counterparts of Baum's acrobatic Lion and companionate Cow.

The work of many hands went into *The Wizard of Oz*, but the most priceless ingredient in its success was Baum's story. Even though on the stage *The Wizard of Oz* was no longer a child's simple fable, but a farce for adults, it had not lost the disarmingly magic moods, or the delicate air of wonderment that still make his books the delight of children and the young in heart. A contemporary newspaper preserves a verse written by May McKenzie, a young woman of the chorus, which shows that even the ensemble recognized how much credit belonged to Baum. Scribbling backstage as she waited to go on with the chorus in the first week of the show, Miss McKenzie wrote:

A nursery magician took all little children by the hand
  And led them laughing through the book
Where Dorothy walks in Ozland.
  Ours is the task with elfin dance
And song, to give to childhood's days
  That merry Land of Oz. And should it chance
To win a smile, be thine the praise.

"A joy for children, a delight for adults, and a happy thing for everybody," was the comment of Cecil Smith, musical comedy's historian, on *The Wizard of Oz*.

The play rolled along through one of Chicago's most humid summers. Patrons disregarded the heat and the rain in their eagerness to pay a dollar fifty for a main floor seat, or fifty cents or a quarter for the balcony and gallery respectively. The newspapers reported that every performance was crowded and that hundreds were turned away at the Wednesday matinees. Manager Hamlin, now certain of a golden future, acted on a suggestion Baum had made to him on the opening night and signed Montgomery and Stone to a five-year contract. After fourteen weeks at the Grand Opera House, the show closed in Chicago and went on tour. During its stay in the city it had played to 185,000 persons and grossed $160,000. At only two of the one hundred and twenty-five performances did receipts fall below one thousand dollars. By today's standards, when a top flight musical comedy will gross fifty thousand dollars a week, this is small business, but in 1902 it was sensational. Advertised as having cost forty thousand dollars to put on the stage, it had quadrupled that sum in box office business in fourteen weeks. Montgomery and Stone got top salaries of two hundred dollars each a week; the scale for other members of the cast ranged down to twenty-five dollars.

After a road trip west and into Canada the company opened again in Chicago after Christmas for a two-week engagement before tackling New York. Chicago welcomed its return with sold out houses, and the *Tribune* called it "the best show of its kind Chicago has seen in many seasons." One gallery devotee recalls that he saw *The Wizard of Oz* for the sixth time during the holidays. In New York a brand new theater, the Majestic, at Broadway and Fifty-ninth Street, was waiting for the players. They took the train after the last Chicago performance Saturday night and opened in New York on Tuesday.

Abraham Klaw, of the mighty theatrical firm of Klaw and Erlanger, had attended the first performance in Chicago. A nice play for the Middle West, he had told Baum, but too innocent and unsophisticated to please New York audiences. New York reviewers were at first in agreement. Their comments were cool and critical. But the box office was busy, and the theater was "drawing crowds nightly," according to the magazine, *Theater*. Two weeks after the opening, Paul West of the *World* wrote in a letter that the show was "an enormous hit." The metropolis was as enthusiastic about Baum's extravaganza as Chicago had been. *The Wizard of Oz* ran for two seasons on Broadway, and when it moved in the fall of 1904, it went no farther than the Academy of Music on Fourteenth Street.

Road companies multiplied; casts changed; Montgomery and Stone played in the show four more years and moved along into *The Red Mill* and other successes. Songs and jokes were worn out and replaced with fresher ones, and still *The Wizard of Oz* ran on and on "like Tennyson's brook, forever" as a New York newspaper remarked. As late as 1911 it was showing at the Castle Square Theater in Boston. In August, 1957, a modern adaptation ran for a week in St. Louis at the Municipal Opera, using music from the 1939 motion picture, and firing Dorothy and the Wizard back to Kansas in a rocket ship. Chicago saw three original versions at Loop theaters in the winter of 1960-61.

Through the mists of half a century it is still possible to discern the complex structure of events and personalities that brought *The Wizard of Oz* to life on the stage. The foundation already existed; for Baum's story of the same name had been published in 1900 and had already begun the extraordinary career that was to make it an all-time best seller. The illustrator of his fantasy, William Wallace Denslow, was the center of a group of artists, writers and bohemian friends who gathered in his studio in the Fine Arts Building. Baum, an occasional visitor, met Isaac (Ike) Morgan there. Morgan, a newspaper cartoonist, later illustrated Baum's *The Woggle-Bug Book*. Through Morgan, Baum met Tietjens, a young musician who had come to Chicago recently from St. Louis. Baum offered Tietjens the opportunity to write the music for *King Midas* and *The Octopus,* two "comic operas" for which he had already completed books and lyrics. Work proceeded far enough for Baum to seek a producer for the shows, but without success. Two melodies from that collaboration, "The Traveler and the Pie," and "Love Is Love," were later used in *The Wizard of Oz*.

A half dozen persons have received credit for first perceiving the musical comedy possibilities of *The Wizard of Oz,* but amid the welter of claims, the most logical presumption is that Baum himself recognized the opportunity to collaborate with Tietjens and make his successful story into something like the Irish melodrama with music that he had staged many years before. Tietjens' diary records that the script that Baum turned over to him was in five acts, and that as soon as he received it he wrote the music for the opening chorus and several songs, including "When You Love, Love, Love."

Frederick R. Hamlin, business manager of the Grand Opera House, became interested in the Baum-Tietjens venture, perhaps through his brother George, a singing teacher and later a member of the Chicago Opera Company. They were sons of John A. Hamlin, who had made a fortune with a linament known as Hamlin's Wizard Oil. With his profits from this remedy, sold to a great extent through traveling medicine shows, the father had bought the Grand Opera House. Ralph T. Kettering, veteran Chicago showman, recalled that Fred Hamlin was only mildly interested until he heard the title of the piece. Perhaps he had a hunch that *The Wizard of Oz* would be as much of a bonanza for him as Wizard Oil had been for his father.

Baum's first script was quite close in plot and spirit to the book version. The characters remained the same, but the dialogue was somewhat more sophisticated. Opportunities had been made to interpolate a number of songs and choral numbers. Percy Hammond, then the Grand Opera House press agent and later the celebrated stage critic, is reputed to have approved the script, and Hamlin then called in Julian Mitchell, stage director for the Weber and Fields shows, whose career as a maker of successful stage spectacles extended from the 1880s right up to the Ziegfield Follies of the 1920s. In January, 1902, Baum and Tietjens, accompanied by Denslow, who had to be included because he was half owner of the copyright for *The Wizard of Oz*, met in New York with Mitchell and made financial arrangements to bring him in as stage director. Tietjens' diary records that Hamlin had agreed to pay Baum and his associates a six per cent gross royalty. Under the new arrangement Mitchell got one per cent of this gross royalty and the other five per cent was split one and seven-eighths per cent each to Baum and Tietjens, and one and one-quarter per cent to Denslow.

On February 6, 1902, the *Chicago Record-Herald* reported that "yesterday a contract was signed by Fred Hamlin and L. Frank Baum to produce an extravaganza founded on *The Wonderful Wizard of Oz.*"

Fortunately, Baum has left behind a record of the process by which his script was remodeled into the version that finally reached the stage. This statement, published as a letter in the *Chicago Tribune* on June 26, 1904, arose out of a press agent's scheme to stimulate attendance at the New York showing of *The Wizard of Oz*. He started a report that Baum was angry because of the "butchery" of his story in preparing it for the stage. The newspapers took up the controversy; the public curiosity improved box office business, and the report having served its purpose, the management decided to squelch it. Accordingly Baum wrote:

As a matter of fact, I am in perfect harmony with both Julian Mitchell and Mr. Hamlin . . . Few authors of successful books are ever fully satisfied with the dramatization of their work . . . This was my own experience. I myself made *The Wizard of Oz* into an extravaganza, and it was accepted by Mr. Hamlin . . . But when Julian Mitchell came to go over the script he declared it would never do in the world for the stage.

Through deference to the opinion of so experienced a stage director, I labored hard to remodel the play and even called in the assistance of professional dramatists. Mr. Mitchell then took a hand in the reformation itself. The original story was practically ignored, the dialogue rehashed, the situations transposed, my Nebraska Wizard made into an Irishman, and several other characters forced to conform to the requirements of the new schedule.

A story has been circulated by the press that I was heartbroken and ashamed of my extravaganza when it was finally produced, but that is not true. I was filled with amazement, indeed, and took occasion to protest against several innovations that I did not like, but Mr. Mitchell listened to the plaudits of the big audiences and turned a deaf ear to my complaints.

I confess, after two years of success for the extravaganza, that I now regard Mr. Mitchell's views in a different light. The people will have what pleases them and not what

the author happens to favor, and I believe that one of the
reasons Julian Mitchell is recognized as a great producer
is that he faithfully tries to serve the great mass of play
goers—and usually succeeds.

My chief business is, of course, the writing of fairy tales,
but should I ever attempt another extravaganza, or dram-
atize another of my books, I mean to profit by the lesson
Mr. Mitchell has taught me, and sacrifice personal prefer-
ence to the demands of those I shall expect to purchase
admission tickets.

Mitchell left the first act of Baum's story relatively in-
tact, except for the introduction of several new characters.
Some of the changes were directed by necessity. This was
before the day of dogs trained for the stage; so instead of
Dorothy's pet dog Toto, Mitchell gave her a pet cow,
Imogene; perhaps because a pet cow had been a great hit
in Edward E. Rice's old time burlesque, *Evangeline*. The
second and third acts have only a passing resemblance to
their original. Into them Mitchell, out of his great experience, threw many time-tested elements, such as the marching choruses so popular in the extravaganzas of the 1890s.
Blackface acts and dialect characters came out of the same
contemporary treasury. The whole thing was embellished
with topical songs and skits by several composers and lav-
ishly mounted in the best Weber and Fields style until
what Baum had originally written as a fairy tale for children became, in Mitchell's adept hands, a farce aimed to
hold the interest and tickle the funny bones of the play-
going public he understood so well.

Stone, in his autobiography, *Rolling Stone*, recalling his
experience in *The Wizard of Oz* and other extravaganzas,
wrote that "a musical comedy isn't written, it is rewritten.
In fact, what happens to the original script is still a puzzle

to me. You cut it down and turn it around; you put in new parts and take out old ones, and after a while you have a musical comedy." Perhaps Stone had in mind that, owing to his insistence, the Mitchell script was remodeled to raise the role of the Tin Woodman to greater prominence so that Montgomery could be his co-star. Only on this condition did the two actors, who were then playing in London, agree to accept Mitchell's invitation to appear in the show.

One striking novelty that contributed greatly to the success of the opening and closing scenes of the first act may have been inspired by Baum's interest in mechanical devices. This was the large revolving celluloid disc which rotated in front of a strong spotlight placed in the balcony. The disc used for the opening scene was painted with stormy black clouds. As it turned, the images giving the illusion of a hurricane were projected on an almost invisible gauze screen. For the poppy field scene at the end of the act, another disc simulated a snowstorm as the flowers nodded and froze.

Baum and Mitchell's work had its influence on the general course of American stage amusements, which in the early years of the century were leaving behind the older pantomimes, burlesques, minstrel shows, and spectacles, and were developing the formula for the modern musical comedy. For example, Victor Herbert's *Babes In Toyland* staged in 1903, and his *The Lady of the Slipper* produced in 1912, both looked back to Baum's work for inspiration and specific plot material. So did *Piff! Paff!! Pouf!!!* of 1904, in which Eddie Foy had a Scarecrow-like role.

Financially, *The Wizard Of Oz* rewarded Baum and his associates liberally. Tietjens' daughter is authority for the estimate that her father received ninety thousand dollars in royalties. One of Baum's sons places his father's share at more than one hundred thousand dollars. According to the reported agreement, Tietjens would have received as much as Baum. Such royalties indicate that *The Wizard Of Oz* during its first eight years took in close to $5,500,000 and that it was seen by more than six million people.

Thus, after having written to please a child, Baum found that he had written to please a good part of the nation.

II

CHITTENANGO AND
ROSE LAWN

THE LONG road that brought Baum to literary and dramatic success started in the comfortable Mohawk Valley hamlet of Chittenango, New York, some five miles south of Lake Oneida and fifteen miles east of Syracuse. The seventh child of Benjamin Ward and Cynthia Stanton Baum, he arrived in the world in the early evening of May 15, 1856.

It was an exciting time to be born, for the expansive period that has become known as the Gilded Age was just ahead. The new baby's sturdy paternal ancestors had come from the Palatinate a century before and had done their part to push the frontier west from New York State, where his Grandfather Baum had been a Methodist lay preacher. His mother was descended from Scotch-Irish farmers who had lived in Connecticut since the seventeenth century.

The new baby was born into an age that would live in cities; that would harvest its wealth from oil wells and factories instead of the soil; whose heroes would be politicians and bankers and plutocrats; an age that would know all the awkward problems of raw new wealth and the

17

temptations of new power. His father was one of those
who grew up in the old ways but soon mastered the new.
Trained to be coopers, Benjamin and his brother Lyman
were the proprietors of a small factory making tight barrels and butter firkins when Colonel Edwin Drake struck
oil at nearby Titusville in 1859. Benjamin Baum was not
slow to recognize that the tight barrels he knew how to
make were just right to hold the liquid treasure gushing
from the earth. By 1861 he had seen that there were even
greater opportunities there and had become a successful
dealer in oil land leases. According to an item in the
Syracuse Herald of October 19, 1885, Benjamin Baum
prospected around Titusville and secured producing
territory at Cherry Tree Run, a tributary of Oil Creek a
few miles south of Titusville. This field was active in the
middle 1860s.

After having made a large fortune there, so the newspaper account goes, he disposed of his interests, opened
an office in New York for stock market speculation, and
returned to Syracuse, where he was a founder and director
of the Second National bank. His next oil field operations
were in the Pennsylvania region near Bradford, where he
was one of a number of independents who tried to break
the tightening grip of the Standard Oil Company by
building a pipe line to Rochester, New York, where
Bradford oil would have been transferred to tank cars and
shipped to refineries in New York and Buffalo. But the
New York Central Railroad, preferring to favor the oil
trust rather than the independents, through its lobbyists
headed by Chauncey M. Depew, helped to defeat a bill in
the legislature to authorize the pipe line.

Benjamin Baum then opened up a field of his own in

Potter County, which adjoins Bradford to the east, but retained some interests at Gillmor, a few miles from Bradford, where he was a member of the firm of Baum, Richardson and Company. In 1882 he built the Cynthia Oil Works at Bolivar, New York, east of Olean, to refine crude oil salvaged at a dam where it collected on the surface of the water from the overflow of the oil field tanks upstream.

Meanwhile his wife, for whom the oil works were named, was busy with what was to be a large family. She and Benjamin Baum had eloped in 1842, while he was still a cooper. Full of faith in Providence, in themselves, and in their future, they had gone to the Methodist Chapel on the first Sunday after their marriage, and Baum had put into the collection plate every cent his pockets contained. In the years that followed, while Benjamin Baum was moving forward in his oil enterprises, Cynthia Baum was bringing her babies into the world and giving them what must surely have been one of the most delightful childhood environments possible. But it was a time of severe infant mortality, and the first two children died in infancy. Then came two girls, Harriet Alvena and Mary Louise, and a boy, Benjamin William. The sixth child, Edwin, died a month after the birth of the seventh, Frank. Another boy, Henry Clay, came along three years later, followed by a ninth child who lived only two years. It was a period when such tragedy was written into the history of almost every family.

The Baums' seventh baby started life as Lyman Frank Baum, a name which at various stages of his life he tailored to his own taste. The Lyman was given to him to honor an uncle, but the boy insisted on being called by his middle name. Nor would he stand for the diminutive, Frankie, used by his mother until he convinced her that it was "sissy." Some years later, he called himself Louis F. Baum in connection with his activities as actor and playwright, and even when he took part in the family oil business. But in his later life as an author he was always known as L. Frank Baum.

Except for games with his brothers and sisters, Frank was a shy and sedentary child. Much of his time was spent alone in some favored spot in the house or a corner of the yard, where he kept happy for hours with the fey playmates his imagination created. Some of this physical inactivity was forced upon him, for he had been born with a seriously defective heart. In early manhood, heart attacks several times caused him to fall unconscious. Later in life he would walk the floor in agony, tears streaming from his eyes as he fought the pangs of angina pectoris.

Family life in the frame house a quarter mile south of Chittenango was a happy one, for despite business and household cares, both parents took a deep interest in their children. When Frank was four years old his father bought a residential farm property just north of Syracuse and the next year the family moved to the new place. Situated on some fifteen acres of rich land, the new house was connected by a winding driveway with the Cicero Plank Road which ran to Syracuse. Because the gardens and drives were planted with hundreds of rose bushes, Cynthia Baum named the estate Rose Lawn. Elsewhere on the place were planted nearly every variety of fruit tree and grapevine that would flourish in upstate New York. It was another such place as the Bolton estate, described with so much affection by Mark Twain in *The Gilded Age,* and in its way the fictional Philadelphia family was akin in simplicity, affection and comfort to the reality of the Baums.

The rooms of the large, comfortable house at Rose Lawn were papered in the fashionable dark brown and black patterns of the 1860s. In the bedrooms stood ornate brass beds and walnut washstands with the customary hand-painted wash bowl, pitcher and slop jar. Under each bed was the china pot that saved the room's occupant a night time trip to the outhouse concealed behind a trellis of roses.

In cold winter mornings in the Baum's country household it was often necessary to break a film of ice in the pitcher before a child could wash the sleep from his eyes. In spite of what today would seem like the most severe inconveniences, but which were the normal way of life for the times, Frank's mother preferred to bring up her children at Rose Lawn rather than in the city. Only in cold weather, or when social obligations called them to Syracuse, did the family occupy the ornate, fretted and curlicued town house.*

Young Frank also had the opportunity of enjoying the diversions of his father's eighty acre dairy lands, known as Spring Farm, which adjoined Rose Lawn on the north. Benjamin Baum had imported his herd directly from the Isle of Jersey and had built a handsome barn and stable for the cattle and fast harness horses which were his pride. North of Spring Farm on a road connecting the Liverpool Road to the Brewerton Plank Road was Baum's third farm, a one hundred and sixty acre commercial grain and livestock enterprise.

* At 1 Rust Street, today Midland Avenue.

From such surroundings Frank developed a deep interest in animals, especially fowl. As a child, he would sit for hours near the chicken yard at Spring Farm watching the birds and before long he had his own flock of Bantams. Throughout his life Frank Baum kept his interest in chickens. A half century later, after he had built Ozcot in Hollywood and was at the height of his career, he kept a flock of Rhode Island Reds to provide meat and fresh eggs for the home table.

In the grain fields of his father's commercial farm, Frank had his first sight of a scarecrow—a sight so familiar to any farm boy that he would never give it a second thought. But on the future writer's vivid imagination it made a lasting impression. In his dreams recurred a nightmare in which a scarecrow was chasing him. Happily, Frank always dashed away while the scarecrow waddled after him and finally collapsed into a pile of shapeless straw. Many years later this dream found enduring expression in *The Wizard of Oz*.

When the boy was eight years old the quiet of one night in the Rust Street home was disturbed by burglars. Frank's mother heard the intruders and wakened her husband, who had just returned from New York. He hurried one of the burglars through a window by firing several shots and, according to the newspaper account, "produced a skedaddle" of the others outside by another shot. Many years later Frank recalled the delicious excitement of that night.

Young Frank's ordinarily placid childhood was occasionally broken by a visit to the oil fields in Pennsylvania with his father. One fall, when he was about eight, Benjamin took him on one of these trips. The child was left to amuse himself while his father negotiated an oil lease. Cold and tired, the boy wrapped his coat around him, rolled under one of the big boilers that supplied steam for the pumps, and went to sleep.

He awoke suddenly. Opening his eyes he saw, by the flickering light of the boiler fires, a huge rattlesnake coiled near his head. Too frightened to cry out or move, he lay still. The minutes seemed like hours; then, slowly, the snake lowered its ugly head. For a tense moment it remained staring into the boy's eyes, then slowly uncoiled and slithered away into the grass.

Until he was twelve, Frank, like the other Baum children, got his schooling at home in the big Rose Lawn farmhouse. He read and reread the books there, and his eager young mind let little escape of what he heard and saw on the farm and in the family circle. In 1868, the doctors, who because of his weak heart had earlier recommended against his going to school, decided he was strong enough to attend Peekskill Military Academy. But his stay there lasted less than two years. After the freedom of Rose Lawn, the confinement and discipline of the military academy were galling. Whenever his father visited him, Frank complained. After every vacation at home he found it more and more difficult to force himself to return to Peekskill.

"I complained to my father about the brutal treatment I felt I was receiving at the school," he remarked many years later. "I said the teachers were heartless, callous and continually indulging in petty nagging. I told father they were about as human as a school of fish. In those days, of course, instructors were quick to slap a boy in the face, or forcibly use a cane or ruler to punish any student who violated in the slightest way any of the strict and often unreasonable rules."

One day Cadet Baum was severely disciplined for looking out of the window at the birds while he should have been preparing his lesson. His resentment of the penalty brought on a heart attack—the first in several years—and he fainted in the classroom. The episode convinced Benjamin Baum that the military academy was not the place for his son. He took Frank home, and the youth completed his education at Rose Lawn and in Syracuse with tutors. From his reading he became familiar with such popular Victorian English novelists as Charles Dickens, William Thackeray and Charles Reade, whose *The Cloister and the Hearth* was always one of his favorites. He also enjoyed memorizing passages from Shakespeare's plays. Of all these authors, the strongest influence discernible in Baum's own writing is undoubtedly Dickens, whose use of caricature for comic and moralistic reasons is mirrored in many of the inhabitants of Oz.

As a young boy, Frank had a keen ability to learn from the life around him. One day when he was fourteen he went with his father into Syracuse. While Benjamin was attending to some business, the youth wandered idly down a nearby street. Presently he found himself in front of the dusty window of a small print shop. He stood entranced watching the elderly owner of the place operate an old-fashioned foot treadle press. Every time the door swung open Frank breathed the odor of ink, lead type, and fresh cut paper. As he watched the man set type in a "stick," lock it up in a form, and run off a batch of cards or handbills, he became so enthralled that he lost all track of time.

His father scolded him when he got back late to the office, but Frank was never to forget the thrill that came from that afternoon's whiff of ink. He decided he would become a printer or a newspaper man when he grew up—a decision that led him into several of the blind alleys he explored before finding his true calling.

Frank talked so much about his experience in Syracuse that his parents soon paid some attention to this new interest. Always an indulgent father, Benjamin sought out a dealer in printing supplies on his next trip to New York and bought a small foot-treadle press, fonts of type, ink, and paper. A few weeks after this equipment was delivered to Rose Lawn, Frank, who throughout his life displayed unusual ability to work with his hands, had mastered the art of "sticking" type, of justifying and making up the forms and of feeding the press without nipping his fingers. He taught these new skills to his younger brother Harry, the closest friend of his youth, and when they were able to turn out an acceptable job, the brothers decided to issue a monthly paper. From surviving copies it appears that the first issue was in May, 1871. Frank christened it *The Rose Lawn Home Journal,* and from his pen came most of the stories and short poems that filled the small, four-page sheet, augmented at times by poems from the pen of his sister, Mary Louise.

Perhaps to these days belongs a more ambitious piece of writing of which the only surviving evidence is a presentation inscription in a book to his sister Harriet. He wrote: "It was you, I remember, who first encouraged me to write. Years ago you read to father an incomplete 'novel' which I, in my youth and innocence, had scribbled, and you declared it was good."

In the newspaper Frank had his first opportunity to display the literary creativeness that found its culmination in his tales for children. One poem written at that time he thought worthy of including, years later, in a small book *By the Candelabra's Glare,* which he was to print and bind by hand in the basement of his Chicago home. It read:

The Romance of a Broken Window

A little kit
On end did sit
To wait for mouse or sparrow.
A little boy
Played with a toy
Known as a bow and arrow.

Intent on game
Near Puss he came
And slyly raised his weapon.
And drew the bow
And then let go
And wondered what would happen.

The little cat
No longer sat
In dreamy contemplation.
The arrow sped
Straight for her head
To her intense frustration.

Roused from her dream
Puss gave a scream
And out of danger fled,
While through the glass
The stick did pass
And injured that instead.

After three years of editing the *Journal,* young Frank joined forces with a friend, Thomas G. Alford, and

founded *The Empire,* which the opening issue announced
would be "a first class amateur monthly newspaper, containing poetry, literature, postage stamp news, amateur
items, etc." Tom Alford, son of a former lieutenant-gover-
nor of the Empire State and later a noted New York City
newspaper man, was publisher and Frank was editor. *The
Empire* was discontinued in 1875, after two years of publication, when its youthful proprietors developed new
interests.

Frank's new interest was the breeding of Hamburg
chickens at Spring Farm. Hamburgs are rather small,
brilliantly plumaged birds of German and Dutch origin
and distinguished by a peculiar rose-colored comb termi-
nating in a sharp point. The boy developed several new
strains and won prizes exhibiting them at fairs and poultry
shows until "Baum's Thoroughbred Fowls" were widely
known throughout the Mohawk Valley. In 1886 Frank
wrote a seventy page pamphlet, *The Book of the Hamburgs,* which was published by H. H. Stoddard in Hart-
ford. One of two known copies, a small volume five by
seven and a half, is in the Rare Book Room of the New
York Public Library. In it the young expert describes
such Hamburg types as the Golden and Silver Spangled,
the Golden and Silver Penciled, the Black, White, Bolton
Greys, and the Creoles; and knowingly discusses plumage
and other show points, care, mating, exhibiting, and judg-
ing of the breed. There is a newspaper reference in the
Syracuse Public Library to indicate that several years before he published his pamphlet on the Hamburgs, Baum
was editing a monthly journal, *The Poultry Record,* for
the Syracuse Fanciers' Club.

One of the express purposes of *The Empire* was to pub-

lish postage stamp news, another of Frank's abiding interests. In 1873, under the name of Baum, Norris & Co., he
published an eleven-page pamphlet, *Baum's Complete
Stamp Dealers Directory*. The pamphlet, 3½ by 6 inches
in size, is described on the title page as "a complete list
of all dealers in the United States, together with the principal ones of Europe, and a list of philatelic publications."
On the back of the title page is a key, listing symbols to
indicate whether the dealer is known to be reliable, not
reliable, or deals in counterfeits. Frank's interest in stamp
collecting continued all his life, and at the time of his
death he owned a large collection.

III

THE GLEAM OF FOOTLIGHTS

In that gilded day of beckoning prosperity the son of a well-to-do business man did not become a poultryman or a printer. But instead of preparing himself for becoming rich, as was the proper ambition of his class and time, Frank, along with his printing, stamp-collecting and poultry enthusiasms, became infatuated with the theater.

The young man had first seen Shakespeare's plays performed in his father's theater in Gillmor, Pennsylvania. While the elder Baum was dickering over oil properties nearby, his son had ample opportunity to sample the wares of the traveling companies whose entertainments were the "culture" of the region. Years later he could still recite long passages from *Romeo and Juliet, Hamlet, King Lear, Richard III* and others. When Frank was eighteen and still living with his parents in Syracuse, he chose what he thought would be his permanent career. He would be an actor. He began haunting the Syracuse theaters, avidly studying the tricks of stage business, and treasuring up in his mind the elocutionary mannerisms and flamboyant gestures affected by the actors of that day.

Several times he approached managers of traveling companies for small parts, but without success. One day, however, the manager of a Shakespearean troupe playing two and three night stands in upstate New York saw "promise" in this well tailored and obviously affluent young man. He agreed to take Frank into the troupe if the aspiring young actor would equip himself with a complete set of costumes for all the starring roles he might be called upon to take in the company's repertoire. Members were required to provide their own costumes, the old manager explained, and if Frank expected to have a place in the company and become an actor, he would have to bring a suitable wardrobe. To the eager youth this did not seem unreasonable, and he agreed. The manager then drew up a long list of the items he said Frank would need. The young man took the list to his father, pleading that the wardrobe be bought at once so he could join the troupe without delay. When Benjamin asked why it was necessary to have such a large number of costumes, Frank explained that the manager had promised to cast him in the leading role of every Shakespearean play the troupe performed.

The older man first tried to make his son see that leading roles would not be given, even in a third rate company, to a young man of no professional experience. But Frank's pleading won over his mother, and together they finally won the consent of his father. Benjamin Baum made only one condition: Frank must not use his own name on the stage, for the name of Baum was respected in the community, and it must not be tarnished or cheapened by association with the theatrical profession, which in those days still had a dubious reputation.

Frank ordered the finest of velvets and silks, the best imported lace and gold bullion fringe, from a noted New York theatrical costumer. The bill totaled several thousand dollars—a much larger sum than it would be today. While waiting for the wardrobe to be delivered, Frank spent most of his hours in his room, stalking up and down before the mirror, practicing grimaces and declaiming the Bard's resounding lines. At last the delivery man brought five large trunks crammed with clothing, wigs, shoes, and properties. Frank, who had taken the name of George Brooks for his stage career, hastened to join the troupe in Oneida. When he got to the theater with his baggage, the manager took him inside, opened the trunks and inspected Frank's purchases, carefully checking each item from a list he drew from his coat pocket. Grinning in high good humor as he appraised the costly materials and fine workmanship, he congratulated the youth on his taste. Summoning other members of the company, the manager introduced the new star to them, and Frank was welcomed into his chosen calling.

As they parted, the manager particularly instructed Frank to be in his dressing room an hour before curtain time. Impatient to set foot on the stage, the youth hurried through dinner and back to the theater. As he was opening his new trunks, which almost filled his tiny dressing room, an old actor came in, sat down on a trunk, made conversation for a few minutes and mentioned casually that he was the Romeo of the night's performance. Unfortunately his doublet was torn and there had not been time to mend it. Might he borrow Frank's—just for the one night, of course. The youngster obliged with one of the shining new garments from his trunks.

By curtain time almost every man in the *Romeo and*

Juliet cast had found his way to Frank's room to borrow
a costume item. Each one had some small emergency.
Within a few days nearly the entire wardrobe, ranging
from wigs to shoes, was in use by other members of the
troupe. Nothing was ever returned. Frank's wardrobe had
plenty of stage experience, but his personal career consisted of a few walk-on roles. Crestfallen, Frank spent a
few weeks with the company, then with empty trunks returned to his family, wiser in the ways of the world and
particularly in the wiles of threadbare actors.

Frank appears to have spent the next year or two as a
salesman for Neal, Baum and Company, importers and
jobbers of dry goods, which Benjamin Baum had organized with William Henry Harrison Neal after the marriage
of his elder daughter Harriet to Neal in 1866. Benjamin
Baum built a block of stores for the concern at 17-19 Clinton Street in Syracuse. Later the company became Sperry,
Neal and Hyde.

But Frank could not forget the fascination of the stage.
He finally left Neal, Baum and Company and managed to
get a bona fide start in professional acting with Albert M.
Palmer's Union Square Theater in New York. Palmer
welcomed new talent and had a coaching staff to train
young actors. Under the name of Louis F. Baum, Frank appeared in one of the company's most notable successes,
The Banker's Daughter by Bronson Howard. First presented on November 30, 1878, this drama of finance and
family ran for one hundred nights. A photograph taken
in New York at the time shows Frank Baum as a handsome
young man with finely molded, regular features whose
youth was poorly disguised by a luxuriant walrus mustache. He was turned out in the very height of fashion. A

velvet collared, double breasted coat was buttoned high on his chest, while a stiff white stand-up collar framed the area from chin to Adam's apple.

According to family tradition, the young actor also served a turn at this time on the *New York Tribune,* to which he had previously contributed occasional articles and humorous verse. This casual connection stimulated his old interest in journalism. Through the influence of his father, he found a job on a weekly newspaper, the *Era,* in Bradford, Pennsylvania, where the elder Baum had considerable oil interests. Since that time the *Era* has become a daily, but back in the eighteen seventies Frank Baum's *Era* was a typical small town, four-page weekly. Front and back pages were filled with news items and advertising collected by the editor on his daily rounds. These outside pages were printed in the paper's shop at Bradford on "stock sheets" bought from a company in New York City which printed the inside pages with what was then known as "patent insides" or "boiler plate"—a miscellany of fiction, comment, foreign intelligence, proprietary medicine advertisements of potent concoctions "good for man or beast," and edifying articles. Such a sheet, when folded down the middle, formed a four-page newspaper with the local news of Bradford on the outside and of the rest of the world on the inside.

After about a year with the *Era,* Frank returned to the stage. His father, who owned a string of theaters in Olean and Richburg in New York State, and Bradford and Gillmor in Pennsylvania, as well as in other small towns throughout the region, made his son their manager in 1880. Later he deeded them outright to Frank, who recalled:

We had a lot of trouble getting shows for the playhouses, hidden away in the oil fields, because the towns were too small to provide profitable patronage for a one night stand. So I decided to organize my own company and produce some of Shakespeare's better known plays.

About that time we were asked to give a special performance of *Hamlet* in the town hall of a small oil settlement. When we got there we found the hall had no stage—not even a raised platform. We asked the oil workers to arrange some saw horses at one end of the room and cover them with one by twelve inch planks that were stacked outside for use in a building under construction.

They soon had a make-shift stage in place, but because they refused to nail the boards to the saw horses for fear of spoiling them for use in the new building, the footing was very uncertain. It was necessary to make this wobbly platform answer the purposes of a stage, but we had to be careful not to walk too heavily or jar the boards, lest they shift under our feet.

That night everything went well until Scene Four was under way. Horatio had just said: "Look, my lord, it comes," and at this cue the Ghost entered and started across the loose planks. I, playing Hamlet, exclaimed: "Angels and ministers of grace, defend us" and jumped back, stumbled and displaced the ends of two of the boards.

The Ghost was covered with a white sheet and could not see where he was walking. He veered to one side and stepped on a plank I had dislodged. It tipped and before anyone could stop him, the Ghost slipped from sight through the floor of our make-shift stage.

None of the oil workers in the audience knew the plot of *Hamlet*. They thought the disappearance of the Ghost in this slapstick manner was part of the play and they roared with laughter. They shouted and whistled, stamped their feet and called "More—more" until we had to repeat the scene five times before we could continue with the show.

The old actor who played the part of the Ghost took his work very seriously, and he was still angry the following morning. He claimed his arms and legs were skinned from the rough boards because he had been required to repeat his performance of the accidental fall so many times. He quit the company in spite of the fact that we tried to make him see he should have felt highly honored. He had received more encores than all the other members of the cast together. But his spirit was bruised, like his body, and we had to get a new man for the Ghost before we could put on *Hamlet* again.

Familiar now with the taste of his audiences, Frank set to work to satisfy it by writing original plays. On February 11, 1882, he entered for copyright in the Library of Congress the titles of three dramatic compositions—*The Maid of Arran, Matches,* and *The Mackrummins.* Application was made from Richburg, New York, where he had a small theater. *Matches* is known only from a playbill and a review in the Richburg *Oil Echo* of June 3, 1882 when it was given in Brown's Opera house there by the *Maid of Arran* company. A performance the night before had been cut short by fire in the theater. Frank played the part of an impecunious fortune hunter who had to outwit a vinegar-faced landlady to whom he owed money so that he could win the heiress of his dreams. "Mr. Baum is to be congratulated," said the newspaper, "not only for his successful interpretation of the leading character, but on his good judgment in selecting such excellent support."

But *The Maid of Arran,* an Irish melodrama, more than made up for these nebulous projects by solid success. The script, music and lyrics were all from the versatile pen of Louis F. Baum, which was the name that the playwright now used for theatrical purposes. It was based on a novel, *A Princess of Thule,* by the Scottish novelist, William Black. A new company was organized so that *The Maid of Arran* might make its bow under the most favorable auspices possible. Frank was leading man and stage direc-

tor. His father's youngest sister, Catherine,* had an important part. Benjamin Baum had persuaded her to join the
company so that she would be in a position to keep a
friendly eye on Frank, who was very young for so much
responsibility.

"Aunt Kate, as we called her, was already well known as
an elocutionist," Baum told his son Frank in later years.
"She had been giving public recitals for many years and
was in demand at social gatherings as an entertainer. She
turned out to be an excellent actress as well and became
a favorite with our audiences. She played two roles in the
show, that of the Prophetess under the name of Kate
Roberts, and that of Mrs. Holcomb under the name of
Katherine Gray.

"We opened *The Maid of Arran* in the opera house at
Gillmor. It was an immediate success. This encouraged
me to engage the Grand Opera House in Syracuse for two
performances. The first was on May 15, 1882, my twenty-
sixth birthday. A correspondent for a New York newspaper sent a favorable account of the play to his editor,
and through this notice the Windsor Theater in New York
booked us for the week of June 19 through 24.

"Apparently our play appealed to the big city folk as
much as it had back home. We had a well filled theater all
week. But I soon found that playing the principal part and
managing the company, too, had become too much for me.
When I asked father what to do, he assigned his brother,
John Wesley Baum, to us as business manager for the road
tour. It started in Ithaca. We played in Toronto and
Rochester and several other cities in northern New York

---

* Mrs. William Bailey Gray.

State. Then we took the train west to Columbus, Ohio, and Milwaukee, arriving in Chicago for ten performances at the Academy of Music beginning October 9. It was my first sight of Chicago, which was very busy and energetic after rebuilding from the great fire."

The young playwright seems to have revised his melodrama and whipped his company into a smooth running organization on the road. At the first Syracuse performance, the newspapers were kind to their fellow townsman; the *Journal,* for example, saying that "instances are very rare of one of his age and experience meeting with the goodly degree of success which he achieved last night." But it spoke of "failures in properly assembling the characters" and of "some filling that needs to be removed," and detected "a vein of crudity running through the play." Baum's aunt was criticised for "continually overdoing the character," but Baum, it said "presented his part very quietly and handsomely." The newspapers also noticed that the opera house was well filled. And when *The Maid of Arran* company returned to Syracuse for a two night stand on February 14 and 15, 1883, at Wieting Opera House, the *Journal* said:

> *The Maid of Arran* . . . was presented with much smoothness and good dramatic effect. Since it was brought out in this city, it has undergone pretty thorough polishing and has been thereby much improved. The company . . . now makes the most of it, giving great force to its principal parts. What the play lacks in strength it made up in superior finish. . . . Tonight autograph albums are to be distributed with the programs.

The play appeared on the boards in Syracuse for the last time on St. Patrick's night, March 17, 1885, when it was played by the Young Men's Dramatic Club. Baum appeared with the amateurs, not as Holcomb, the hero, however, but as Con O'Mara, the patriarch of Arran.

A copy of the script of *The Maid of Arran* has survived to evidence the flavor and the craftsmanship of Baum's first major literary work. From Black's quietly plotted novel, rich in the atmosphere and folklore of the Hebrides, Baum made a period-piece melodrama of rapid action, sure-fire situations and sentimental characters calculated to win the tears and the applause of the sentimental audiences of the time. The mood was established by this opening invocation chanted by the Prophetess to the strains of "The Harp That Once Through Tara's Halls":

The picture lives, breathing ruin where once was magnificence and kingly splendor. And this fair-haired stranger comes not to paint Arran in her palmy days, but in desolation. Aye! And more than this. He comes to woo our last treasure in whose soul is centered all the sweetness and honor of a kingly race. Would I could save her. But I can not! The Hand of Fate is here, and we must bow to her will.

The first act, laid in the Hebrides, introduces Shiela O'Mara, daughter of Con O'Mara, who is descended from the Kings of Arran. The high dignity due melodrama faltered a bit here, for Baum could not resist giving him a punning name. Also present on the island is Hugh Holcomb,* London society man on a painting excursion, and Holcomb's false friend and the villain of the piece, Captain John Ingram. Both fall in love with Shiela, but Hugh wins and weds her and takes her to London as his bride.

* This was the part Baum played in the original performance.

Shiela cuts an unpolished figure in London society, and in the second act a quarrel arises from her country manners and from Captain Ingram's crafty efforts to break up the marriage. In the same act, Hugh introduces her to his aunt, a hypochondriac whose many eccentricities are capped by her constant quotation of maxims from Marcus Aurelius, but whose money enables Hugh to live as a gentleman. This was the major role of the two played by Baum's Aunt Kate.

Shiela, her heart broken by Hugh's growing indifference, takes refuge with his aunt, despite an impassioned speech by a follower of her father who has come to London to bring her a piece of the "old sod"—a plea that must have made the rafters ring with applause. He argues:

> My poor, poor girl. You are scarce a woman yet, and you have learned so soon the bitterest lesson of life—to be scorned by the man you love. But cheer up, Mavourneen, you are young yet and life is before you. Thy father waits by the fireside for his darling child, his little Shiela. It's cold and dark here, God knows, but there are warm hearts in Arran to welcome you. . . . Come with us, Shiela. Come back to the old isle where the shamrock is green and life is bright as in the old days, Shiela. Come, Shiela.

Mrs. Holcomb, Hugh's aunt, whose heart is golden despite her gruffness, first disinherits her nephew and leaves her fortune to Shiela; then, when Hugh rushes in, remorseful and determined to make a man of himself by shipping as a common sailor, she leaves half to each and conveniently dies.

Act Four is pure melodrama with Hugh in the power of Ingram, who sees that by Hugh's death he can have Shiela and the fortune. (The stage setting aboard a full rigged

man o' war was much admired by reviewers.) Hugh reveals
his understanding of Ingram's true character in these
words:

> The seeds of discord which separated me from the
> woman I love were sown by this man under the guise of
> friendship. Behind that quiet smile is a heart that all hell
> cannot match for falsehood and deceit. Watch him, and
> he is harmless. Trust him and he will bury his fangs into
> the deepest recesses of your heart.

Captain Ingram puts Hugh in chains and sentences him
to be hanged from the yardarm for mutiny. But the faithful follower of O'Mara frees Hugh, and Captain Ingram
dies like the villain he is. The fifth act brings Hugh back
to Arran and to the arms of his ever-loving Shiela.

The young playwright composed seven songs which
were interpolated in the quieter moments of the play. The
seven—"The Legend of Castle Arran," "A Rollicking Irish
Boy," "When O'Mara Is King Once Again," "A Tuft from
the Old Irish Bog," "Ship Ahoy," a choral number "Waiting for the Tide to Turn," and "A Pair o' Blue Eyes"—
were published in 1882 in New York with an appropriately
melodramatic lithographed cover. This score was presumably hawked in the lobbies of theaters both in New York
and on the company's road tours.

The *New York Mirror* reviewer called the songs
"pretty." Following is a sample verse from the hit song,
"When O'Mara Is King Once Again":

> In the days, when our Isle was a Kingdom
> And O'Mara was King over all,
> Then the fairest of Arran's fair daughters
> Reigned a Princess in that castle hall.

> Oh, her face was the brightest,
>   Her hands were the whitest,
> And heart of the lightest had she.
>   And she had a lover, but he was a sailor
> And roamed the seas over did he.

The same reviewer wrote that "Baum, as Hugh Holcomb, was quiet and effective and held the sympathies of the audience." And the *New York News* remarked: "Taken all in all, the drama that came to us unheralded and un-puffed is a gem of dramatic thought, and will, no doubt, prove a bonanza to those who have it in possession."

New York saw *The Maid of Arran* for a second time when it played on March 26, 1883 at the Lee Avenue Academy of Music in the Brooklyn district known as Wil-liamsburg.

IV

GOLD DAYS AND GRAY

———————————

BAUM SPENT the Christmas holidays of 1881 with his family in Syracuse. One of his first calls of the season was at the home of his sister, Harriet Neal. "I was glad to see Frank home for the holidays," Mrs. Neal recalled later, "for there was a certain girl I wanted him to meet. I had known her through Aunt Josephine, wife of my father's brother, Adam Clark Baum. Both of us were very fond of her, but when I mentioned the subject to Frank he was less than enthusiastic.

" 'I'll be glad to meet her, just to please you,' he said, 'but remember, Hattie, show business doesn't leave me much time to run around with girls. You know I've never found one yet I could stay interested in.'

" 'You come over tomorrow night, anyhow,' I told him. 'You may change your mind when you meet this girl. I am having the younger crowd in for a little party and she will be among them. Her name is Maud Gage. She comes from Fayetteville and she and your cousin Josephine room together at Cornell University. They're home for the holidays.'

" 'Tell me what she's like,' Frank said.

" 'Well, she's different from the girls you've known around here. Pretty, but independent, with a mind and will of her own. She's twenty years old and lots of fun.' "

The following evening Baum found his friends gathered in Harriet's home. As he came across the drawing room and greeted his sister, his Aunt Josephine took the arm of a young woman standing nearby, brought her over, and said, "This is my nephew, Frank. Frank, I want you to know Maud Gage. I'm sure you will love her."

"Considered yourself loved, Miss Gage," was Baum's smiling acknowledgment of the introduction.

"Thank you, Mr. Baum," she replied as she held out her hand. "That's a promise. Please see that you live up to it."

Before the week was out Baum knew that he had at last found the girl he could stay interested in. But several other swains divided her attentions, and he and Maud were no more than good friends when he returned to *The Maid of Arran* company after New Year's Day and she went back to her sophomore year at Cornell University.

"During the following summer," Baum remembered later, "my show had some free time between bookings. At every opportunity I returned to Syracuse, borrowed a horse and buggy from father, and drove the eight miles to Fayetteville. The Gage home there was an attractive house with colonial pillars, built in 1805, roomy and comfortably furnished. There were front and back parlors with sliding doors between. We were in the front parlor when Maud finally consented to become my wife. Then she asked me to wait there while she told her mother.

"Mrs. Gage was in the back parlor and, although the

doors were closed, I could not avoid hearing what was said. The old lady told Maud in no uncertain terms that she objected to her marrying an actor who was on the road most of the time, jumping from town to town on one night stands, and with an uncertain future.

"I heard Mrs. Gage say: 'I won't have my daughter be a darned fool and marry an actor.' Maud snapped back: 'All right, mother, if you feel that way about it, good bye.' 'What do you mean, good bye?' Mrs. Gage demanded. 'Well,' Maud replied, 'you just told me I would be a darned fool to marry an actor, and you wouldn't have a daughter of yours do that. I'm going to marry Frank, so, naturally, you don't want a darned fool around the house.'

"Then Mrs. Gage laughed and said: 'All right, Maud. If you are in love with him and really determined to marry him, you can have your wedding right here at home.' "

This clash of wills is indicative of the family into which Baum was planning to marry. Maud's grandfather, Dr. Hezekiah Joslyn, had brought his bride to the big house* in Fayetteville in 1825. He was an ardent abolitionist, and his house became a station on the Underground Railway; a series of refuges that passed from one station to the next, fugitive slaves seeking safety in Canada. He instructed his daughter, Matilda Electa Joslyn, born in 1826, in Greek, Latin, mathematics and medicine. She grew up in the company of such notables as Susan B. Anthony, Elizabeth Cady Stanton, William Lloyd Garrison, Wendell Phillips, Julia Ward Howe, Lucretia Mott and Henry Ward Beecher, who at various times were house guests of the Joslyns, and, later, of the Gages.

* 210 East Genesee Street.

Miss Anthony was such a frequent visitor that one of the bedrooms was reserved for her use. In the course of her visits she scratched her signature, with a diamond ring, on a pane of glass in one window of the room. This is still preserved. Joslyn's daughter Matilda threw her crusading spirit into the cause of women's suffrage, and with Miss Anthony and Mrs. Stanton, wrote the four volume *History of Woman Suffrage* and edited *The National Citizen and Ballot Box*. She also wrote *Woman, Church and State,* a book which attacked governments, and particularly the Roman Catholic church on the grounds that they did not grant rights or dignity to women.

Married at nineteen to Henry Hill Gage, merchant and Erie Canal boat operator, Matilda had four children, of whom Maud was the youngest, the darling of the family and greatly indulged. Maud had long dark hair, merry mischievous eyes, a slightly retroussé nose and skin remarkably clear and soft—a quality which she retained until her death at the age of ninety-two. She was above average in height, had a singularly well formed figure, and was accounted a beauty.

She became Baum's bride on November 9, 1882 in the handsome Victorian front parlor of the Gage home with its heavy, carved, black walnut furniture, horsehair upholstered chairs and sofa, and a bookcase topped with a stuffed owl. The minister was the Reverend William H. Hawley of the Fayetteville Baptist Church. The young couple spent their honeymoon in Saratoga Springs, a fashionable resort north of Albany, where Maud could parade her wardrobe with its wasp-waisted gowns, tight skirts and high heeled shoes so small that a mincing gait was not only fashionable but compulsory.

Baum had interrupted his western tour with *The Maid*

of Arran company for the wedding and honeymoon. Immediately afterwards, he and his bride headed west with the company to Kalamazoo, Michigan, made a swing down into northern Indiana through Elkhart and South Bend, and into chilly Kansas for a December performance at Lawrence. On the company's return trip, it stopped off in London, Ontario, in January of 1883, and completed the tour with bookings in Massachusetts, Connecticut, Pennsylvania, and New Jersey.

After these months of living out of suitcases in small and often distasteful hotels and theatrical boarding houses, Maud decided that it was time to establish a permanent home where their first child would be born. Baum engaged a new leading man for *The Maid of Arran*, broke in a new manager, and rented a house at 8 (now 107) Shonnard Street in Syracuse, where their first baby—a boy —arrived on December 4, 1883. He was named Frank Joslyn—Frank for his father and Joslyn from the family name of Maud's mother.

Frank Baum was from the first a devoted parent. He played with the baby for hours, until Maud protested he was spoiling the child. Nevertheless he spent whole evenings rocking his son in his arms and crooning him to sleep with the old nursery song:

> Bye, Baby Bunting,
> Papa's gone a-hunting;
> Just to get a rabbit skin
> To wrap his Baby Bunting in.

From this the baby's family and kinfolk nicknamed him Bunny—a name that clung to him until he entered grammar school.

With the income from *The Maid of Arran* and his chain of small theaters, Baum had leisure to enjoy his new family and support it in comfort. He and Maud also became active in Syracuse's social life. Some years later a Syracuse newspaper, in mentioning his success as a writer, commented that "while in Syracuse, he was popular in society. A writer of short stories, a poultry fancier, a musician and actor and a jolly, good-hearted fellow, he is remembered by hundreds of friends as a witty and droll but most enjoyable companion."

Despite all these advantages of situation and fortune, Frank and Maud Baum did not settle down into a placid, Gilded Age domestic routine without some temperamental difficulties and stresses. His early years had been sunny and carefree, spent in a family that had adjusted early to the new industrialism and materialism of the era. He was adventurous, easygoing, and as his sister Mary once remarked, a dedicated optimist who saw the silver lining in every cloud. Years of living in the shadow of a heart ailment had taught him to avoid upsets that might bring on an attack.

His young wife, however, had grown up in a sterner school which for all its advanced social ideas was actually truer to an older tradition than to the bustling and more carefree present. In the long years of her widowhood, Maud Baum often mentioned that peace and harmony had always graced her home, but those who knew the family best felt that this was true only because Frank, from the time of their marriage until his death thirty-seven years later, allowed her to have her own way with the household, the children, and the family purse. Only because of his easy nature and because he remained all

those years very much in love with her, was he able philo-
sophically to accept her often unpredictable temper.

Together they knew lean times and times of prosperity
as Baum, an exemplar of the versatility and enterprise
demanded from men in those times, tried many avenues to
success until he hit upon the one that brought him recognition and economic security. Through it all, Maud managed the household capably and reared four sons into
successful adulthood, not, however, without occasional
storms. More than one incident remembered from these
early days in Syracuse illustrate the adjustment problems
of the young parents.

When Frank Joslyn Baum was about three years old he
disappeared from sight while the Baums were visiting the
Gage home in Fayetteville. Frank and Maud searched the
house until they found their son sitting very still in a small
closet under the hall stairway. As he smiled shyly at them
from his cramped hiding place, they saw to their horror he
was clutching two open razors—the old-fashioned, keenly-
honed, broad-bladed sort—one in each little fist. Afraid
that they might startle him and cause him suddenly to
close his tiny hands on the sharp edges, both feared to
move. Then Maud slowly turned away, and running to
her mother she burst into tears. But Baum began to sing
a lullaby and simultaneously to creep into the tiny closet
on hands and knees until he reached the boy's side. Then,
as he caught the child's attention by whispering a little
story, he carefully opened the baby's hands, finger by
finger, until he was able to remove the razors without dam-
age. Maud's reaction on her return, however, was to scold
her husband for leaving the razors where little hands could
reach them.

On another summer day in Fayetteville, Maud and her

mother were busy in the big kitchen making fans of wall-paper—a current fad. The fans were about two feet high with a spread of some forty inches. They were made of strips of fancy, highly-colored wallpaper held together with paste of cooked laundry starch. Such fans were tacked up in living rooms for decoration, and there was quite a rivalry to see who could combine the greatest variety of patterns and colors to get the most "elegant" effect.

Maud and her mother had just prepared a batch of starch paste and put it in a large dish pan to cool on the back steps. While it cooled, Maud dressed her two small sons, Frank and Robert, in white sailor suits for their father's arrival by horse and buggy from Syracuse. The two women were cutting strips of wallpaper when they heard a scream. Rushing to the back steps, they saw that Frank had fallen into the pan of paste and rolled down the steps into the dirt. Garden soil was literally glued all over his hands, face, and what had shortly before been an immac-ulate white suit. Maud scrubbed him, spanked him and dressed him in his last clean white suit. Presently Baum drove up, and she topped off her account of the day's events with the incident of the paste.

Baum took the child by the hand, walked with him to the kitchen and asked how the accident had happened. His son said: "I'll show you," and walked to the kitchen door. On the same steps a new pan of paste was cooling. The boy turned to smile up at his father, one foot slipped, he tumbled into the paste and rolled again into the dirt. This was too much for Maud. She rushed the child to her room, scrubbed and spanked him again—this time with the back of a hairbrush until his little bare bottom was fiery red—and put him to bed without his supper.

The child's sobs echoed through the house, and the family ate dinner in strained silence. After the meal was finished, Baum disregarded Maud's protest and took a plate of food to the child's bedroom. Then while he fed his namesake, he told one of his stories of enchanted countries, and watched beside the bed until the child drifted off to sleep.

To conform with fashions of the day, this same young man, until he was six years old, wore long yellow curls and a Scotch kilt with a black velvet jacket. In such a costume he had to learn early how to take his own part against the mobs of boys in knee breeches and long black stockings who mocked his appearance whenever he went down the street.

Another long remembered matrimonial crisis became known in the family as "the affair of the Bismarks." One evening during his first year of married life, Baum brought home a dozen of the round, fried, jelly-filled pastries known as Bismarks. When he put the sack on the kitchen table, Maud bristled and tartly demanded to know whether he was dissatisfied with the food *she* bought and prepared. He assured her he liked her meals but, with a smile, he also liked Bismarks for breakfast.

Now a Frank Baum breakfast was a hearty meal by any standard. After several kinds of fruit he liked a dish of hot oatmeal with sugar and heavy cream; then either a steak, lamb chops, fried ham, fried codfish or finnan haddie. With the meat or fish he demanded thick gravy and a plate of fresh hot bread with plenty of butter and fried potatoes. All this was floated down with five or six cups of coffee fortified with sugar and cream—coffee strong enough "to float a spoon on it without sinking" as he expressed it.

The first morning after bringing home the Bismarks,

Frank topped off his breakfast with two of them. The second morning he had two more. When Maud slapped a plate with eight Bismarks before him on the third morning, he suggested they were getting stale. Maud replied coldly that he had bought them and he would have to eat them. She refused to have anything to do with such indigestible stuff. Baum pushed them aside and went on with his breakfast.

The eight stale Bismarks came to the table on the fourth morning. After breakfast Baum wrapped them in a newspaper and hid them in a kitchen cupboard. When they showed up at breakfast on the fifth morning, Maud's only comment was: "It seems as if we are playing games, doesn't it?"

After breakfast he wrapped them again and buried them in a corner of the garden. But Maud dug them up, washed off the dirt, and had them on the table on the sixth morning. Baum protested, "For Heaven's sake, Maud, let's stop this nonsense. Those things are not fit to eat and you know it."

"You bought them without consulting me," she replied, "so you will have to eat them. I am not going to have food wasted. But I'll let you off this time if you will promise never again to buy any food unless I ask you to get it."

He agreed and "the affair of the Bismarks" was over. But it had taught him a lesson he never forgot: that Maud in her way was as stout a battler for "women's rights" as her mother had ever been and that around the house she was the boss.

V

THE TROUGH OF THE WAVE

ONCE SETTLED in Syracuse, Baum was drawn into the family oil business. *The Maid of Arran* company seems to have gone on without him for the rest of the 1883 season, for in 1885 the *Syracuse Journal* mentions that it had "experienced two successful seasons in the principal cities of the United States." An advertisement in the *Courier* of July 9, 1883 announced a new oil store, dealing in all grades of machine, engine, cylinder and paraffine oils, as well as sperm, lard and neat's foot and sewing machine oil, hoof ointment, petroleum (U.S.P.), (presumably for medical use), family safety oil and axle grease, "at bottom prices." Proprietor of the store at 70 East Water Street was L. B. Baum, doubtless a misprint of the initials of the erstwhile playwright.

Baum had suffered one heart attack shortly before his marriage, and in the summer of 1883 his uncertain health was indicated by nausea and dizzy spells. According to family tradition, he had been working long hours to complete a new play, *Kilmourne,* which was never copyrighted, or, so far as is known, professionally performed. On April 4, 1883, however, an amateur group in Syracuse, the Young

52

Men's Dramatic Club, gave *Kilmourne, or O'Connor's Dream,* at the Weiting Opera House. The playbill invited theater goers to "come and enjoy a night in Ireland with the Irish."

Even though the routine of running a retail outlet for his father's Bolivar Oil Works was far removed from the excitement and glamor of trouping with his own road company, Baum seems to have settled down successfully into this conventional life. Actually he was about to enter the first crisis of a long series. He was twenty-eight, and behind him lay a happy childhood in a privileged home, flattering success as actor, playwright and producer, a happy marriage and a young son to carry his name. Beyond the present crest of his wave of happiness, however, lay the trough, which was to toss him violently on the cross-currents and riptides of the Gilded Age.

Sometime in 1884, John Wesley Baum, Frank's uncle and business manager of his theatrical enterprises, became seriously ill, and a bookkeeper was employed to take over his responsibilities. Frank habitually paid little attention to money, but the more practical Maud soon noticed that the weekly checks were becoming smaller and smaller. She kept after her husband and Uncle John to investigate. But Baum was busy writing another play, *The Queen of Killarney,* which had been commissioned by Joe Scanlon for production in Rochester,* and by the time Baum's Uncle John was well enough to return to the office, he and Baum found gross mismanagement and such inadequate bookkeeping that it was impossible to make an audit. While the investigation was under way the bookkeeper disap-

* Scanlon died while the play was in rehearsal, and it never reached the stage.

peared. At this critical point, the affair reached a climax worthy of a melodrama of the times, when word came that the town of Gillmor had burned, and with it Baum's theater and the costumes, scenery, and properties for *The Maid of Arran* and other plays. By the time all accounts had been settled, Baum's realty holdings, including the string of small theaters acquired from his father, the production rights of *The Maid of Arran* and all his other ready assets had been sacrificed.

Baum's elder brother, Benjamin William, had organized a chemical manufacturing company in Buffalo, which he had recently moved to Syracuse under the name of Baum's Castorine Company. An advertisement in the *Syracuse Journal* of January 14, 1885, describes the company as "manufacturers of the great lubricant, Castorine, the best axle oil in use," which was to be had at drugstores and hardware stores and at the manufactory, 70 East Water Street, which was the address of Frank Baum's oil store. Frank's uncle, Dr. Adam Clark Baum, was listed in the advertisement as manager, and Frank, under the name of Louis F. Baum, was described in city directories as superintendent. Thus Baum was rescued by acquiring a place in another business, and a thriving one at that, for this was the heydey of the horse-drawn vehicle—wagon, cart, dray and coach—all with squeaky wheels. Tallow, whale oil, and other lubricants used on the axles had drawbacks. The petroleum lubricant, however, which Brother Will had developed had a consistency like castor oil and, as the Castorine Company advertisement boasted, "will not gum or chill and is ever ready for use."

Frank Baum, despite his title, appears to have become head salesman. He went on the road to tell druggists and hardware men about the new product, while Uncle Doc, as Adam Baum was called by the family, remained in the office to look after the books and oversee the factory. Frank presumably was energetic and enthusiastic, and the product must have had merit, for it seems to have sold well. Presently the little company had enough retail outlets to create a thriving demand for Castorine.

But despite fortune's apparent favor, ill luck had not yet run its course. Frank's father, the elder Benjamin, financial mainstay of two generations, was injured while driving a colt recently broken to harness. The colt shied at a piece of paper blowing in the street, ran away, and wrecked the buggy against a hitching post. Benjamin Baum and a fourteen-year-old boy riding with him were thrown out. Baum suffered a severe injury when his head struck the cobblestones. He was ill for weeks until, dissatisfied with his slow recovery, he went to Germany for medical treatment. Brother Will also became ill at about this same time.

Benjamin Baum's affairs were badly administered while he was in Germany, and he returned to find that his wealth had dwindled. The one hundred and sixty acre commercial farm was sold to the Crouse family of Syracuse. Rose Lawn* was also disposed of, and Benjamin, his wife, and their son Harry moved to a smaller house in town, where two years after his accident, Benjamin Baum died, on February 14, 1887.

After Benjamin's death, Cynthia Baum and Harry moved to Spring Farm, which Harry operated for his mother for several years before he opened medical offices

* Where Rose Lawn stood is now the suburb of Mattydale, named for a hog-raising Syracuse alderman.

in Syracuse. The death of the elder Baum and the illness of Benjamin threw heavy responsibilities on the remaining brothers, and Frank's responsibilities had also been growing elsewhere. In February 1886, Maud gave birth to their second son in their new house on Slocum Avenue, where they had moved the year before, and seventeen days later Brother Benjamin died. Maud named the baby Robert Stanton Baum—Robert because her own grandmother had been born in Scotland, and Stanton from Grandmother Cynthia Baum's family name. In the midst of the rejoicing over the birth of her son, however, Maud became seriously ill of peritonitis and lay in bed for months, a drainage tube in her side, while she fought for life with all the resources of her superb constitution. Her husband, deeply worried and distracted by this latest misfortune, had little time to give to the Castorine business. Instead, he spent many hours at home every day so that he would be near if Maud needed him. He whiled away the time playing with their two children, singing to them, rocking them in his arms, keeping them quiet so that Maud would not be disturbed, and finding in them his refuge from anxiety.

Some months after Robert's birth, Maud was able to leave her bed long enough to be moved. Baum rented another house at 43½ (now 268-70) Holland Street, so that Maud and the two children could be near his sisters. There she could have companionship and help while he was absent, sometimes for weeks, selling Castorine on the road. As her convalescence lengthened into two years, Maud found it convenient to make many visits to her own family in Fayetteville. Often she and the two boys would be at the Gage home for several days at a time.

While Baum was busy developing the sales territory for his new lubricant, the office and manufacturing were left in the hands of Uncle Doc. More than two years of service in the Civil War as a surgeon* had left Uncle Doc with shattered health, and he was unable to give his full attention to the office of the Castorine Company, which was left to a clerk. In the spring of 1888 Baum returned to Syracuse early one morning from a sales trip and went directly to the office. He unlocked the door, entered, and was stunned to find the clerk sprawled across a desk—dead. The revolver with which he had shot himself was still in his hand. An audit disclosed that much of the firm's capital had been gambled away while bills had been allowed to pile up, unpaid. Baum's Castorine, despite its success in the trade, was barely solvent. Finally Frank sold the business to Marcus and Howard Stoddard, manufacturers of a scouring powder. Some thirty years later the Stoddards were still selling Baum's Castorine with the signature, "L. F. Baum" on the label.

This time Baum was left with some capital, but with the responsibility of planning a new course of his own. He and Maud talked it over. Her sisters, Helen (Mrs. Charles H. Gage) and Julia (Mrs. James D. Carpenter), and her brother, Thomas Clarkson Gage, were living in Dakota Territory. Their letters glowed with accounts of the prosperity to be found in the West where, they reported, vast fortunes were being made from cattle raising and wheat. It was an age when the eyes of the young, especially those who as yet had had no more than a glimpse of good fortune at home, were turning to the glowing promise of the fron-

* With the 50th Engineers.

tier. Maud urged that their future lay there. Baum hesitated. He liked Syracuse, his friends and relatives were in the East, and he was confident he could rebuild his fortunes there as he had done before. But at his wife's urging he agreed to make a trip and look things over.

Baum changed trains in Chicago, where six years ago he had come as the head of his own successful stage company. Fortune had treated him well then; now it had turned against him. But as he breathed the strong winds of the booming city by the lake, he regained some of his self-confidence. How much more optimistic he would have felt if he could have known that Chicago would be the cradle of his greatest success; that here, at last, he would find the pot of gold at the end of the elusive rainbow!

He spent ten days in several Minnesota towns and in St. Paul and Minneapolis but found little to lure him away from Syracuse. Then he took a train for Dakota Territory to see what the vast expanse of prairie so recently wrested from the Sioux had to offer.

VI

PIONEER DAYS IN
THE DAKOTAS

BAUM ARRIVED at Aberdeen in Dakota Territory on a warm
day in July, 1888. He swung off the train into a treeless
country town of three thousand persons—a town laid out
seven years before on the dry, flat prairie. Its settlers had
been drawn from the East by the discovery of gold in the
Black Hills in 1876 and by the distribution of free home-
stead lands. All of them were young, many were couples
with young children, and they included an unusually high
proportion of professional people and college graduates.
The first settlement had been abandoned when the Milwaukee Railroad came through the territory, and the
town was relocated on the railroad's right of way. It was
named after the native city of the road's general manager,
Alexander Mitchell.

For two weeks after his arrival Baum was a guest of his
brother and sister-in-law. Although the first flush of prosperity following the gold rush was past, the Gages and
their friends were convinced the decline in business was
only a lull. They gave Frank glowing accounts of the
Territory's natural advantages. As an inducement to move

to Aberdeen, Maud's elder sister, Helen, and her husband offered to rent Frank a store on a business property they owned. It was easy to catch their enthusiasm—the optimism of the frontier with its open spaces and fertile unfenced land. After talking with the town's business leaders Baum decided to move to the new country.

While he had been on the road with his stage company he had stopped in Utica, in New York State, and there had seen the first F. W. Woolworth store. Aberdeen had nothing of this type, and Frank felt sure that here was a splendid opening for a general notions store handling inexpensive merchandise. He leased space in the Gage Block at Fourth and Main Streets, and left late in July for Syracuse. On the way he stopped in Chicago long enough to place orders with wholesale houses for merchandise.

When he arrived home and told Maud of his decision she was greatly pleased. She at once went to work getting their household goods ready for the long trip West. After a number of farewell parties they left early in September and reached Aberdeen with their two babies a week later; tired, travel-worn but happy.

As soon as his family was sheltered as guests of Maud's brother, Clark, Baum began buying fixtures for his store. An old ledger records that he purchased:

Glass for signs	$ 3.50
Gum letters	1.60
2 Showcases	22.28
2 Iron stands	10.00
2 Counters	15.69
Money drawer	8.30
Freight (Show cases)	15.69
Cartage	.25
	77.31

Within a short time the Baums found a house on Ninth
Avenue and put into it the furniture they had brought
from Syracuse. Baum hired a clerk at five dollars a week
and a boy to make the fires at seventy-five cents a week,
and began to prepare for the grand opening of Baum's
Bazaar. But while the novelty of the new store attracted
patronage at first, Baum soon found that Aberdeen and
its back country were too sparsely settled for such a specialty as a "5¢ and 10¢ Store." Almost at once he began
adding higher priced goods to his stock, as may be seen
from one of the surviving early advertisements:

BAUM'S BAZAAR

Always in stock—

G.A.R. Flags	Japanese Goods
Chinese Lanterns	Children's Carriages
Express Wagons	The Grendon Velocipede
Crockery	Girls and Misses Tricycles
Glassware	Spalding's Sporting Goods
Tinware	Store and House Awnings
Lamps	Household Goods
Books-Stationery	Fancy Goods
Toys	Cigars and Cigarettes
Confectionary	Ice Cream and Sodas
Candy	Cuspidors, Hand Painted and Solid Brass

Adults who came to the store noticed that the tall, slim
proprietor was exceptionally well dressed. They admired
his tailor-made suits and high-button, black patent-leath-
er shoes, and they took as a sign of prosperity the heavy
gold watch chain spanning his waistcoat. On one end was
a large hunting case watch and on the other a well-worn

silver cigar clipper. Children, however, ignored the costume, and simply came to the store because they loved their genial friend behind the counter. The Bazaar always was crowded with youngsters after school. Some bought a penny's worth of candy or ice cream; others bought bottled pop. Many came just to hear the stories of magic and enchantment that Baum could be persuaded to tell.

Baum quickly made friends in Aberdeen, and he and Maud enjoyed the card parties and dances that constituted the social life of the town. Soon after his arrival, Baum organized and managed a baseball team that won the South Dakota championship. He also found time to become stage manager of the Drama Club of St. Mark's Episcopal Church. The little prairie town first became acquainted with the quality of his acting when he appeared in the play entitled—rather appropriately—*Everybody's Friend*. Later he was in charge of the Baby Show at the Opera House during the town's "Grand July 4 Celebration."

The Bazaar was busy the first month, and cash sales totaled $531.16. Not only, however, did the novelty wear off, but Aberdeen was sinking into depression which followed its first boom. Even well-to-do families leaned more and more heavily on credit. Baum continued to carry customers on his books until he had one hundred and sixty-one accounts past due. Of these, one hundred and five were never collected. Under such conditions, he could only watch helplessly as his stock dwindled and his capital disappeared. On New Year's Day, 1890, he closed the doors of the Bazaar for the last time.

Two weeks before, on December 17, the Baums' third child had been born. Frank and Maud had been so con-

fident that the baby would be a girl that they had chosen
the name Geraldine. But the baby was a boy and was
christened Harry Neal. A week later, there was a big
Christmas celebration at the house on Ninth Street. It was
one in a long line of family dinners, for Baum and Maud
enjoyed making occasions of holidays, just as later they
welcomed their son's wives and children into the family
circle at Christmas, New Year's, the Fourth of July, and
Thanksgiving. No matter how lean the purse—and it was
lean in Aberdeen at that early celebration in 1890 just as
it was to be many times later in Chicago—there was always
money enough for a family celebration.

After Baum closed the Bazaar, he faced 1890 with less
than a hundred dollars to his name. He was without a job
and without any prospect of one, but several times previously he had been in the same fix and he had always
come out all right. In spite of the economic depression of
that year, he refused to worry. He trusted his versatility.
And he was right; for events opened a new pathway in his
meandering course.

John B. Drake, a former resident of Syracuse, had established the *Dakota Pioneer,* a weekly newspaper, in Aberdeen in 1881. Now he was going to Kiel, Germany, as
United States consul. Drake had been appointed by President Benjamin Harrison as a reward for his services to
the Republican party in Dakota Territory. Drake knew
Baum from his Syracuse days, and he knew that Baum
had closed the Bazaar. Drake did not need his newspaper
any more; Baum needed an occupation. When he suggested that his fellow townsman buy the *Pioneer* on small
monthly payments, the opportunity seemed providential
to a young man who had never lost his boyhood liking for

the smell of printer's ink. Completing the deal did not take long. In January, 1890, less than a month after Baum's Bazaar had closed, its former proprietor issued the first number of his paper, whose title he enlarged to *The Aberdeen Saturday Pioneer.*

For a small prairie community, Aberdeen was generously supplied with newspapers. Besides the *Pioneer* it had two other weeklies, the *Star* and the *Republican,* and a daily, the *News.* Keeping up with the competition, especially in a depression, called for all the enterprise and talent at Baum's command. Few printers were available because the flow of land seekers to the West had almost ceased. Many times Baum found himself literally a one-man newspaper. He collected and wrote the news and editorials, solicited advertisements, set type by hand and ran off the edition on an old flat bed press. In his leisure hours he took care of work in the job printing shop where, traditionally, a small town weekly makes most of its profit.

Busy though he was, however, he did not forget the junior patrons of the Bazaar days, and they did not forget him. Often, as Baum would walk down the streets of Aberdeen on his rounds for news and advertising, he would be stopped by children demanding a story. He would sit down on the edge of the dusty wooden sidewalk, gather the children around him, perhaps make room for a curious adult or two, and spin one of his yarns of magic countries. Whenever he went near the Red Front Store, a popular place with the children of Aberdeen, he could be sure of a group waiting for him to drop a few pennies in the candy machine near the entrance and pass out "red hots" or jaw breakers to his junior following.

Baum's most memorable contribution to journalism

Benjamin Ward Baum (above, left) and Cynthia Stanton Baum (above, right), parents of L. Frank Baum; drawing of a Castorine can from a Syracuse directory (center); Dr. Henry Clay Baum (below, left), Baum's favorite brother, and Adam Clark Baum (below, right), his "Uncle Doc."

L. Frank Baum in his New York days as an actor, from a picture taken in 1881 when he was 25 years old.

Advertisement for L. Frank Baum's first literary success, *The Maid of Arran,* in which he played the leading part on the stage for several years. John W. Baum was his uncle, and Katharine Gray his aunt.

William W. Denslow at his drawing board (above). Book jacket of *Father Goose His Book* in background dates picture about 1900. Paul Tietjens, composer of the music for *The Wizard of Oz,* at his desk (below).

Dave Montgomery as the Tin Woodman and Fred Stone as the Scarecrow in
The Wizard of Oz, 1902 (above). Dorothy, played by Anna Laughlin, with
her cow, Imogene, played by Fred Stone's brother, Edwin, as they discover
Fred Stone as the Scarecrow, in a scene from the same production (below).

Bessie Wynn as Sir Dashemoff Daily (above, left), and Jeanette Lowrie as the Lady Lunatic (above, right) in *The Wizard of Oz*, 1902. Chorus girls in their costumes from the 1902 production (below).

Anna Laughlin, the Dorothy of *The Wizard of Oz*, 1902, in her costume.

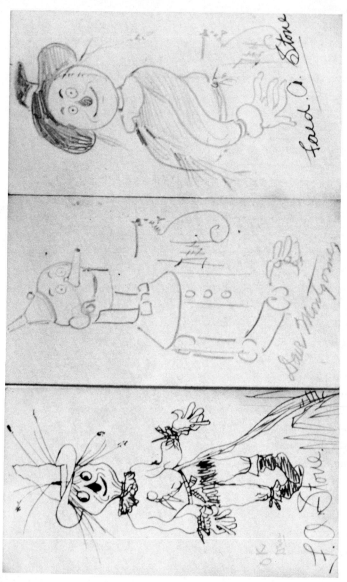

Sketches made by William W. Denslow at rehearsals of *The Wizard of Oz* in 1902, showing Fred Stone and Dave Montgomery in costume. The drawings, signed by the two stars, were made on calling cards of W. T. (Biff) Hall, police magistrate and noted Chicago newspaper man.

and to the gaiety of Aberdeen was a column, "Our Landlady," which he started during January, 1890. In the form
of what purported to be dialogue between residents of
a boarding house—the sort of wry exchange made famous
by Oliver Wendell Holmes in *The Autocrat of the
Breakfast Table* and imitated later by John Kendrick
Bangs in *Coffee and Repartee,* and by other humorists—
Baum commented on affairs close to the hearts and purses
of Aberdeen readers. It was a device he used for humor,
social satire, character portrayal, personal comment, and
fantasy. A typographical error involved him in the only
frontier style personal encounter of his journalistic career.
According to the tradition still alive in Aberdeen, Baum,
in reporting a wedding, described the bride as having a "roguish smile," but unfortunately this appeared in
the *Pioneer* as a "roughish smile." The bridegroom took
offense and challenged Baum to a duel. As the challenged
party, the editor chose revolvers as the weapons. Their
seconds arranged that the duelists were to walk away from
each other, proceed around the block and fire whenever
they came within sight of each other. Both duelists, it is
remembered, while on their way around the block chose
to retreat down the first alley they came to, and made up
their differences later in a more peaceful fashion.

On December 6, 1890 appeared an "Our Landlady"
column that barely conceals under its clowning the bitter
feelings in Aberdeen over hard times and the apprehen-
siveness of the citizens at the threat of the "Messiah War,"
which was the last Indian uprising in the West. The "Messiah War" took shape when a Paiute Indian, Wawoka,
started a religious movement aimed at driving out the
whites. He had the original idea of enlisting the ghosts

of braves gone to the Happy Hunting Grounds and summoning them to the aid of the living. Wawoka and his followers had gathered in the Black Hills to evoke the departed spirits by means of a "Ghost Dance." The whites paid only cursory attention until they learned that Sitting Bull, one of the chiefs who had wiped out General George Custer's command at the Battle of the Little Big Horn, was preparing to join the ghost dancers.

It was against the background of these events that Baum sent his fictitious Landlady, Mrs. Bilkins, to interview the Indian chief. When the redskin saw her coming he started to run away. She reported the encounter in this fashion:

"Here you, Hole-in-the-Face," says I fiercely, "what do you mean by running away?"

Now Hole-in-the-Face comes up kinder sad an' says: "Don't hurt me, Miss Bilkins, an' we'll never do it again."

"Why should I hurt you?"

"Why, the scouts is all bringin' in word that the whites is all risin' against the Injuns. Candidate Afraid-of-his-Pocketbook was in camp this mornin' an' said the rumors o' the whites risin' that we'd heard was all true. He said the whites was all starvin' in Dakota, an' the givernment wouldn't give 'em any rations, an' they was comin' to rob us Injuns o' what we had. I tell you, the Injuns is pretty skeert an' they're leavin' their homes an' banding together for mutual pertection."

"But what about the ghost dance?" says I.

"Why," says he, "we live in a free country. We Injuns can vote an' you wimmin can't. Religion is free as water, an' much more plenty. Here we Injuns has been drawin' rations from the givernment an' layin' by our savin's 'tell we got in pretty fair shape, an' jest when we least expect it, here comes a risin' o' the starved whites, an' they're liable to swoop down on us at any minit an' rob us o' all we possess."

"No," I says, "they're afraid o' you swoopin' down on them."

He laughed sourkastically. "What have they got we want?" says he. "Nothin'! But the Injuns has got lots that the givernment has give 'em that the whites would like to have for themselves. My braves is gettin' anxious to move their property out o' harm's way, so good day ter you."

Baum would not have been a small town newspaper man if he had passed up the opportunity to bludgeon the other Aberdeen editors with a closing jibe. As Mrs. Bilkins returns and recounts her Indian adventure to the rival newspapers, she is curtly rebuffed with the remark, "We ain't lookin' for truth—can get all we want for a cent a line, but a good lie is worth a dollar a word to us any minit."

Ten days after the column appeared Sitting Bull was killed by army Indian police sent to restrain him from leaving for the Black Hills. A few days later, Custer's old regiment, the Seventh Calvary, slaughtered an entire village of Sioux—three hundred men, women and children—at Wounded Knee Creek when the villagers attempted to escape from a roundup to return them to their reservation.

On February 8, 1891, the "Our Landlady" column dripped gall on the only big business in the Dakotas—the railroad, which totally dominated the local economy, and in the same issue looked forward with prophetic relish to a day of air transportation. Although Samuel P. Langley had started investigation of heavier than air craft in 1887, he did not make a flying model until 1896, and the Wright Brothers did not make a successful flight until seven years later, in December, 1903. Nevertheless, Baum had a true vision of what might occur in the future. When the results of Langley's studies were published* in 1891, Baum wrote:

"I read in the papers," said our Landlady, as she finished sewing a button on the doctor's overcoat and bit off the thread as a woman will, "that the great airship is going ter be a success, after all."

"If it does," said Tom, "the railroad will be ruined."

"An' serve 'em right," exclaimed our Landlady, taking her gum from the inside band of the Colonel's Sunday hat. "They beat the people long enough and tyrannized over 'em with a rod o' iron, an' I, fer one, will be glad ter see 'em shut up shop. An airship can call fer ye at your own residence, whenever ye hoist a signal flag. People will own their private ships too, an' go where they pleases, an' if anyone wants ter quit Dakoty, why then they can step inter their airships an' float around till they come to a place as is got a crop. There's other things that private airships is good fer. You can go on a picnic any time you like an' take the whole family. The hired man can use it to go arter the cow with, an' it will save the labor o' leadin' her home by hitchin' her to the ship an' skimmin' along the surface o' the ground. At election time they can make the pollin' places airships, an' when the ballot closes the ship can rise ter a moderate distance where the candidates can watch 'em, an' the votes can be counted without any chance o' further contests. Stanley won't be anywheres. If a feller wants to explore Africa he can do it with neatness and dispatch in his airship. If he wants to go to the North Pole, he can do so—pervided he don't freeze. A trip to Europe will be as cheap as livin' at home, for all you need is a stock of provisions."

The Landlady's best claim to the interest of posterity, however, rests on her visit to Downditch Farm, a fiction in which Baum let his imagination wander so happily that

* "Experiments in Aerodynamics."

many conveniences of today, but unknown in his time, were foreshadowed. Three years before, Edward Bellamy's *Looking Backward* had held out the vision of a utopia made possible by the wonders of mechanical invention as well as by social reorganization. Baum's column may have been half meant as a gentle satire on Bellamy's popular novel. In the issue of January 3, 1891, Baum wrote:

"Gentlemen," said our Landlady, as she entered the room in which the boarders were at supper and threw her hat on the sideboard and hung her shawl over the doctor's head. "This kind o' life ain't worth the livin', an' if I ever were sick of this air boardin' house, I am this minit."

"What's wrong?" inquired the colonel wonderingly. "I thought you had been on a visit to the Updyke Farm, and to have you come home in such a humor as this is astonishing."

"Updyke!" cried our Landlady with an unmistakable sneer. "I ain't been near that wretched hole; but I've been to a much more wonderful place."

"Indeed," quoth Tom, "here—sit right down in this chair and let me feed you scalloped oysters while you tell us all about it."

"All right, but don't interrupt me, for every word I'm goin' to say is gospel truth. Well, you know I set out fer the Updyke Farm. I got the best directions I could an' traveled over the prairie 'til I most thought I'd lost my way. By and by I come ter a feller swiftly ridin' along in a wagon. I rubbed my eyes in amazement fer a minit, 'cause there was no hoss ner beast o' any kind hitched to it.* Then I yells 'hullup.' He did, comin' to a period right by me."

"A period?"

"Well, a full stop. I asked him how in blazes he made his wagon go by itself."

* The first "horseless carriage" in the United States was manufactured by Charles and Frank Duryea in 1892—almost *two years after* Baum wrote this. Ford's first experimental car was made in 1893.

" ' 'Lectricity,' says he: 'ye see the machinery is stored under the seat. All I have to do when I want to go is press a button an' she rushes.'

" 'How do you guide it?' said I.

" 'By this little wheel—like steerin' a ship. It beats bicycles 'cause you can carry a load an' it ain't no exertion.'

" 'Who invented it?' says I.

" 'Downditch,' says he.

" 'Well,' says I, 'can you tell me where this Updyke farm is?'

" 'Updyke,' says he, thinkitively, 'why he used to work for Downditch but his farm's a good way off—on the other side of Aberdeen.'

" 'Dear me,' says I, 'then I've walked all this way fer nothin! I wanted ter see all the wonders he does with 'lectricity an' a artesian well.'

" 'Humph,' says he. 'Why don't you go to Downditches? Beats Updyke's all holler. Jest take this trail to the right an' it'll fetch ye there. So long!'

"He teched his button an' the wagon whirled away, an' I thought my best plan was ter follow his advice, so I took the path ter the right, an' by and by I come to a lot of buildings all clustered together an' painted pure white.

"The biggest one, all wings an' angles an' coverin' about a acre o' ground, I tuk to be the house, so I wandered up to the front door, an' seein' a 'lectric button, I pushed it.

"Instantly the door flew open an' I started to step inside, but my feet went out from under me an' I went kerflop inter a big armchair, which was on rollers an' started at once to move down the hall with me in it. A door opened as we come to it, an' jest as we passed through, some little steel arms jumped up an' untied an' took off my bunnit an' jerked off my shawl, an' away we glided to another door. This opened automatically too, an' we entered a small room that I took ter be a study. In it was a thoughtful lookin' man who looked up and bowed pleasantly as my chair stopped alongside o' his'n.

" 'How do, Mrs. Bilkins,' says he.

" 'Howdy,' says I, 'but how did you know my name?'

" 'It was written inside your shawl,' says he, 'an' the machine that took it off read it and telephoned it ter me.'

"I looked at him in wonder. He smiled and teched a button on his vest. Instantly a handkerchief flew out of his pocket, wiped his nose an' went back again, all of its own accord.

" 'May I ask your name?' says I.

"He touched another button on his vest an' a card flopped out of his buzzom which read *Aesop Downditch, Scientist. Born Ipswitch, 1821, graduated at Redfield College; fur further particulars, see biography, price $1.00. For sale here.*

" 'You must be my guest until tomorrow, Mrs. Bilkins,' says he. 'Let me interjuice ye to my wife an' dorter.' He teched a button on the table an' instantly two doors opened on opposite sides o' the room, an' his wife an' dorter rolled in on chairs an' smiled and bowed. Mr. Downditch interjuced me an' soon we was all buzzom friends.

" 'It's time fer dinner, papa,' says Clarabel, his dorter.

"Mr. Downditch teched a buttom on his vest an' his watch flew outer his pocket an' opened in front o' him.

" 'So it is,' says he, 'how tempus does fugit.'

"He an' his wife an' dorter then all teched a little button that was on the outside of their chairs, an' a wash rag o' satin came out an' washed an' dried their faces quickly an' gently. I did the same thing an' I must say such an invention removes all the terrors o' wash day.

" 'How is this did?' says I.

" 'All 'lectricity,' says he, smilin'. 'The power to run the motor is furnished by our artesian well, an' by a little invention I have arranged so that all the little household and personal duties are performed by 'lectrical apparatus. It saves us no end o' trouble.' He teched a button on the table as he spoke an' at once the table sunk through the floor an' another rose in its place, all set fer dinner an' kivered with the most luxuriest meal you ever heard of. There was nineteen courses an' eatables o' every description, from peaches an' cream to fried manna with nectar sauce. I tell you, fellers, such board is worth a hundred

dollars a week. We ate and drunk all we could—that is, I
did, an' when we was through the table disappeared
through the floor again.

"'Who washed the dishes?' says I.

"'We employ the same agent that prepares the food an'
sets the table—'lectricity,' says Missus Downditch. 'But it's
time fer the theater; would you like to attend it, Mrs.
Bilkins, afore you retire for the night?'

"'You bet,' say I. 'I want to take in the whole aggrega-
tion afore I leaves. It'll make the folks in Aberdeen sick
when I tells 'em about it.'

"Mr. Downditch touched a button on his vest an'
shrugged his shoulders by 'lectricity.

"'It ain't any mor'n any of 'em can have,' says he, 'if
they puts down artesian wells and utilizes the water properly. I bid you good evenin', Mrs. Bilkins.'

"As the chairs of us three ladies moved away I saw Mr.
Downditch press a button an' open his mouth, an' the
next instant a lighted cigar was in his mouth, an' he was
puffin' away contentedly. I tell you I wished I could bring
that vest home to you boarders. It would surprise you, but
I 'spose Downditch couldn't spare it. Well, the room we
was wheeled to was furnished just like a Oproar House.

"'It's a model o' the Madison Square Theater,' says
Missus Downditch. A big phonograph played the over-
ture, an' then characters o' the play came out an' acted.
They was all dummies with phonographs inside 'em, an'
the power was furnished by the artesian well. It was a
good show, though, an' after it was over I bid the ladies
good night.

"'When you get to your room,' says Missus Downditch,
'tech that air button on the side o' yer chair.'

"Then the chair started and wheeled me through the
halls till it finally entered a good sized room. The only
piece o' furniture in it were the bed, but it was a corker.
The head of it was as high as the ceiling, an' was sunk
inter the wall, an' jest above the pillars was a row of buttons. It had a lace cover an' looked so soft I wished I didn't
have to undress afore I got inter it. But I remembered
what Missus Downditch had said, so I pressed the button
on the chair.

"Instantly a number o' steel arms shot out an' undressed me in a jiffy an' flung a embroidered nightgown over my head, an' there I was! Afore I recovered from my surprise the blamed thing lifted me up an' shot me inter bed, the bedclothes turning down jest afore I landed. The bed was nice and warm, being heated by 'lectricity. As my head teched the pillar it set off a music box that played 'Hard Times Come Again No More' until I was fast asleep. I woke up in the morning, feelin' as happy as a editor who'se got a new subscriber, and lay there thinkin' what a glorious thing artesian wells is. As I did so my eye caught the row o' buttons on the headboard. I teched one an' a large, box-like lookin' thing swooped out in front o' me, with a rubber tube hanging to it which plumped inter my mouth. The box had several buttons labeled coffee, tea, chocolate, rum punch, water, an' so forth. In spite o' me I winked at the one what said rum punch, an' it was so delicately adjusted that it set the thing off, an' I tell you it was a drink worthy o' Taubman.*

"I teched the next button an' my face was washed in a jiffy. The next one brushed my hair an' done it up; the next one shot me outer bed plump inter the chair. By techin' the same button I did last night, I was dressed an' then the chair moved away toward the breakfast room.

"Mr. Downditch greeted me with a smile an' asked if I had rested well. I told him I had an' then I set to work on the best breakfast I ever tackled. Mr. Downditch then excused hisself as he had some business to tend to, an' he bid me good-bye with a smile, an' left.

" 'What a nice man your husband is,' says I to Missus Downditch, 'he is allus smilin'.'

" 'Oh, yes,' says she. 'He smiles by 'lectricity.' "

Frontier journalism is usually deadly personal or deadly dull. Baum managed to avoid both evils by his sprightly column and his deft way with social news, while he kept his personalities under better control than most editors of his time.

---

* E. T. Taubman was an Aberdeen attorney noted for his familiarity with liquor.

But readability was not enough. Business was depressed; lack of rain had ruined the crops and the farmers were broke. When the federal farm agent asked a farmer whether he had feed for his horses, according to Baum's Landlady the farmer replied, "No, I put green goggles on my horses and feed 'em shavings an' they think it's grass, but they ain't gettin' fat on it." Later, when he wrote *The Wizard of Oz*, Baum must have recalled this column; for he prepared Dorothy and her companions for entrance into the Emerald City by putting green spectacles on them.

In spite of Baum's ingenuity, however, the pulse of the *Saturday Pioneer*—its circulation—grew more and more feeble. By February, 1891 the advertising revenue could no longer be stretched to pay even the running expenses of the paper and buy food and shelter for the Baum family. A surviving letter from that period makes clear the desperate straits of the paper and the unfailing humor and good spirits of its proprietor.

An Eastern patent medicine manufacturer had written Baum, asking why advertising rates in the *Saturday Pioneer* were higher than those in other Western weeklies and whether the size and scope of the circulation justified the rates. Baum replied that the circulation of his weekly had dropped from three thousand five hundred to one thousand four hundred with most of the circulation concentrated in the West, except a few copies to the East and one to Drake in Germany. It was with the greatest difficulty, he added, that he managed to keep the whole circulation from going to hell. Finally, at the end of March, Baum recognized that "the sheriff wanted the paper more than I did—so I let him have it." On March 24, three days after the sheriff took possession of the *Saturday Pioneer*, the Baum's fourth son was born in their house on Kline street. He was named Kenneth Gage. To well-wishers the father remarked that although he had lost a paper he had gained a son.

Thus, the lean Dakota years had defeated him twice. There seemed no likelihood of returning prosperity in the new state for some time, and Baum looked back East, remembering particularly the bustling city by the lake where he had stopped on his trips and where he had bought merchandise. Chicago, preparing for the glory of the World Columbian Exposition, seemed the most likely place to find a job. He turned his back on Aberdeen and took the train to Chicago. Years later, when success had come, he could look back on his Dakota experiences with "mingled sighs and smiles," but the day he left there in that bleak spring of 1891 it needed a brave heart to be optimistic.

VII

ON THE ROAD TO SUCCESS

BAUM'S FIRST thought on arriving in Chicago was to look for work on one of the city's newspapers. He tried the *Tribune, Times, Morning Herald, Daily Journal, Mail, Inter-Ocean, Globe,* and *Daily News* without success. But he had better luck at the *Evening Post,* which was celebrating its first anniversary.

James W. Scott published the *Post* from an office at 128 North Wells Street, then in the heart of newspaper row. Scott looked over clippings of Baum's year as publisher of *The Aberdeen Saturday Pioneer* and offered him a job as reporter and editorial writer, starting May 1 at twenty dollars a week. Baum at once wrote Maud in Aberdeen, asking her to come with the children. His next concern was to find a place for the family to live. A stranger, baffled by the size of the city, he put his problem in the hands of chance. In later years he liked to tell how he did it:

> One afternoon I was walking slowly down State Street. I stopped at the corner of Adams to look in the windows of the Fair department store and admire the skillful window decorating.
> As I looked I was half aware that a street car had passed me and stopped where the rails ended at State Street. The

driver unhitched the horses, led them to the other end of the car and hitched them again for the outbound trip.

Just as the car started, I impulsively ran into the street and jumped aboard. I had no idea where I was going as I paid my five cent fare and looked out the window. We left the business district, crossed a bridge over the river, and were soon in a residential neighborhood. Later I learned that I had taken the Harrison Street line and ridden into Chicago's great West Side.

When we came to a section of good average American homes, about as far from the business district as I desired to live, I got off and began walking. A half hour later I discovered quite an attractive street only a block long. Down the center of a wide thoroughfare was a grassy parkway; large shade trees grew along the curbs, and the street radiated a feeling that here lived warm-hearted, contented folks. A sign post on the corner was lettered Campbell Park and halfway down the block was a cottage with a *For Rent* sign in the window.

This was before the day of electricity in houses and very few, including this cottage, even had gas fixtures. However, in most respects it was the sort of house I wanted and felt I could afford. I hunted up the owner and signed a lease.

From neighborhood stores Baum bought such furniture as was necessary to make the cottage habitable, although the small amount of money he had brought from Aberdeen was nearly gone. The furniture left in Dakota was to be sold there to avoid moving charges.

Baum had been at work on the *Post* only two weeks when Maud and the four boys arrived in Chicago, thoroughly exhausted from the long train ride with Kenneth, a sickly baby only six weeks old. Baum met them at the station and took them directly to the cottage where they were destined to live for the next four years.*

* The house at 34 Campbell Park is long since gone, and the site is now numbered 2233.

But if fortune had so far served him well in getting settled in Chicago, luck was less kind at the newspaper office. At the end of his first week the *Post* cashier handed him a pay envelope containing $18.62. He protested to the cashier, explaining that he had been hired at a salary of twenty dollars a week. The cashier insisted, however, that Baum's salary was eighty dollars a month, figuring four weeks to a month. Then dividing eighty dollars by thirty days per month made his pay $2.66 a day, or for a seven day week, $18.62! Every dollar was precious just then, but Baum was forced to accept the cashier's accounting. The injustice rankled every time he drew his pay, especially as Baum was sure the man who had hired him knew nothing of the circumstances. Maud kept the resentment keen by her comments on pay day. Driven by his own feelings and her urging, he hunted up a new job a short time after going to work for the *Post*.

His contributions in the few short months on the *Post* have disappeared into the anonymity characteristic of newspapers of the day. An editorial published May 9, 1891 about a Syracuse woman who had an appetite for hardware, and two on June 16 and June 19 about small doings back in South Dakota may be from his hand.

By fall he capitalized on his experience at the Bazaar in Aberdeen, persuading the Siegel, Cooper and Company department store to make him buyer for the crockery department. Siegel, Cooper had suffered a disastrous fire in August and had restocked and reorganized its entire store in a new location at Adams Street and Wabash Avenue. Later it returned to State Street and continued to be one of the leading department stores of Chicago until it was absorbed into the Boston Store in 1918. Siegel, Cooper turned out to be a pleasant place to work, although the salary level was low. As buyer, Baum had an opportunity to develop acquaintance with executives of the wholesale houses from which he purchased crockery. One of these was Pitkin and Brooks, a wholesale company whose salesmen showed its stock of fine china and glassware throughout the Middle West.

Baum and the sales manager of Pitkin and Brooks became somewhat more than casual business acquaintances. One day an unexpected opening developed, and Baum was offered a tryout as a traveling salesman, working on a liberal commission with railway and hotel expenses paid. Starting shortly before Christmas, 1893, he would have until the following April to demonstrate his abilities. "If everything is satisfactory then," he wrote his mother, "they will keep me the whole year. I am starting in very well and have not much fear but what I shall be able to get bread and butter anyhow, although I'm afraid we can't indulge in many luxuries." Baum and Maud searched their souls for several days before deciding that exchanging the certainty of a salary for the uncertainty of a commission was a good gamble. Both knew that the new job would keep him away from home for weeks at a time, but this drawback could be overlooked in the bright prospect of an adequate income after the lean years they had just been through. In this spirit Baum left Siegel, Cooper after a year's employment and took over a sales territory extending through central and southern Illinois, Iowa and Missouri.

This was the heyday of the traveling salesman, who was the vital link between the small town retailers and the big city wholesalers before chain organizations and easy

communications made him less important in American
merchandising. Baum's routine, like that of thousands of
his peers of the road, was to start a tour of his territory by
expertly packing six to ten trunks with samples of fragile
china and glassware. These were shipped by railroad to the
first town or city on his route, where they were drayed to
a hotel. Here he would unpack his wares, display them in
a big, bare sample room and arrange for visits from the
local merchants, who had been apprised by mail of his
coming. After they had given their orders he would repack
the hundreds of delicate pieces for shipment to the next
town.

In those pre-automotive days a traveling salesman was
at the mercy of railroad timetables. Often he would have
to stay overnight in some small town hotel, waiting for
the morning local to take him to his next stop. The hotel
lobby with its pot-bellied coal stove was his club, and the
type of humor known as the traveling man's story was expected to be his diversion. Baum wearied quickly of the
company of his fellow salesmen and would retire to a
corner, find an old envelope or scrap of hotel paper, and
pass the tedious hours jotting down jingles and bits of
stories.

Baum's first year with Pitkin and Brooks coincided with
Chicago's greatest gesture of the century—the World
Columbian Exposition. One Saturday noon the firm entertained visiting customers at a formal luncheon. Baum was
present to be host to an important Kansas City buyer who
was in town to see the fair. Because of the nature of the
affair he was properly attired in striped trousers, Prince
Albert coat and tall silk hat. After the luncheon, Baum
in all his finery boarded the horse cars to visit the exposi-

tion grounds in Jackson Park. He arrived just as an enormous crowd gathered to watch the arrival of the Spanish Ambassador and his retinue. It was impossible to get near the entrance gate. Baum was pushing his way vainly into the crowd when the police arrived. They soon made an opening for the day's guest of honor. Through it marched the party of Spaniards, all attired alike in striped trousers, Prince Albert coats and top hats. As they neared the gate, the dignitaries took off their hats and held them breast high in their right hands.

"I quickly removed my silk hat," Baum reported later, "and holding it over my breast, fell in at the end of the procession. After we had gone through the gate, I slipped away into the crowd.

"Just as I reached the entrance, I glanced up. Above the heads of the crowd, clinging to a telegraph pole, was my friend, the sales manager of Pitkin and Brooks. He had reached the fair grounds in his own carriage well ahead of me and had climbed the pole for a good view of the visiting Spaniards.

"Recognition was instantaneous. Later he told me he was so surprised to see one of his salesmen doubling as a Spanish dignitary he nearly dropped off the pole."

Such fancy dress episodes were uncommon in the quiet obscurity of Campbell Park. Life was routine, and in many ways not even comfortable. The little cottage lacked a bathroom and running water, and Saturday night meant a tin bathtub placed on the kitchen floor and filled from the kettle simmering on the back of the coal range. Toilet facilities were decidedly rustic.

Baum was making good on his new job but money was always scarce. Maud helped out by giving embroidery

lessons at ten cents each to groups of neighborhood women.
In later years Baum explained how he managed to get
through the early 1890's:

Prices were in line with my income. Steak cost us ten
cents a pound, chickens were twenty-five cents each, eggs
ten cents a dozen, and butter a dime a pound. Ice cost us
three cents a pound, but we did not use much of it. Food
that had to be kept cool we buried in a box of clean sand
from the shores of Lake Michigan. When we wanted a
cold drink on a hot summer evening we would send one
of the older boys down to the corner to 'rush the growler.'
A quart pail full of cool, foaming beer was a nickel, and
it tasted mighty good as we sat on the small front porch
hunting for a stray breeze.

Clothing for myself and boys was comparatively cheap,
too. Boys in those days wore what were called combination
suits—knee breeches that buttoned to a shirt, with coat
and cap to match. When I told one of the boys that I was
buying him a combination suit he wanted to know what
it was like. Jokingly I told him it was a combination of
green pants, yellow coat, purple hat and blue shirt. Pic-
turing himself parading to school in such an outfit while
his classmates jeered, he began to sob. He was not much
comforted until I explained what I really planned to get
him and let him see it.

Years later Baum's son Harry recalled that he was six
years old before he knew a chicken did not have four legs.
He and Kenneth, the two younger boys, received the wings
when they asked for legs. The legs always went to the two
older boys. But the Baums were not too poor at that time,
or too affluent in later years, to be without a cat and dog
and other animal pets for the children. Both parents were
fond of animals, and always had at least one, preferably
a small dog, around the house.

Family circumstances eased gradually as Baum developed into a seasoned salesman. Maud was even able to think of having a maid. Through a Swedish girl working for a neighbor she arranged to bring a girl over from the old country. A few months later the girl arrived—strong, pretty, energetic and totally ignorant of the English language. She gave the name of Sigrid Swanson, and it was not until some years later that the Baums learned that her true name was Sigrid Prinze. Friends in Sweden had told her that Americans expected a Swede to be named either Swanson, Olson or Johnson, and Sigrid conformed. For a dollar fifty a month, later increased to two dollars, Sigrid did most of the housework, helped with the care of Harry and Kenneth, and gave a hand with the marketing. Every day she carried a tin pail to the milk depot in the back yard of a nearby house, where for five cents it was filled with a quart of raw milk dipped from a large can which had never known sterilization. This was the girl's life and routine for eight years until she married a fellow countryman and left the service of the Baums.

A lesser luxury of the Campbell Park days was a crayon portrait of Baum which Maud had commissioned from a door to door artist. For two dollars she got a recognizable likeness, drawn from a photograph, of his head and shoulders, with cheeks of startling pink. Removing an old steel engraving of *The Stag at Bay* from a heavy oak frame, she replaced it with the portrait and hung it on the wall of the living room. One day when Baum had been gone for several weeks on an exceptionally extended sales trip, Kenneth, then age five, began to cry convulsively. Nothing could stop him. "I want my daddy," he wailed. Finally Maud picked him up, carried him into the living room and showed him the crayon portrait, saying: "Stop your

crying. There's your daddy." Kenneth choked back his
sobs, raised his head, took a quick look at the portrait
and screamed, "I-want-a-daddy-with-legs!"

After four years in the Campbell Park house Baum
moved his family in 1895 to a more modern home in the
same neighborhood. It had a bathroom and gas lights and
was only a block away from the Campbell Park cottage, so
that contact with old friends remained unbroken. For
Baum the new house* had one advantage he particularly
appreciated; it was a little closer to the old Cubs baseball
park at Wolcott and Polk Streets. Baum rarely missed a
Sunday game when he was in town and could get away
from home. His mother, Cynthia, who was quite elderly
by this time, had convictions which had been part of
"religion" in an earlier day. She felt strongly that sports
and other worldly diversions should have no place in the
Sabbath activities. Baum had been brought up in this
strongly Methodist atmosphere but had grown away from
it after leaving home. While in Aberdeen he worshipped
at the Episcopal Church, and Maud, who had been reared
in a free-thinking household, made her only concession
to formal religion by sending Frank and Robert to the
rather avant-garde Ethical Culture Sunday School.

One Sunday while his mother was visiting the family
in Chicago, Baum slipped away after early dinner. During
the afternoon loud cheers and boos from the ball park,
less than a mile away, were distinctly heard in the Baum
home. After one prolonged burst of cheering, Frank's
mother asked the occasion of this unseemly noise on the
Sabbath. Robert, eager to be helpful, spoke up, "That's

* It was 120 Flournoy Street, now 2149.

Daddy, yelling at the baseball game!" There was stunned
silence. Maud was embarrassed. The elder Mrs. Baum was
shocked. That evening she lectured her son with all the
fervor of her lifetime convictions, and after that he passed
up Sunday baseball whenever she was a visitor. But he had
another habit which annoyed his mother and which he
did not give up. He would tease her by glibly quoting
imaginary passages from the Bible—passages which, in
fact, did not exist. For example, she once said to him,
"Frank, you are telling me a story," and he replied at once,
with a straight face, "Well, Mother, as you know, St. Paul
in his Epistle to the Ephesians said 'All men are liars.' "
His mother pondered a minute and said, "Why, Frank,
you are wrong. I don't recall that." But, although she had
been fooled many times before, she got out her Bible and
looked it up before she realized that she was being teased
again.

Not long after moving, Baum took a brief interest in
politics. Stirred by William Jennings Bryan's "Cross of
Gold" speech at the 1896 Democratic Convention, he
marched in torchlight parades in behalf of Bryan's candi-
dacy. Again in 1900 he took part in Bryan's second cam-
paign. But aside from these two campaigns and from vot-
ing regularly in elections, usually for Democratic candidates, he ignored the problems and personalities of public
life. Other matters always seemed more important.

In the new house the family would gather in the early
evening, after supper and shortly before the boys' bedtime,
to read, study and talk around the big kerosene lamp on
the dining room table. This lamp had been brought from
the cottage and remained the family's favorite because
the unsteady and flickering gas light was trying to the eyes.

Whenever Baum was home at this family hour he would
recite to the boys favorite Mother Goose rhymes. Harry
Baum recalls that he sat on one knee and his younger
brother Kenneth on the other as their father told them
stories. They would ask him, for instance, how blackbirds
baked in a pie could later come out and sing and got what
Harry remembered as a satisfactory answer.

Often neighborhood friends of the two older boys would
drop in for the storytelling hour. On cold nights they
would cook molasses taffy on the coal range and pull it
until it was the right texture, while the younger children
would pop corn in an iron basket over the coals. Then
Baum would make the popcorn into balls, and they would
all sit and munch while he told stories. On warm nights
they took turns cranking the ice cream freezer by hand in
preparation for a feast during the story hour.

As he entertained the youngsters, Baum began to em-
broider details on Mother Goose verses and weave them
into little episodes. Many of the rhymes he had memorized
from a pamphlet picked up in a secondhand book store.
This was a facsimile published by Joel Munsell's Sons at
Albany, New York, in 1889, of Isaiah Thomas' reprint
(about 1785) in Worcester, Massachusetts, of John New-
bery's London edition (about 1760), entitled *The Original
Mother Goose's Melody*. Mrs. Gage, Baum's mother-in-
law, who spent nearly every winter with the Baums, enjoyed the little stories and often told her son-in-law she
felt sure thousands of children would also enjoy them if
they were written down and published. After much urging from the strong minded Mrs. Gage, Baum began putting his stories on paper.

He had kept one connection with his newspaper days

through the Chicago Press Club, on the second and third floors of the building at 3 North Clark Street, where working newspapermen mingled with their kind and with former reporters who had gone into other lines of work. He made it a habit to drop into the Press Club whenever he was in Chicago between trips for Pitkin and Brooks. Early in 1896, while making one of his occasional visits, Baum mentioned in conversation with Opie Read, the popular novelist, that he had written some Mother Goose stories and was looking for a publisher. Read was the club's greeter and character, always present and conspicuous both because of his geniality and his attire of a collarless starched white dress shirt over which Opie's jaws moved rhythmically in enjoyment of his "eatin'" tobacco. Read was already well known as a novelist of the South and as editor of the humorous newspaper, *The Arkansaw Traveler,* when he came to Chicago in 1887. Among his best known novels were *The Jucklins* and *A Kentucky Colonel.*

When he heard that Baum had a book manuscript in hand, Read turned around and introduced him to another Club member, Chauncey L. Williams, junior partner of the publishing firm of Way and Williams. Williams was then thirty-five. He had come down from Madison, Wisconsin, following the sudden death of his father. With an inheritance of one hundred thousand dollars he had formed a partnership with W. Irving Way "to spend Chauncey's inheritance in publishing fine books," as William Allen White expressed it in his autobiography. Way was a former Santa Fe Railroad official who had come to Chicago in 1890 and had broken into publishing by issuing Harriet Monroe's "Columbian Ode," the Muse's greet-

ing to the World Columbian Exposition, in 1893. Way
was active in organizing the Caxton Club and other
bibliophile enterprises in Chicago. Later, when he went
to Los Angeles to live, he was a dealer in rare books and
an advisor to well-to-do collectors.

Way and Williams, like several similar firms, of which
Stone and Kimball was the most notable, flourished briefly
in the cultural ferment of the "Chicago renaissance" of the
90's. The new publishers gave new writers an opportunity to be heard, and their books were singularly well designed. Around the publishers gathered a coterie of young
artists and writers, stimulated to expression by the cos-
mopolitanism of the Columbian Exposition, although
most of them were dedicated spokesmen for the Middle
West. They included Hamlin Garland, George Ade,
George Barr and John T. McCutcheon, H. B. Fuller, Harriet and Lucy Monroe, Wallace Rice, Eugene and Roswell
Field, Stanley Waterloo and Elia Peattie, and the artists
Will Payne, Frederic Goudy, Bruce Rogers and Will Brad-
ley. Williams held open house for these talented people
at his home in River Forest, which had been designed for
him in 1895 by Frank Lloyd Wright.*

Williams, who was on the lookout for new writers, encouraged Baum to submit his Mother Goose stories. They
were accepted, and *Mother Goose in Prose* was put on the
firm's 1897 list along with books by such established
authors as Kate Chapin, Mrs. Peattie,† and Read and
Octave Thanet. Maxfield Parrish was commissioned to
draw a pictorial title page and twelve full page illustra-

---

* At 530 Edgewood Place.

† Mrs. Peattie was the mother of Donald Culross Peattie.

tions in black and white. This was the first book that Parrish, who was then twenty-seven, had illustrated. His drawings succeeded in keeping the traditional flavor of Mother Goose within the framework of a distinctive and decorative style. Unhappily, he had to sue for his fee. It was reputed to have been twenty-five dollars a page, and the publisher had run out of money. *Mother Goose in Prose* appeared sumptuously in folio with large type and heavy paper, handsomely bound in decorated white cloth. It was a ridiculous children's book, too big for childish hands, too fine and expensive for rough use, and too white for grubby fingers. But even today a well-cared-for copy is a thing of beauty, and sixty years have failed to "date" it.

Publication of *Mother Goose in Prose* in October, 1897, was the slender thread that would lead Baum out of the labyrinth of the Gilded Age. After following the false paths of actor, newspaperman, salesman, and frontier merchant, he at last held fast the clew that stretched to his goal. Henceforth he would make children happy. This is implicit in the preface of *Mother Goose in Prose,* where Baum wrote, "I have thought the children might like the stories told at greater length, that they may dwell the longer upon their favorite heroes and heroines." *Mother Goose in Prose* was in many ways a foretaste of the books that would follow from the same pen. Here was the enchanted outdoors of flowery meadows and animals who talk, the romantic atmosphere of princesses and castles, the bright world of gentle children and happy endings. In "Little Bun Rabbit" there is even a Dorothy, who is memorable only because a more famous Dorothy was to appear within a few years in *The Wonderful Wizard of Oz.* When Baum included "Little Bun Rabbit" in his

Snuggle Tales in 1916 he changed Dorothy's name to Doris.

Most of the twenty-two stories were original creations displaying considerable ingenuity in building a fluent narrative upon the "bare suggestions" of the jingles. "Sing a Song of Sixpence," for example, became a Dick Whittington tale of a poor boy who makes his way in the world; "Mistress Mary," an elaborate and sentimental story of a lonely little girl who grows flowers to mark the days until her brother and father return from the sea; the shoe in which the "Old Woman" lives is a house whose ramshackle additions furnish the thread of a plot. "Three Wise Men of Gotham" and "The Wondrous Wise Man" poke fun at pretentious learning, an innocent source of merriment that Baum would exploit time and again in his Oz books. If one were to be chosen for an anthology, it would probably be "Humpty Dumpty" with this bucolic beginning by Baum, the chicken-fancier: "At the top of the hay mow in the barn, one speckled hen made her nest, and every day for twelve days she laid in it a pretty white egg—and she called the twelfth egg Humpty Dumpty." From the nest Humpty rolls into a whimsical chain of adventures.

Mother Goose in Prose was popular enough to be printed several times, although its author once confessed that it had been more of an artistic than a financial success. Way and Williams went out of business in 1898 and transferred its list to Herbert S. Stone and Company. Its copyrights were sold to Doubleday and McClure in 1900. The book was reissued by Stone in 1899 and reprinted by George M. Hill Company in 1901, then by the Bobbs-Merrill Company in 1905. The Hill and Bobbs-Merrill editions were in smaller format. Duckworth and Company of London published an English edition in 1898 which was in every way a duplicate of the original folio edition produced by Way and Williams. In 1901 individual stories from the book were given as premiums in exchange for the "three bears cut from Pettijohn's Breakfast Food package and eight cents in stamps to pay for mailing."

VIII

SHOW WINDOWS AND SUCCESS

"I HAVE BEEN more worried than usual over business matters this summer," Baum wrote his sister, Mary Louise, wife of Henry D. Brewster, New York State tax assessor, on October 3, 1897. "Writing of all kinds I have been forced to neglect and the result, after all my labors, has profited me but little. I have wanted to quit traveling and find some employment that would enable me to stay at home, and I conceived the idea of a magazine devoted to window-trimming, which I know is greatly needed and would prosper if ever I could get it going.

"I wrote Mr. Neal [his brother-in-law] to loan me the money to start it, but he bluntly refused. Next I interested a Chicago man who promised to put ample means into the business and when the first number was ready to go to press he failed in business and left me just where I started. I have been nearly a month now trying to find someone with money to pick up the enterprise and carry it through. . . .

"My book [*Mother Goose in Prose*] will be out sometime this month and I expect it to make a success, for it

92

will be beautifully printed and bound. The same publisher will produce my 'Phunniland' book next year."

Ever since his shopkeeping days in Aberdeen and the
year with Siegel, Cooper, Baum had made a practice of
studying show windows. He had lingered in front of the
big Loop windows in Chicago and the smaller ones in the
towns where he sold chinaware for Pitkin and Brooks.
Most merchants, he observed, had no notion of effective
display and no medium through which to become acquainted with the work of merchants and windows trimmers in other cities and towns who did.

When a Chicago heart specialist, consulted after Baum
had suffered several severe nasal hemorrhages and grip-
ping chest pains, advised him to find a more sedentary occupation than the heavy, fatiguing routine of a traveling
salesman, Baum resigned the job he had held for five years
with Pitkin and Brooks. At the age of forty-one he took
another step in the path which was leading him blindly
toward success and started publication of a monthly trade
magazine, *The Show Window*. Offices of the Show Window Publishing Company were opened in Room 1130 in
the Caxton Building, 500 South Dearborn Avenue, with
Baum as editor and Chauncey Williams as publisher. Presumably Williams was the man who finally put up the
capital for the enterprise. The first issue, eight by eleven
inches in size, appeared November 1, 1897. It was issued
monthly, two volumes a year, for an original subscription
price of one dollar a year or ten cents a copy. This was
doubled for the third volume, in July 1898.

Describing his magazine as "a journal of practical, up-
to-date window trimming" for the merchant and professional, Baum presently proclaimed in its pages that

"more merchants read *The Show Window* than any other periodical published. It is the recognized authority in window trimming throughout the civilized world." Offices were listed in New York, St. Louis and Boston in this country, in Canada, and in London, Paris and Dublin abroad. By the second volume it advertised a monthly circulation of ten thousand. Editorially, *The Show Window* had two definite aims: (1) to teach the techniques of window trimming to its readers, by articles and by some twenty-five full page photographs in each issue, and (2) to raise the vocational standing as well as the standards of window trimmers. Training and a professional association, Baum reasoned, would enable window decorators to demand more salary than the twenty to twenty-five dollars a week they were getting. Two prizes, of ten and five dollars in gold, were awarded monthly for the best photographs of outstanding show windows.

The first few issues were rather uninspired, but Baum was soon able to make his magazine more lively by publishing short stories by Stanley Waterloo and Gardner C. Teall, and by writing himself about the values of window advertising in specific trades. This and similar material, plus some readable correspondence on window displays in Europe gave the publication a certain "tone," while a feeling of group solidarity was created by signed articles from window trimmers, by free use of names in the business, and by organization of the National Association of Window Trimmers of America. This organization, conceived by Baum, was originally mentioned in the issue of February, 1898. The idea met with such favorable response that it was expanded in the next issue, and at a national convention held that August, Baum was elected one of three directors. By 1899 the Association had grown to such size that two hundred members attended a convention in the Palmer House.

By these devices Baum built up the advertising revenue and the subscription list of his magazine. In the beginning only professional trimmers in the big cities subscribed, and for a time after that the list grew slowly. In the meantime, advertising also was light, and the expense of obtaining pictures of fine displays and of making a large number of plates for each issue was heavy. To swell revenues, Baum induced Way and Williams to advertise their latest offerings, including *Mother Goose in Prose,* and the April issue for 1898 contained a full page photograph of a Carson, Pirie, Scott window full of copies of that book. William's brother-in-law, Harrison H. Rountree, advertised for his Turner Brass Works, and Gordon Selfridge, president of Marshall Field and Company, endorsed the new magazine in a full page advertisement.

In those early days Baum often took Maud and the two older boys to the office on the day that copies arrived from the printer, and the four of them would work busily all evening wrapping and addressing the magazines for delivery to the post office.

To a historian of taste, Baum's pages are a gold mine, for fashionable decorations are illustrated in page after page, showing shop windows packed with goods arranged in elaborate and often fantastic patterns which are veritable period pieces. Illustrations and articles from the magazine were gathered together in 1900 into a book, *The Art of Decorating Dry Good Windows and Interiors,* which was described in the July, 1899 issue of *The Show Window* as a "complete manual of window trimming, de-

signed as an educator in all details of the art according
to the best modern methods, and treating minutely of
every important subject. Five hundred illustrations." It
was published by the magazine at four dollars a copy when
the subscription list for the book had reached one thousand. Baum continued to publish *The Show Window*
until 1902, when it was sold to Nickerson and Clark, publishers of another trade journal. In their hands it became
The Merchant's Record and Show Window. It was finally
absorbed into the *Display World,* which is still published
in Cincinnati.

As a magazine editor Baum had more occasion to frequent the Press Club than in his mercantile days. In the
course of rubbing elbows there with newspaper men,
writers, and artists, he whiled away many hours with his
colorful friend Opie Read. One day as they were talking,
Read introduced him to a gruff, walrus-mustached artist
who had just illustrated Read's novel, *An Arkansas
Planter.* William W. Denslow, the artist, and Baum found
immediately that they had interests in common, but certainly neither could envisage that from their almost casual
meeting would come the most fruitful years of both their
lives.

Denslow had been born in Philadelphia in 1856. Thus
he was exactly the same age as Baum. After studying
drawing there and in New York, Denslow sold his work to
Harper's, Cosmopolitan and *Puck,* as well as to newspapers
in New York, Chicago, Denver, and San Francisco. He
came to Chicago in 1886, drew for the *Herald* and *Tribune,* and established a downtown studio and a home on
the lake shore in Highwood, a North Shore suburb. He
became the first artist employed by Elbert Hubbard in

the Roycroft Shops in East Aurora, New York, where he spent several winter months each year, drawing up a stock of cartoons and initial letters for Hubbard's publications. He also illustrated editions of *The Ancient Mariner* and *Omar Khayyam*, and drew the macabre cartoon, "What's The Use," a skull crowned with a laurel wreath and resting on a book, which is still a stock in trade of postcard vendors. For several years around the turn of the century, Denslow's cartoons in *The Philistine* poked genial fun at Hubbard, its editor, and his critics alike. Somewhere in each of his drawings would appear his sign, a stylized sketch of a sea horse. From this he was nicknamed by his friends, Hippocampus Den.

Denslow was far more widely known than Baum in the Chicago publishing world, and his studio on the eighth floor of the Fine Arts Building on South Michigan Avenue was a gathering place for such established artists and writers as George Ade, Kirk La Schelle, Ray Browne, Ike Morgan, and the McCutcheons. Denslow's bride, Ann Waters, a sunny blond whom he had married the previous year, provided good food and a congenial atmosphere for the visitors. Mrs. Denslow was a daughter of Martha Holden, a Chicago newspaperwoman who wrote under the name of Amber. Mrs. Denslow also was a contributor to newspapers and by her contacts and social ability had helped advance her husband's career as an illustrator.

Baum read to Denslow some of the jingles and verses he had jotted down on the backs of hotel envelopes and scraps of paper while he was on the road for Pitkin and Brooks. Baum's family circle, gathered around the big oil lamp on the dining room table, had liked them, and Baum thought Denslow might enjoy them too. Amused by several of the verses, Denslow sat down and sketched illustrations. In the winter of 1897-8 Denslow became a frequent visitor at the house on Flournoy Street, where in the evenings he and Baum would sort over the scraps of paper and select the jingles that appealed to both. Denslow would then draw an appropriate picture.

What moments were left, from the demands of his magazine and the book, Baum devoted to dabbling in printer's ink in another form. He revived a boyhood interest by borrowing a foot power press and a few fonts of type to run off a book of his poems, *By the Candelabra's Glare.* In the foreword he commented, "My best friends have never called me a poet . . . nevertheless this little book has an excuse. Unassisted I have set the type and turned the press and accomplished the binding. Such as it is, the book is 'my very own.' " Ninety-nine copies, five and a half by seven and a half inches in size, and made up of seventy-five pages, were printed. Most of them were bound in an off-white cloth ornamented with a candelabrum and the title stamped in dark brown on the cover. A few were bound in brown leather with the ornamentation and title stamped in gold. The end papers are gold with a Chinese design. Denslow and several other artists drew the illustrations, and friends contributed the paper, ink and binding materials; so Baum could say the book had cost him only his labor. All the copies were given away to friends and members of his immediate family. *By the Candelabra's Glare* is now one of the rarest of his books.

The author was being modest when he apologized for his poetry. Certainly most of it is conventional, in a light amatory vein, but it is readable and has vitality and wit. A dialogue between a wife-mother and a "New Woman,"

that phenomenon of the Nineties, has its overtones of
seriousness. Another, born of Baum's memories of hard
times in the Dakotas, touches on very harsh reality indeed.
Most of the pieces are addressed to adults, but there is a
small group of children's poems, including "Where Do
They Go?" which he valued enough to reprint later in
Father Goose, His Book. One of these poems epitomises
Baum's belief that children's stories should be without
horror, a belief that he later stated in the introduction of
The Wonderful Wizard of Oz. It is entitled: "Who's
Afraid?":

> Ev'ry giant now is dead—
> Jack has cut off ev'ry head.
> Ev'ry goblin, known of old,
> Perished years ago, I'm told.
>
> Ev'ry witch on broomstick riding
> Has been burned, or is in hiding.
>
> Ev'ry dragon, seeking gore,
> Died an age ago or more.
>
> *
>
> Lions now you only see
> Caged in the menagerie;
>
> And the grizzly bear can't hug
> When he's made into a rug.
>
> Who's afraid?

While Baum was completing the printing of *By the
Candelabra's Glare,* Maud's mother died March 18, 1898,
at their house.

On the advice of Williams, whose own publishing firm

was no longer active, Baum took his typed jingles and
Denslow's illustrations to the George M. Hill Company at
166 South Clinton Street, west of the Loop. This was a
young book jobbing and binding firm which up to that
time had been more interested in manufacturing than in
the editorial end of publishing. Hill, then thirty-eight,
was the president; Frank K. Reilly had recently joined the
company as production manager, and Sumner S. Britton
was secretary and head salesman. Hill looked over the
Baum-Denslow collaboration and called in Reilly and
Britton. Reilly saw no promise in the book. Britton, on
the other hand, favored a small edition of about five thousand copies but said the book would need a catchy title
to make it sell. Britton commented that the book was on
the order of a Mother Goose book. He, Reilly, and Hill
all felt it would have to compete with cheaply produced
Mother Goose editions while suffering from the handicap
of a higher price made necessary by the expense of color
illustrations and unconventional typography.

Baum objected that he did not wish his book to be
regarded as an imitation of Mother Goose. He told them
Mother Goose was old-fashioned and lacking in novelty,
but he felt there would be an advantage in selling his
American jingles if they could be subtly associated with
the classic Mother Goose in the minds of book buyers. He
suggested that it be called Father Goose. Reilly snorted
but said nothing. Britton nodded his head, sat a minute
in silence, then slowly rolled out the words. "Good. Let's
call it *Father Goose, His Book*." Hill wound up the discussion by declining to undertake publication. Instead,
he offered to print, bind and sell a small edition if Baum
and Denslow would pay for making the printing plates
and for the manufacturing costs.

The author and illustrator pondered this proposal for some days and finally hit upon an expedient that promised to make publication possible within their limited means. Denslow knew a young artist, Ralph Fletcher Seymour, who had recently come to Chicago and was struggling to live on a few dollars a week. He agreed to hand-letter the jingles into the pages with Denslow's drawings, using a technique that made the finished pages resemble a series of small posters. When Denslow assured him that he and Baum had very little money to spend, Seymour agreed to do the job for fifty dollars, which amounted to fifty cents a page. Seymour hired another young artist, Frederic Goudy, later famed as a type designer, to help him. After lettering a number of the pages Seymour protested that there was too much work for such a small sum of money; so Baum and Denslow gave him a page advertisement—the last page of the book.

The first edition of *Father Goose* was published on September 25, 1899. To the astonishment of Hill and the delight of Baum and Denslow, it was so quickly sold out that a second edition of ten thousand copies was printed on October 16. By Christmas, 75,700 copies had been run off to meet the demand. On a single day, December 18, 1899, there were sold 3,934 copies. Nor did interest in the book die with the holiday season. During 1900 this best seller required the printing of an additional thirty thousand copies, and the *Tribune* reported in June, 1900, that "*Father Goose, His Book* last year achieved the record of having the largest sale of any juvenile in America."

From this it was evident that Mother Goose now had a formidable rival for attention in the nursery despite Baum's guileless remark in the introduction that he "had no intent to imitate or parody the famous verse . . . of

Mother Goose." Father Goose with his old-fashioned skirted coat and twinkling eyes, like a comic Ben Franklin, was popular alike with the public and the book reviewers. "Father Goose is the new philosopher of the cradle and the fireplace," wrote the *Times Herald*. "As he comes in fancy masquerade, with clever yarns, bright ditties and assurances that he will take off from Mother's shoulders a good deal of work, give him double welcome."

"The humor of both text and pictures," wrote the *Tribune*, "is clean, bright and spontaneous. Author and artist have succeeded in being genuinely funny." Even William Dean Howells unbent from the pedestal where his fame as novelist, critic, and editor had placed him and took a copy of *Father Goose* to a young niece in the country so that, he said, he could share with her the joy of reading it. Elbert Hubbard, whose *A Message to Garcia* was one of the popular literary landmarks of the day, read Baum's verses for his own entertainment and then read them to his baby daughter. She explained all the pictures back to her father, and each night after that would bring the book at bedtime and insist on having it read to her. Hubbard claimed it was the highest praise that could be given a book when it interested adults and fascinated children. But perhaps sweetest of all to Baum was the excitement one night in the household of Edward Pitkin, president of the chinaware firm for which Baum had once traveled, when Pitkin brought the news that "that fellow Baum who worked for us is the author of a book that is selling like hot cakes."

Father Goose set the pattern in some ways for the format of the Oz books that were to come. This elder brother in the family is nine by eleven inches, contains more than

one hundred pages and is bound in boards decorated on
the front cover with Denslow's drawing of a jolly old fellow, his greatcoat pockets stuffed with papers and quill
pen in hand, while he talks to an attentive goose. The
seventy verses are the kind of agreeable nonsense which
seems artless because of the simple words and the familiar
themes, but which, in fact, is the product of an adult mind
which has the freshness of a child's and the sense of wonderment and enchantment that is God's gift to the
young in heart. With such qualities the awkward rhymes
and lines padded for the sake of meter, which make many
of the verses something less than poetry, can be overlooked.
Baum was under no illusions about his art, for in the letter to his sister quoted at the beginning of this chapter he
had remarked that "poetry doesn't pay today—especially
good verse" but went on to say that "doggerel will sometimes command a price, if it is witty and pointed and on
humorous lines."

Denslow, too, excelled himself in the high spirited and
decorative illustrations that make every page a delight.
Thus both men contributed to enjoyment of the whimsical lilt of:

> Did you ever see a rabbit climb a tree?
> Did you ever see a lobster ride a flea?
> Did you ever?
> No, you never!
> For they simply couldn't do it, don't you see!

Cows are standard fare in children's books but none was
quite like the *Father Goose* cow:

> The Bossie-Cow is big and red,
> Her eyes are round and bright—

And those great horns upon her head
　　Are quite a horrid sight.
And yet the Bossie's very kind
　　And good to us, I think;
She's full of beefsteaks, you will find,
　　And gives us milk to drink.

Baum liked puns almost as much as he liked cigars, and he must have known that children liked them, too, for he slipped them slyly into his stories and verses. One of the first that he put into print appears in the *Father Goose* verse about the Clockwork Man:

Now once I owned a funny man,
　　A clockwork was inside him;
You'd be surprised how fast he ran
　　When I was there beside him.
He was the pride of all the boys
　　Who lived within our town;
But when this man ran up a hill
　　He always would run down.

A reviewer's riposte to this read: "The jingles that the fellow, Baum, has put into this masterpiece are, for blues and biliousness, a real Baum of Gilead!"

Father Goose was one of the books published by Hill which were taken over by the Bowen-Merrill Company, later the Bobbs-Merrill Company, when Hill went out of business in 1902.

So popular did the book remain that more profit was skimmed from it in 1900 by issuance of *The Songs of Father Goose* (George M. Hill Company), in which the hand-lettered pages for twenty-six of the verses were reprinted facing pages of music setting the rhymes to compositions for the piano by Alberta M. Hall.* Denslow drew a new title page and a new cover design for *The Songs of Father Goose* showing the old man seated comfortably and singing while accompanying himself on a goose-necked mandolin. Two flanking geese sing along with him. According to family recollection, Mrs. Hall called on Baum at his home, proposed to him that she set some of his jingles to music, and played him several that she had already composed on the old square piano in the living room. Baum saw that she had succeeded in keeping her songs within the voice range of a child, and he and Denslow made a three-way contract with her to share the royalties. Not only did *The Songs of Father Goose* sell very well, but during the summer of 1900 many of the songs were printed separately in four page folders, eleven by thirteen and a half inches, and used as a music album supplement to Sunday newspapers throughout the country.

---

* Mrs. Hall later was married to a man named Burton, became a Christian Science practitioner, and died in Boston in 1956. Bobbs-Merrill reprinted *The Songs of Father Goose* from the original plates in 1952.

IX

ANNUS MIRABILIS

ONE EVENING, while the thunder of Admiral George Dewey's guns was still echoing in Manila Bay, Baum was sitting in his Chicago home telling stories to youngsters. The two events brushed each other briefly in the course of manifest destiny and children's literature. Baum was sitting on the living room floor to be close to the neighborhood boys and girls who, joining his sons, clustered around him. He smiled at the eager faces and began a new episode of a story he had been spinning for them whenever they could get away from home chores and lessons for the precious interval Baum had made customary between supper and bedtime.

"You remember that little Dorothy found the Scarecrow stuck on a pole in a cornfield," he began. "When she helped him down, the Straw Man thought it would be a good idea to go with her to see the great Wizard. The Scarecrow said he needed brains because the farmer who made him had stuffed his head only with straw.

"While they were walking along the road of yellow bricks, through a great forest on their way to the Emerald City where the Wizard lived, they discovered the Tin

Woodman. The poor fellow had gotten wet and was so
rusted he couldn't move. So they oiled his joints and the
hinges of his jaw and he soon was able to walk and talk
again."

With an actor's instinct for a dramatic pause, he stopped.
At once several voices piped up: "Don't stop, Mr. Baum.
What happened next?" Baum smiled and went on with
his story:

   " 'It must be inconvenient to be made of flesh,' the
Scarecrow said thoughtfully. 'For you must sleep and eat
and drink. However, you have brains and it is worth a
lot of bother to be able to think properly.'
   " 'After all, brains are not the best thing in the world,'
said the Tin Woodman. 'Brains do not make one loving;
and love is the best thing in the world. Once I had brains
and a heart, too; so, having tried them both I shall ask
the great Wizard for a heart.'
   " 'All the same,' said the Scarecrow, 'I shall ask for
brains, for a fool would not know what to do with a heart
if he had one.' "

As the story teller stopped to rest his voice, Tweety Robbins, a little girl who lived nearby, cried:

   "Oh, please, Mr. Baum! Where did the Scarecrow and
the Tin Woodman live?"

Baum looked around the circle of his young audience,
tugged at the end of his dark brown mustache, and slowly
scanned the room as if it held the answer to the little girl's
question. He did not see an answer in the big, old-fashioned square piano in one corner of the room, or in the
well-worn rug that covered the pine floor. Nor was it in
the pot-bellied iron stove with its isinglass windowed
doors that stood waiting to be put away for the summer.

   His gaze moved on, past the heavy oak dining table;

past Millet's "Angelus" in its ornate gilt frame that concealed a faded spot in the dark wall paper; past the chair where Maud sat in the light of the kerosene lamp, head bent as she embroidered colored silk pansies on a doily. At Maud's feet lay a copy of the *Chicago Journal* for May 7, 1898. Baum could read the headlines, and they attracted his attention to that corner of the room:

WAR EXTRA
DEWEY, HERO OF THE GREATEST
NAVAL VICTORY OF THE AGE!

The outer corner of Baum's left eyelid dropped, a sign the family knew meant inner satisfaction or merriment, as he repeated the child's question!

"Where did the Scarecrow and the Tin Woodman live? Where did they live?" He paused a moment to give suspense to his reply.

"Why," he exclaimed, grinning at the squirming youngsters, "the Scarecrow and the Tin Woodman, and the Cowardly Lion and the great Wizard, all lived in the marvelous Land of Oz!"

"Where *is* the Land of Oz, papa?" demanded his seven-year-old son, Kenneth.

"Oh, it's a long way off and none of us could ever get there," was the reply. "It's surrounded by the Deadly Desert, and the Great Sandy Waste, and the ——"

Just then a knock on the front door interrupted him. Maud opened it to admit Patrolman Jamieson, whose beat was the Flournoy Street neighborhood. He made a habit of dropping in to see that visiting children got home safely after dark. As the door closed on the policeman and the children, Maud spoke to her two younger sons:

"It's bedtime for you boys. You've heard enough tall tales for one night."

Kenneth turned to the bedroom, but Harry turned in the doorway. "Please, papa," he pleaded, "tell us a good night story before we go to sleep."

Maud put down her embroidery and helped them undress. When she returned to the dining room, Baum went to the bedroom and leaned back in the big oak rocker, worn by years of hard use.

"Tell us about the chickies, papa," said Kenneth sleepily, as he hugged "Eddie Riley" the rag doll who was his companion every night. "Where do the chickies go when it gets dark?"

"That's a good question," replied his father. Then his voice filled the room as he repeated his own little poem:

> Where do the chickens go at night?
>   Heigh-Ho! Where do they go?
> Under the breast of their mother they rest,
>   Finding her feathers a soft, fluffy nest;
> And there's where the chicks go at night,
>   Heigh-ho!
> Yes, there's where the chicks go at night.

He started a second verse in a softer voice but stopped when he saw both boys were asleep. Kissing them gently, he returned to the dining room. As he did so Maud looked up from her embroidery.

"Frank Baum," she said severely, "where did you get that absurd name of Oz?"

The two older boys, Frank and Rob, stopped their studying to listen for the answer.

"Absurd?" said Baum as he chuckled. "I thought it a rather good name for a magic country. When Tweety Robbins asked me where the Scarecrow and the Tin Woodman lived, I was stumped. Then I noticed that old filing case over there in the corner."

"For goodness sake!" exclaimed Maud. "What does an old filing cabinet have to do with it?"

"Take a look at it," he explained. "On the front of the top drawer are the letters A-N. On the bottom drawer are O-Z. The minute I saw it tonight I knew that OZ was just the right name for the country where the Wizard lived in the Emerald City. The more I think of it the better I like it.

"I know at times you get impatient with me for telling stories instead of working at other jobs when we need money so badly. But we have broken the ice with *Mother Goose in Prose*. I hope to publish other books that will please the children—and make life easier for us, too. Right now I am thinking of writing a long story about Dorothy and the Scarecrow; something like the story I was telling the children tonight. Now that I have coined a good name for my magic land I am sure it will make the extra money we need."

"Well," said Maud thoughtfully, "I have to admit the children keep coming here to listen to your stories, and some of their parents are interested, too. Mother was usually right about things, and she kept telling us your stories would sell if you would only write them down."

"I would like nothing better than to spend all my time that way," Baum confessed, "because I, too, like to hear about my funny creatures. I never know what strange characters are going to pop into my head when I begin telling a story. You know, I think up things for them to do, but when I start telling the story to the children, these characters seem to develop a life of their own. They often surprise *me* by what they do—just like living people."

But Baum was busy getting out his *Show Window* magazine each month, working long hours at the office and involved in heavy correspondence with window trimmers and merchants. He did not get around to writing his story about the magic Land of Oz, but years later, he would remember the exact day he thought of the title because it was the day the news of Dewey's victory reached Chicago.

As Baum's magazine prospered, he was able to move his family into a larger house on a corner of Humboldt Boulevard, a wide, quiet street with a wooded parkway on Chicago's west side.* As soon as they were settled, Baum began to work evening after evening on the book length story which he had decided to call *The Emerald City*. In the new house he had, for the first time since his marriage, the luxury of a den where he could write and keep his papers.

The main elements of the story were already so clear in his mind from its slow growth as he had tried out the episodes on his circle of young listeners that the writing proceeded rapidly. He wrote in longhand on letter size typewriter paper, using a soft, thick lead pencil. In the study of the home which he built more than a decade later in Hollywood hung a picture frame containing the stub of a pencil attached to a sheet of paper. On the paper is written: "With this pencil I wrote *The Emerald City*."

Baum was left-handed and wrote back hand, but his manuscripts were unusually legible. As a rule he sat in a

* It was Number 68, now 1667.

large, leather-upholstered armchair with a pad of paper on his knee. As he became engrossed in the story he would swing first one leg, then the other, over the padded arm of the chair and write in that position. He typed the final versions of his stories, with two fingers, on an L. C. Smith typewriter, revising them as he worked. The only book which he did not type as he revised was *The Wonderful Wizard of Oz,* which was submitted to the publisher and set in type from his original longhand copy.

As soon as he had some of the story written, Baum called in Denslow, and as they discussed the travels of Dorothy and her little company through the Land of Oz, Denslow sketched out ideas for illustrations. The air in the den grew heavy with smoke from Baum's strong cigars and Denslow's pipe, for the artist was the writer's close rival as a human volcano. Baum chain-smoked cigars as he wrote, lighting one from the butt of the last. Elbert Hubbard II recalls that Denslow "smoked a corncob pipe, with a big bowl of tobacco on one side of his drawing board and another bowl of burnt matches on the other. He'd get about two or three puffs out of a match and then have to relight. He smoked more matches than tobacco."

Outside the closed door of the den, in the living room, Maud and Denslow's young wife, Ann Waters, chatted away the long evenings.

By fall, 1899, Baum and Denslow were knocking at Hill's door with several chapters of *The Emerald City* and specimen drawings. Hill kept the material for six weeks, then declined to invest any money in publishing it. He advised the author it was the consensus of the book trade that children were satisfied with the fairy tales already on the market, and that their parents would not buy anything as unconventional as an American fairy tale. Their enthusiasm dimmed but not dashed by this cold reception from their own publisher, Baum and Denslow trudged to other offices with their samples. At each they got a rejection—and also lost a few weeks of time. One publisher turned Baum down with the comment that if there had been any profitable market for an American fairy tale, it would have been written and published long ago.

This remark discouraged both author and artist, but one day when they were in Hill's office to pick up royalty checks on *Father Goose,* they ventured to raise the subject of *The Emerald City* again. Reilly, Hill's production man, and Britton, his head salesman, were also present. When Baum brought up the topic they got into a heated argument about the merits of American fairy tales in general and of *The Emerald City* in particular. Part of the argument hinged on Denslow's illustrations. He had made his drawings in black and white, but both he and Baum wished to have them appear in color. Hill felt that color plates were an extravagance in a child's book. Presently, however, Hill stopped the argument and made Baum and Denslow a proposal.

"I'll tell you what I'll do," he said. "If you think so much of *The Emerald City,* why don't you gamble on it as you did on *Father Goose?* I mean, put up the money to pay for engraving the illustrations in color, for setting the type and for printing and binding a few thousand copies."

"I'm in favor of that," broke in Britton. "I'd be willing

to bet I could place at least fifteen hundred copies the first year, and we might even be able to sell five thousand before the public tires of it."

"If you agree to my proposal," continued Hill, "I'll put the title in our catalog and our publicity department will do all it can to promote the sale of the book."

"What sort of a contract will you give us?" Denslow inquired.

"Oh, like the *Father Goose* deal," Hill replied. "You and Baum pay the publication costs and you get all the profit from sales except a small percentage for the firm to cover costs of promotion, advertising and review copies."

Baum and Maud, Denslow and Ann talked over this offer for several days. Finally they decided to invest some of their royalties from *Father Goose* in publishing *The Emerald City*. Thus, in a very real way, the story that was to make Baum and Denslow famous owed its being to the verses the chinaware salesman had jotted down during his idle hours on the road. But after the agreement with Hill had been reached, a new complication arose. Reilly flatly told Baum that his title was unsuitable and would have to be changed. The publishing trade, he said, had a superstition to the effect that a book with the name of a jewel in the title was bound to fail. Baum argued that this was silly, but the whole Hill organization, already prejudiced against the book's prospects, refused to foredoom it further by what they firmly believed to be an unlucky title.

The Fairyland of Oz was Baum's second choice for a title, and as late as January 19, 1900, James O'Donnell Bennett in a column of comment in the *Chicago Journal* wrote:

"With the opening of the spring book trade, the George M. Hill Company will conduct book publishing operations on considerably broader and higher class lines than it hitherto has followed. . . . Another issue by the Hills to follow a month or so later will be a fairy story by Frank Baum with pictures by Denslow. In the light of the success of their first book, *Father Goose,* the second seems bound to go. It will appear under the title, *The Fairyland of Oz,* and will run to some forty thousand words."

Evidently Bennett was copying a piece of press agent material, perhaps from the pen of Britton himself, for the article mentions that the book had been "gravely pronounced the right sort by a jury of two children" and a kindergarten teacher, and that an advance royalty of one thousand dollars had been paid. Both remarks, especially the latter, were in the realm of fancy.

The Hill Company was still dissatisfied with the title, and the author shortened it to *The Land of Oz.* It was mentioned under that name in the *Chicago Journal* on January 27, 1900. Meanwhile Baum had his heart set on something more colorful—more descriptive—more eyecatching. Thinking the matter over, and talking with Maud and Denslow, he finally came up with another, and final, title—*The Wonderful Wizard of Oz.* For once, everyone concerned was enthusiastic, and the collaborators diligently set about completing the story and illustrations.

Meanwhile, Hill asked Baum to write verses for twin alphabet books—*The Army Alphabet* and *The Navy Alphabet*—which Hill proposed to issue while the Grand Army of the Republic held its encampment in Chicago during the summer of 1900. The books, ten and a half by twelve and a half inches, were illustrated in color by

Harry Kennedy, a page to each letter, and the verses were hand-lettered by Charles T. Costello. Baum had met both men at Denslow's studio. The *Chicago Post*'s reviewer reported that the verses were an improvement on those "Mr. Baum had perpetrated for *Father Goose*" and commented that Baum would be a very clever versifier if he were more critical of his work. The reviewer also praised the illustrations but objected to the color printing, while the reviewer on the *New Orleans Picayune* said the books "are printed in the best manner and illustrated with a richness and skill that reflects the highest credit upon American draughtsmen."

Not long after the agreement had been made with Hill to issue *The Wonderful Wizard of Oz,* Baum was introduced to Robert Howard Russell, a New York publisher who was in Chicago on business. Russell was familiar with *Mother Goose in Prose* and had paid *Father Goose* the compliment of publishing an imitation of it. He commissioned its author to prepare a book length story for him. Baum had one ready, for in the back of his desk lay a manuscript he had prepared in 1897 to be published as a successor to *Mother Goose in Prose* on the 1898 Way and Williams list. When that firm had gone out of business he had made no further attempt to market his Phunnyland book, as he had called it in a letter to his sister. The fourteen stories of which it is composed have little organic unity except that they are all laid in the Valley of Phunnyland. This is a typical Baum paradise where the rivers of milk and cream run past banks of granulated sugar, candy grows on bushes along the streams, and an island in Rootbeer River is a rich block of fruit cake. Even the rain in Phunnyland is lemonade, and it falls to the thunder of a chorus from "Tannhauser." The people, of course, are always young and beautiful. In this perfection, only the prince has anything to complain of, for he must remain a prince always because the king, like all his subjects, is immortal.

This confection was published under the title, *A New Wonderland,* in October 1900. Russell issued it in a large, handsome volume bound in pictorial boards. Frank Verbeck, whose reputation had been made by his comic animal drawings, brightened the pages with color plates and crisp text illustrations. The book was well reviewed, but Russell seemingly was not aggressive in promoting it. Sales, consequently, were disappointing. Nevertheless, in 1903, the Bobbs-Merrill Company reissued the stories under a new title, *The Surprising Adventures of the Magical Monarch of Mo and His People.* Baum rewrote the first chapter and changed the Valley of Phunnyland to the Valley of Mo; otherwise the stories are the same as those in Russell's edition.

The title page describes *A New Wonderland* as "a laugh book for children of all ages." Despite the high calorie count of Phunnyland, most of the stories are only mildly amusing and rather skim-milk fare. But in the history of Baum's evolution as a writer, they are important because they foreshadow many of the characteristic elements which would appear later in the stories about Oz. For example, the most memorable of the Phunnyland episodes concerns a princess' adventures during her efforts to regain her big toe, which had been stolen by a wicked wizard, who "lived in a cavern of rubies." Equipped by her good fairy with an odd arsenal of magic weapons, she overcomes a giant snake, a witch, a cave of daggers, and a monster, then

destroys the wizard—all in a fashion which Baum here
invented and made his own. Another story recounts the
adventures of Timtom, a poor boy in love with the capri-
cious Princess Pattycake. His experiences in passing over
a gulf and surmounting a jasper wall in quest of a golden
pill to sweeten the princess's disposition strikingly antici-
pate some of Dorothy's adventures in *The Wonderful
Wizard of Oz,* and in *The Lost Princess of Oz.*

Baum wrote a letter on April 8, 1900, to his favorite
brother, Harry, in Syracuse. At that moment *The Wonderful Wizard of Oz* was in the hands of the printers. Like
many letters written for the eyes of a family circle, it is
part confession, part bravado. But it is worth notice because at that moment the author was standing on the brink
of success. It is a long letter, and much of it is trivia of
family affairs. With these omitted, it reads:

The boys are growing wonderfully and I sometimes
think I must be a kid no longer, when I behold the stal-
warts around me and hear them call me "dad." There's a
mistake somewhere, for I have failed to grow up—and
we're just five boys together. . . .
Here I have my acquaintances but, outside my home,
no intimates. I do not make friends easily, nor does Maud
. . . Probably I shall make Chicago my home. The boys
have grown up here and Maud likes it . . . her wishes are
the most sacred. . . .
The financial success of my books is yet undetermined,
and will only be positively settled after the coming fall
season. We only had three months sale of *Father Goose,*
and though it made a hit and sold plenteously we cannot
tell what its future may be. . . . I have been grateful for
its success. The money has been a pleasure to me and my
work is now sought by publishers who once scorned my
contributions. Harper Bros. sent a man here last week to
try to make a contract for a book next year. Scribner's

write offering a cash advance for a manuscript. Appletons, Lothrops and the Century have asked for a book—no matter what it is. This makes me proud, especially as my work in *Father Goose* was not good work, and I know I can do better. But I shall make no contracts with anyone till next January. If my books succeed this year I can dictate terms and choose my publishers. If they fall down I shall try to discover the fault and to turn out some better work.

A lady here, Mrs. Alberta N. Hall, has written some charming music to the *Father Goose* verses. *The Songs of Father Goose* was the result and is now in preparation, being announced for publication June 1st. *The Army Alphabet*, wonderfully illustrated by Harry Kennedy, will be issued May 15th. The book surely *ought* to catch on. *The Navy Alphabet*, also illustrated by Kennedy will appear August 1st. I have received some proofs of the illustrations Frank Verbeck has made for my Phunniland book, which appears July 1st from R. H. Russell's, New York. The work is splendid. This is the same man who has illustrated Kipling's new book of animal stories, having been selected over all the other American artists to do that work. The title of the book will be *A New Wonderland*. Then there is the other book, the best thing I ever have written, they tell me, *The Wonderful Wizard of Oz*. It is now on the press and will be ready soon after May 1st. Denslow has made profuse illustrations for it and it will glow with bright colors. Mr. Hill, the publisher, says he expects a sale of at least a quarter of a million copies on it. If he is right, that book alone solves my problem. But the queer, unreliable Public has not yet spoken. I only need one hit this year to make my position secure, and three of these books seem fitted for public approval. But there—who knows anything! I'm working at my trade, earning a salary to keep my family and holding fast to a certainty until the fiat has gone forth.

The apprehensive author did not have long to wait. Advance copies of *The Wonderful Wizard of Oz* which Baum inscribed and presented to his brothers and sisters are dated June 20, although there is a sewed but unbound copy with an inscription to his sister, Mary Louise, on the fly leaf and dated May 17—two days after his forty-fourth birthday. It reads: "This 'dummy' . . . was made from sheets I gathered from the press as fast as printed and bound up by hand. It is really the very first book ever made of this story."

Hill did an excellent job of bookmaking for his two clients. The first edition of *The Wonderful Wizard of Oz* is six and a half by eight and three quarters inches—an oddly squarish book of two hundred and sixty-one pages bound in green cloth stamped in red and green, with the Cowardly Lion on the front cover and panel heads of Dorothy, the Scarecrow, and the Tin Woodman on the back cover. It sold for $1.50. Denslow's illustrations, twenty-four of them full pages in color, were brilliantly printed, and the press work was good. A color scheme in harmony with the episodes of the story—gray for the dusty days in Kansas, blue for the Munchkin adventures, green for the doings in the Emerald City, yellow for the progress through Winkie land, brown for the China country and red for the Quadling affairs—gave variety to Denslow's decorative drawings. What is generally accepted as the first issue is distinguishable from subsequent ones by an eleven line colophon on the inside back cover which reads:

Here ends the story of the Wonderful Wizard of Oz, which was written by L. Frank Baum and illustrated by William Wallace Denslow. The engravings were made by the Illinois Engraving Company, the paper was supplied by Dwight Brothers Paper Company, and Messrs. A. R. Barnes & Company printed the book for the publishers, the George M. Hill Company, completing it on the fifteenth day of May 1900.

In later issues of the first edition, the colophon is thirteen lines long, and when the book was published by the Bobbs-Merrill Company, the colophon was dropped. There are at least three states of the first edition and several variant forms, distinguishable by minor differences in the type and binding. Baum dedicated his masterpiece to "My good friend and comrade, my wife," and dated the short introduction April, 1900. Copies of the first issue appeared with the copyright notice printed on page 6 instead of on the back of the title page, as is required by copyright law. This defect was remedied in some copies by rubber stamping the notice in the proper place, so that it appears twice in these copies. In later issues of the first edition the notice is printed in both places. Although the notice reads: "Copyright: 1899, by L. Frank Baum and W. W. Denslow," the Copyright Office, despite years of searching, has failed to find any evidence of application for copyright in that year. The official copyright date is August, 1900. The Library of Congress received its copies on December 12, 1900.

Publication date of the first edition of ten thousand copies was August 1, but distribution was not actually made to the trade until the middle of September. The Wizard's magic began to be felt at once. Orders from bookstores came in so rapidly that twenty-five thousand more were printed in October, and thirty thousand in November. A fourth edition of twenty-five thousand copies was printed in January, 1901, making a total of ninety thousand copies published by the Hill organization before it went out of business. It was the best seller on the publisher's list that Christmas season of 1900. Now six decades

and several million copies later it has become one of the
best sellers of all time.

The *Chicago Post* received its review copy about September 15 and ran a short, mildly enthusiastic review on
September 21. "Mr. Baum has written by far his best book
and Mr. Denslow has illustrated it in a way that is more
than half the battle for success." Despite a snide remark
that the artist could not draw a childlike child, the reviewer intimated that if the book were a success Denslow
would deserve more credit than Baum.

In spite of Baum's optimistic remark in the letter to
his brother that Hill expected a sale of at least a quarter
of a million copies, the success of *The Wonderful Wizard
of Oz* obviously was a complete and most welcome surprise
to him, to Maud, to Denslow, and to the publisher. Son
Harry, a teen-ager at the time, recalls that his mother
asked Baum to go to Hill a few weeks before Christmas
to request an advance on royalties so that she could buy
presents for the family. Baum demurred, explaining that
royalties were paid twice a year and that he disliked asking
for money in that way. But Maud insisted, and her husband took the streetcar downtown and went to Hill's office.
After some casual conversation, he asked whether he might
have whatever royalties had accumulated. Hill called in
his auditor and told him to make out a check for the
money due Baum.

Baum took the check, passed the season's greetings with
Hill and without looking at the check, buttoned it in his
coat pocket and went home. Maud was in the kitchen,
ironing her husband's best shirt.

"Did you get it?" she inquired.

"Yes," was the reply.

"How much is it?" she asked eagerly.

"I don't know. Didn't look at it," said Baum as he took off his overcoat.

"Well, give it here and let me see," she demanded, and Baum handed over the check. As Maud glanced at it, she clutched the ironing board for support.

"Look," she said in a small voice. "It is for $3,432.64."

"What?" replied Baum incredulously. "You must be mistaken," but a glance verified the figure, and he and Maud stood looking at each other in astonishment.

A few years before her death, Maud herself recalled the incident and the mark it had made on her memory.

Why did *The Wonderful Wizard of Oz* have such an impact on its time; what is the wizardry that survived translation into a stage spectacle and an equally successful motion picture; what was there in the time and the writer from which it drew such amazing vitality? The book's basic strength obviously lies in its ability to capture the imagination of children; but that is not all. An important factor in its success was that the time was right. The high tide of romantic fiction was flooding into the book shops. *When Knighthood Was in Flower* was the novel to read in 1898; *Monsieur Beaucaire* came along two years later, and *Graustark* was the best seller of 1901. If the grown-ups were reveling in novels of imaginary kingdoms and glittering courts, why should not the children want to escape into Wonderland, too? The country was tired of coping with the problems left by the Gilded Age. The growth of big industry and ruthless riches threatened the democracy of farmers and small shop-keepers on which the nation had built its government and ideals. Capital and labor had gone to war; a disquieting gulf was growing between the new rich and the new poor; the cities knew the problems of slums; and the farmers felt an unaccustomed financial stress. Particularly, the farmers of the plains were in revolt—a folksy revolt of Sockless Jerry Simpson of Kansas and of the woman leader who advised the farmers to raise less corn and more hell.

The serious novelists of the era reflect the brassy glare of the nation's social problems. They were necessarily sober—Edward Bellamy in *Looking Backward,* William Dean Howells in *Through the Needle's Eye,* and Mark Twain in his satire, *A Connecticut Yankee in King Arthur's Court.* Between 1888 and 1900 more than sixty utopian novels, that favorite form of the social critic, were published. But crops improved, money was easier, and Dewey's guns signaled America's entry into world affairs with the close of the Spanish-American War. Readers forgot reform, and Maurice Thompson, Booth Tarkington, and George Barr McCutcheon, with their pretty romances, became the new literary lions. Like these men, Baum was a story teller, not a social critic. Despite the Never-Never Land setting of his fable, his utopian days were to come later, when he had fully discovered the Land of Oz. He had marched in torchlight processions for Bryan, the spokesman of agrarian discontent; he had felt the bitter breath of failure and hard times in the Dakota Territory; there had been long, lean years in Chicago that he would never forget, yet he did not turn to resentful social criticism.

Once in a while, as in the first pages of *The Wonderful Wizard of Oz,* drab with the dust of Kansas and the defeated farmers, the troubles of this world intrude. More indirect is the casual reflection on modern "civilization" when the Good Witch of the North is made to say to Dorothy, "In the civilized countries I believe there are no witches left, nor wizards, nor sorceresses, nor magicians. But, you see, the Land of Oz has never been civilized. . . . Therefore we still have witches and wizards among us."

So it was not utopia, but a golden story of color and imagination which set the middle-aged magazine editor on fire. The air of Chicago tingled with excitement in those days; the spirit was contagious. The city was on fire, too; not the Great Fire of thirty years before, but an artistic and creative fire that had inspired William Jenney to build the first skyscraper, led Louis Sullivan to the prairies for plant motifs for the ornaments on his great Auditorium Building, created the Chicago Symphony Orchestra, laid the foundations of the Art Institute, built the great Gothic towers of the University of Chicago on the Midway. All this was fueled by the growing wealth of the city, and by the Columbian Exposition of 1893, which Henry B. Fuller called "the city's intellectual and social annexation to the world at large."

But backgrounds are only the setting. The center of interest lies in the book itself. The youngsters who found *The Wonderful Wizard of Oz* under their Christmas trees in 1900 had a new kind of story—a native American fairy tale—in their hands. Until that time, children's reading had come chiefly from European authors who retold Greek and Latin myths, such as those Andrew Lang collected in his Red, Green and other fairy tale books; from the Mother Goose stories of Charles Perrault, such as "Little Red Ridinghood," "Bluebeard," "The Sleeping Beauty" and "Cinderella," augmented by many jingles that attached themselves to the Mother Goose tales; from Hans Christian

Andersen's stories such as "The Ugly Duckling," "Red Shoes" and the like; and from the collections of folk tales made by Jacob and Wilhelm Grimm. Then there were John Ruskin's "King of the Golden River," Charles L. Dodgson's *Alice in Wonderland* and *Through the Looking Glass* with fancy of a more original strain, and the American imitation of Alice, *Davy and the Goblins,* by Charles E. Carryl.

In the United States the Puritan insistence on the "terrible reality of invisible things" long cast odium on reading for enjoyment. As a result, moral tracts were only gradually superseded for child reading by the Rollo books with their educational emphasis and by the scarcely less purposeful Peter Parley and Oliver Optic. Even the Horatio Alger books drove home the moral lesson of the growing industrial age—Get Ahead! Nathaniel Hawthorne in *Tanglewood Tales* (1853) and *The Wonder Book* (1852) reworked the rich vein of classic myth, but only a few of his stories on native themes, such as "The Snow Image" and "The Great Stone Face," were made of the stuff that enthralls the minds of the young. Otherwise the landmarks of children's reading of the period were sober: Louisa May Alcott's *Little Women* (1868); Samuel Clemens' *Tom Sawyer,* actually written for adults; such regional literature as Joel Chandler Harris' *Uncle Remus* (1883); and Washington Irving's *Legend of Sleepy Hollow* and *Rip Van Winkle.*

In looking back for prototypes of *The Wonderful Wizard of Oz,* one finds little except two long forgotten tales by a Boston poet and painter, Christopher C. Cranch. *The Last of the Hugger Muggers* (1856) and *Kobboltozo* (1857) derive their American flavor from their hero, a New

England boy who sets out from his native shore (somewhat like Gulliver or Robinson Crusoe) on an imaginary voyage to an island ruled, in real Baum fashion, by a benevolent giant and his wife.

Dorothy's journey from Kansas to the Land of Oz and home again is in the tradition of great imaginative quests, from Homer's *Odyssey* to Maeterlinck's *Bluebird*, but it is distinctively American. Dorothy has good Kansas dirt on her shoes and she is blown into Oz by a real Kansas cyclone. Her companion, the Scarecrow, comes straight from a mid-west cornfield. Even the Tin Woodman is essentially a mechanical toy, so dear to the heart of every gadget-minded American boy.

An editorial in *Collier's* (February 6, 1946) suggested that *The Wizard of Oz* keeps on selling year after year "because it is a fairy tale of a strictly American kind with a deep appeal to the best of American characteristics," which the editorial described as realistic, inquiring, and fearless attitudes of mind. Dr. Edward Wagenknecht, professor of English at Boston University and academic troubador of the Baum wonderlands, emphasized the same fundamental quality when he remarked that "Baum taught American children to look for the wonder in the life around them, to realize that even smoke and machinery may be transformed into fairy lore if only we have sufficient energy and vision to penetrate to their significance and transform them to our use."*

Children in 1900, like the children of today, were familiar with machine-made wonders. There seemed no limit to the impact of invention on all aspects of American life.

* *Utopia Americana,* by Edward Wagenknecht, University of Washington Chapbooks, 1929.

But Baum touched machines with magic and with imagination; his Tik-Tok and his Tin Woodman are this power
personified—the humorous essence or the soul of the bene-
ficient aspects of the machine. His story telling gave
warmth and meaning to a materialistic, industrial age.
Baum has one of his own characters, the Shaggy Man,
say: "All the magic isn't in fairyland. There's lots of magic
in all Nature, and you may see it as well in the United
States, where you and I once lived, as you can here," and
he cited the magic of a blooming flower, or of a cow making milk for children.

While striking out on new paths, Baum made another
break with the grim European tradition. In his introduction he wrote, "The time has come for a series of newer
'wonder tales' in which the stereotyped genie, dwarf, and
fairy are eliminated, together with all the horrible and
bloodcurdling incidents devised by their authors to point
a fearsome moral." He went on to say that the story was
written "solely to pleasure children of today. It aspires to
be a modernized fairy tale, in which the wonderment and
joy are retained and the heartaches and nightmares are left
out."

When the golden ingredients in the making of *The
Wonderful Wizard of Oz* are being assayed, too much emphasis cannot be placed upon Baum's inborn talent as a
story teller. He told stories to the children in Aberdeen
who came to his store and entertained his own sons and
their friends with the tales that teemed in his mind. As a
story teller he always kept in mind the motto that hung
above his desk, "When I was a child, I spake as a child,
I understood as a child, I thought as a child." (I Corin-
thians 13:11) His wife once told a group of Hollywood

women, "Frank knew how to cater to the tastes of children. He wrote their language. . . . He had two strong facets of character—humility and patience. Both were strongly in evidence in all his contacts with children and grown folks alike. Youngsters live in a world of half make-believe—talking with imaginary people while at play—people who are very real to the children, but whom the grown folks can neither see nor hear. . . . Even Santa Claus is a very substantial person to them."

In appraising the appeal of *The Wonderful Wizard of Oz* to the child, the age-old and ageless form of the story—a journey—should not be forgotten. A journey is lively, it is chronological, and it is easy to follow. It is full of suspense, and it is a convenient device to bring together a lot of otherwise disconnected incidents and persons. Dorothy's journey is told in simple words and short sentences, without distinction of style, but without the conscious repetitions and limited vocabulary which irritate an adult, and even a child, in many modern "children's stories." No sociological or pedagogical theory cramped the vigor of Baum's pen; it had only one aim, to keep alive in his readers' minds why Dorothy and her companions were going to see the Wizard.

The pace of the story is well fitted to the comprehension of children from six to twelve, and incongruity—the kind of humor they like best—is plentiful. Adults may read the book for its color and movement and the undercurrent of irony, but it was not written for them. The child wants incident, melodrama rather than emotion, a tingling sense of conflict and the satisfaction of conquest, but he does not care to have his fantasy get too far from the earth. Style is secondary; for the child is not critical of language, although he will not accept prosaic story telling. But Baum's greatest skill was the deftness with which he interwove realistic, everyday materials so intimately with fancy and fantasy that even the unreal seems familiar, and the obvious wears seductive new colors. The story has the enchantment of the remote, but simultaneously the "mystery of the near at hand."

Dorothy's predicament is not unreal to a child. Dorothy is lost and is trying to get home. Home is a weather-beaten Kansas farm where she lives with her drab, defeated uncle and aunt. In Oz, where the grass is always green and the meadows are carpeted with flowers, she is surrounded by all the color and excitement of the Emerald City. But she knows that Aunt Em and Uncle Henry are worried about her, and she can think only of getting home to them. When the Scarecrow asks her why she wishes to "leave this beautiful country and go back to the dry, gray place you call Kansas," she replies, "No matter how dreary and gray our homes are, we people of flesh and blood would rather live there than in any other country. . . ."

There are obstacles—the Deadly Poppy Field, the Fighting Trees, the Kalidahs, the Winged Monkeys and a wicked witch or two—but she overcomes them, and she is never alone or in real terror. Like the heroines of the comic strips, she bears an enchanted life. But unlike most comic strip folk, Dorothy's course is untainted by moralizing or sentiment. She is fond of her stuffed and tinny companions, but the affection is implied, not expressed. None of the sticky sentiment of love or marriage, death or illness, diverts her from her steady purpose of returning to Kansas. Best of all, from the child's point of view, there is no grownup nonsense about rationalizing the whole business as a dream, as the motion picture did several decades later.

Proper nineteenth century children had been dosed with moralizing in their reading as regularly as they got sulphur and molasses in the spring. But *The Wonderful Wizard of Oz* was a refreshing exception. True, it has a moral, but it is a whimsical moral which really has nothing to do with the story. The Scarecrow, who lacks brains and goes along with Dorothy to get some from the Wizard, is the one who thinks out the solutions to the company's little problems. The Tin Woodman, who is desperately troubled because he has no heart, is so kind and gentle that he cries when he accidentally steps on a beetle. The Cowardly Lion has plenty of courage when danger threatens. The all-powerful and awesome Wizard turns out to be very human, a Colonel Sellers and P. T. Barnum all in one; and Dorothy's talisman to take her safely home is the pair of silver slippers she has worn all the time. What we want, the moralist whispers, is within us; we need only look for it to find it. What we strive for has been ours all the time.

Was not this the lesson of Baum's life? After half a lifetime stumbling through the Gilded Age and half the vocations a man could try, he had found his fortune within himself, in the humble gift of story telling. Perhaps he even thought of himself as the Wizard, for as the saga of Oz extended itself through book after book, the Wizard of Oz who began as a Prince of Humbug became a genuine wizard.

A poster printed to accompany the stage version of *The Wizard of Oz,* and perhaps intended as a frieze in a theater lobby, puts all this into doggerel:

Next came a lion cowardly, as timid as a bird;
Yet if some danger threatened Dot, his mighty roar
   was heard.
The lion wished that he were brave;
   The Scarecrow wanted brains;
The Tin Man craved a loving heart,
   With all its joys and pains.
Fair Dorothy would fain go back to Kansas and her
   folks. . . .
'Twas thus the four got all their wish;
   His heart the Tin Man got,
The Scarecrow had his brains, and home went Dot.

What would the book have been without Denslow's
illustrations? Certainly it would have lacked one of its
most enchanting features, for Denslow's simple homely
figures are as solid as Baum's story, just as the mock heroic
drawings that Sir John Tenniel made for *Alice in Wonderland* wonderfully reflect its delightful nonsense. Most
nineteenth century children's books were illustrated by
artists who, for the most part, appeared more interested
in beautiful composition and drawing than in pleasing the
child's taste. Furthermore, color illustrations had been too
costly for inexpensive books until after the introduction
of the halftone, about 1893. Denslow splashed the entire
text of *The Wonderful Wizard of Oz* with color. Bright
hues enlivened the story, and he was lavish with full page
pictures. He was not a great draughtsman; he did not have
a soaring imagination, but he had humor, and his characters made friends at once with readers of every age. There
were no barriers of fancy drawing or pretense between the
Scarecrow or the Tin Woodman and little Johnny-Oz-fan.
In the coming years Baum was to work with a number
of illustrators, several of them more talented, but none

ever won greater loyalty from the readers than Denslow.

There are many reasons for the success of *The Wonderful Wizard of Oz*. The time was right. The story was pure enjoyment and had the vitality to survive. The illustrator did his part. But perhaps the real secret was put into words nearly forty years later when the dedication of the Metro-Goldwyn-Mayer motion picture version of the story said of it:

"Time has been powerless to put its kindly philosophy out of fashion."

X

THE WIZARD MARCHES ON

As *The Wonderful Wizard of Oz* became first a best seller and then an institution of American childhood, it drew to itself not only a large army of fans, but also—surest testimony to its worth—a small army of Dorothys. At least a dozen young women made some claim that they had inspired Baum, or that he had them in mind when he wrote. Among others was a matron in Grand Rapids who, by her own account, as a child had been surprised by Baum in his garden at Macatawa Park, Michigan, while she was picking a flower. In later years she recalled that he had told the four-year-old child stories about her namesake which were later used in the Oz books. Unfortunately, Baum did not have a garden at Macatawa; only a cottage on the waterfront. In those days it was common dinner table conversation of the Baum family to discuss each claimant as a phenomenon of their new literary prominence. The author laughed them all off with the remark that he had liked the name of Dorothy long before he had used it in one of his Mother Goose prose stories, and that when he came to write *The Wonderful Wizard of Oz* he "just picked it out of the air."

While Dorothys came and went and were forgotten, *The Wonderful Wizard of Oz* was not. It was destined to go on for half a century, then get its second wind and make a good start on a new half century. No other children's book of its day has been continuously in print until the present; perhaps no other American book has shown greater vitality.

The George M. Hill Company went into bankruptcy in February, 1902, and the receiver, Robert O. Law, took possession of "a modern book bindery . . . several hundred set of plates . . . juvenile books, including a number of the famous Baum—Denslow copyrighted juveniles . . . and books in sheets and in 'process,' " as the sale advertisement in *Publisher's Weekly* of March 29, 1902 put it. Baum's royalties immediately stopped, and he and Denslow could not persuade the receiver to release the plates of their books, which were their property and not subject to the bankruptcy proceedings, so that they could find another publisher. In May the assets and good will of the Hill company were sold to George W. Ogilvie and Company, 166 South Clinton Street, Chicago, who advertised in *Publisher's Weekly* in the same month that *Father Goose, The Wizard of Oz*, and *Mother Goose in Prose* would be on their list. No copies of these books with the Ogilvie name on the title page are known, but that company may have bound and sold some from the sheets which were part of the Hill assets. In June, Ogilvie sold the manufacturing plant of the Hill Company to the Hill Bindery Company, of which George M. Hill was manager.

In September, 1902, the Bowen-Merrill Company, of Indianapolis, Indiana, bought the printing plates for *The Wonderful Wizard of Oz* from Baum and Denslow and forced the receiver to release them. On February 23, 1903, Bowen-Merrill and the two copyright owners signed a contract, giving the company an exclusive right to publish the book. On July 15, 1903, the Bobbs-Merrill Company, successor to Bowen-Merrill, published its first edition under the title, *The Wizard of Oz.* The success of the stage extravaganza, which had made the shortened form of the title familiar to Americans, dictated the change in title for the book. At the same time and in the same way, the Bowen-Merrill Company acquired rights and plates for *Father Goose, The Songs of Father Goose, Dot and Tot of Merryland, American Fairy Tales, The Army Alphabet* and *The Navy Alphabet*—other Baum titles that Hill had published. The firm also took over *A New Wonderland* from R. H. Russell.

The nine thousand nine hundred copies of the 1903 Bobbs-Merrill edition were bound in dull green cloth ornamented with the Scarecrow and Tin Woodman in black and the title in yellow. This edition contained sixteen color plates instead of the twenty-four in the Hill edition and dispensed with some of the ornamental text drawings. This edition, however, was still highly decorative and attractive, especially as compared with later Bobbs-Merrill printings in which the text was reset, and most of the text illustrations eliminated. The color plates gradually disappeared, and a paper label of the Scarecrow and Tin Woodman in colors became the principal feature of the binding.

When the Chadwick Pictures movie version of *The Wizard of Oz* was released in 1925, a special edition containing illustrations from the movie was published for a short time, and, similarly, when the M-G-M color film appeared in 1939, an edition appeared with special end papers of scenes from the movie and a new jacket.

In 1944 the Bobbs-Merrill Company brought out *The New Wizard of Oz,* which retained Baum's story but was illustrated by Evelyn Copelman. She freely adapted Denslow's drawings, changing Dorothy materially, and bringing the dress and appearance of the characters up-to-date for today's children at the sacrifice of much of the charm and fantasy of the original pictures.

Between 1913 and 1920 M. A. Donohue and Company of Chicago issued an edition almost identical with the early Bobbs-Merrill edition under license from the publishers. In 1950 Random House published an adaptation of the story for younger children with new and sleeker illustrations by Anton Loeb.

The copyright on *The Wizard of Oz* expired in 1956, placing it in the public domain. Grosset and Dunlap promptly issued three editions, which they supplemented with a charming Italian-made one in 1958, while Reilly and Lee, publishers of all the other Oz books, brought the title under their imprint for the first time with illustrations by Dale Ulrey. An edition reprinting some of Denslow's plates in black and white and with a history and commentary by Martin Gardner and Professor Russel B. Nye, Chairman of the English Department of Michigan State University, appeared from the press of that institution in 1957. Since then editions have multiplied with the Junior Deluxe edition illustrated by Leonard Weisgard; the Looking Glass Library edition illustrated by Rita Fava, which also includes *The Land of Oz;* and three paperbacks—the Crest book with the Denslow illustrations, the Tab Books edition illustrated by Paul Granger, and the Dover edition which is virtually a facsimile in color of the first edition.

Life, in the issue of December 28, 1953, carried an eight-page article about *The Wonderful Wizard of Oz*, illustrated with what the magazine described as "rare original drawings" retelling Dorothy's amazing adventures. The drawings were fifteen of the full page color illustrations from the 1900 edition.

Translations, usually somewhat abridged, have been published in Holland, Hungary, Portugal, Germany, Rumania, France, Spain, Japan, Italy and Scandinavia. Editions have also appeared in Great Britain and Canada. In addition the book is one of the three Oz books available in Braille for the blind. Under license from the publisher, the durable story has not been too proud to shed some of its sales magic on such varied trivia as pop-up books, paint books, coloring books, cutouts, games, jig-saw puzzles, dolls, mechanical toys, balloons, stationery, and the vending of everything from clothing to peanut butter and ice cream.

According to figures compiled by the Bobbs-Merrill Company, sales of all editions while it was copyrighted totalled about four million. In the six months of 1903 Bobbs-Merrill sold only 9,900 copies, but thereafter, until August, 1956—the latest figures available—it published or licensed for publication the following editions and adaptations:

Trade Editions:

December 31, 1903 to December 30, 1922....	88,827
August 1923 to December 1938 (includes 5,000 movie edition)......................	134,719
January 1939 to October 1943................	116,266
School edition (Special library binding).......	8,484
New 1954 edition to August, 1956...........	262,100

Popular Editions:

Blue Ribbon Waddle Books	38,336
Grosset & Dunlap 50¢ edition	50,000
Animated Duenwald edition	393,767
Wonder Books edition	1,365,026
Random House edition	361,196
Grosset & Dunlap	66,058

Foreign Editions:

English	199,240
Dutch	4,933
Hungarian	1,141
Portuguese	2,000
Canadian	4,574
German	2,000

Special Editions:

Paint book	243,000
Picture book	165,000
Story book	259,000
*Cocomalt edition	430,000

These total 4,195,667, and with the Hill Company editions, and sales that have been running into six figures a year, the total swells into an awesome testimonial to the abiding qualities of the American fairy tale that nobody wanted to publish.

After many years on the stage, *The Wizard of Oz* underwent four metamorphoses on the screen. The first was a one reeler made by the Selig Polyscope Company in Chicago under the title of *The Wonderful Wizard of Oz*. It was released March 24, 1910 and was described in the *Moving Picture World as* "an excellent film, well acted

* Forty-eight page adaptation given as a premium with a beverage powder made by Penick and Ford Limited.

and clearly photographed." A month later Selig released another one reeler, *Dorothy and the Scarecrow in Oz*, in which Dorothy and the Scarecrow meet Oz the Wizard in the Emerald City, the Scarecrow gets brains, the Tin Woodman a heart, and the Cowardly Lion courage from Oz himself, and then all undergo some of the adventures of *Dorothy and the Wizard in Oz*. Late in May, Selig released a third one-reel film, *The Land of Oz*, which moved the *Moving Picture World* to rapture about the spectacles in the Emerald City and the assault on Oz's capital by General Jinjur's soldiers. "It would draw a week anywhere," was the magazine's verdict. Selig had made an Oz movie in 1908 for Baum's Radio-Plays lecture tour, and it appears certain that these one reelers derived most of their material from that film.

Four years later a group of Los Angeles business men, operating as the Oz Film Manufacturing Company, made a five reel version under the title of *His Majesty, the Scarecrow of Oz*. This potpourri from several of the Oz books was later issued as *The New Wizard of Oz*. In 1925 Chadwick Pictures brought out a full length silent movie of *The Wizard of Oz*. Larry Semon was the Scarecrow and Oliver Hardy was the Tin Woodman. Dorothy Dwan played her namesake. The producer depicted Dorothy as a somewhat vampish young woman in short skirts and flapper costumes. The film found little favor with audiences and was soon withdrawn. Twenty-four years later Hollywood tried again, and the result was a resounding success. The Metro-Goldwyn-Mayer Technicolor feature, released August 15, 1939 with a premiere at Grauman's Chinese Theater in Hollywood, offered spectacular settings and a star-studded cast: Judy Garland as Dorothy,

Ray Bolger as the Scarecrow, Jack Haley as the Tin Woodman, Bert Lahr as the Cowardly Lion, Frank Morgan as
the Wizard, and Billie Burke as Glinda the Good Sorceress. Few films have had such a tuneful musical score, including the hit song, "Over the Rainbow," and the marching song, "We're Off to See the Wizard," by Harold Arlen
and E. Y. Harburg.

The producer, Mervyn LeRoy, recognized early in the
game that he faced the same problem that had come up
when *The Wizard of Oz* was adapted for the stage. He
would have to make a picture which would entertain
adults as well as children. He would have to add music
and spectacular color and dramatic effects, but above all,
would have to keep the fantasy down to earth. "We had
to make even a Scarecrow, a Tin Woodman, a Cowardly
Lion, a Witch, a Wizard, and such strange people as
Munchkins and Winkies seem like real personalities," he
said. "In other words we had to put realism into the fantastic. No matter how strange our character, or how weird
our events, they had to be believable and plausible." The
M-G-M version deliberately conformed to Baum's story
"to please every Baum fan," as Victor Fleming, the director, put it, except in one respect. The producers caused
Dorothy to be knocked unconscious in the cyclone. In that
condition she was made to dream the story of her adventures in Oz, peopling that dream world with hired men
and neighbors from her Kansas farm home. At the end
she awakens to find them all at her bedside. In 1956 the
Columbia Broadcasting System reran this Technicolor
motion picture as a television spectacular for which the
sponsor is reputed to have paid a single performance royalty of $250,000, and it played a return engagement in

1960. The picture has been re-released several times for showing in movie houses throughout the United States.

In the late 1920's a puppet version was produced by Ellen Van Volkenburg, and the Cornish School of the Theater in Seattle toured with its own highly acclaimed dramatization for puppets in 1955. Nancy Kelly was Dorothy and Parker Fennelly was the Cowardly Lion in a radio network series from September 25, 1933 to May 24, 1934. It was sponsored by the makers of Jello. A form in which the story of *The Wizard of Oz* has been much used by amateur and school dramatic groups is Elizabeth Fuller Goodspeed's dramatization published in 1928 by Samuel French for Junior League Plays.*

The plump, squarish green book that hit the stores in the fall of 1900 was too successful and too original to be overlooked by other writers. Presently it became the fashion to make children's books American in setting and benevolent in mood. The most slavish imitation is Eva Katherine Gibson's *Zauberlinda*, which was published by the Robert Smith Printing Company in Chicago in 1901. The Black Hills of Dakota take the place of Baum's Kansas settings; Annie and her cat stand in for Dorothy and her dog; and the action revolves around a wise witch against a background of gnomes and other fairyland folk. *Zauberlinda*, which is self-described as "an attempt to unite the rich legends of Older Lands with the Fact and Fancy of the New World," found an avid juvenile public

---

* *The Land of Oz* was also dramatized in 1928 by Mrs. Goodspeed. It was followed by *Ozma of Oz* (1935) and *The Enchanted Island of Yew* (1937) from the pen of Mary Isabel Buchanan, and *The Patchwork Girl of Oz* (1930) by Mrs. James Waller Marshall. All are in French's Junior League Plays series.

prepared for it by the success of its more memorable predecessor. In physical appearance, from the cover decorations to the illustrations and florid text drawings by Mabel Tibbitts, the book as closely follows Denslow's designs as its story parallels Baum's.

Worthy of briefer mention in this connection is Grace Duffie Boylan's *Yama Yama Land,* a tale of considerable original merit now remembered only because it inspired the musical comedy in which Bessie McCoy was "the Yama Yama Girl."

Baum himself paid little attention to his imitators and literary disciples. He was delighted with the success of *The Wizard of Oz,* and he was even more delighted with the response of the children to his fable. Scarcely a day passed without a letter from a boy or girl demanding "more about Dorothy," or asking "what became of the Scarecrow," or "where did the Cowardly Lion live?" The letters came singly and in bundles of fifty and one hundred. Whenever a teacher read the story to her pupils— and it happened far more frequently than one would suspect—Baum would receive letters from some of the children, or on occasion, a joint letter signed by the whole class. For years he answered them personally, recalling that when he was a boy, a letter from an author whose book he had enjoyed would have made him the happiest child alive.

One little girl wrote wanting to know whether he had any little girls of his own. She added: "If you had it would be nice for them to be sick because then you could tell them such nice stories."

"Please, Dear Mr. Baum," began a letter from another, "write another story about the Tin Woodman, the Scarecrow and the Wizard. They are grate. Your friend, Marcus."

"My teacher has read us *The Wizard of Oz,*" asserted one child correspondent. "The picture I like best is the Scarecrow. I think he is very funny. Our family likes it very much. I don't know where you get all the nice stories." Another child wrote: "I am going to write you a letter. You wrote a nice book. It's called *The Wizard of Oz.* I couldn't write a book like that. I think I love you."

Again and again the children demanded more books about Oz. "I just love *The Wizard of Oz,*" wrote one typical fan. "I have read it three times and the pictures are just lovely. My name is Dorothy, too. And the Scarecrow and Tin Woodman were so nice to Dorothy and all of them. I would like very much to have you write another story about Dorothy. You don't have to make it very long and, of course, you don't have to do it if you don't want to. We had a cyclone here once but I wasn't born. If I were born then maybe I would have gone to the same place as Dorothy did."

A letter from another Dorothy said: "I read *The Wizard of Oz* every rainy day. I thank you very much for the lovely book. I think the pictures are fine, too. I hope lots and lots of girls and boys will read the book, too."

One of the most touching was from a nine year old boy from Brooklyn. Perhaps with some help from his uncle, he wrote: "My uncle told me to write you and ask if you would make me a sequel to *The Wizard of Oz* which I have read with great interest. My grandma, with whom I have lived since my papa died, has lost her eyesight and likes to have me read to her so I read some every day. I think she would like to have me read her a new book you write."

One group of letters came from grownups, telling of the therapeutic value of these stories. One in particular, from a young mother whose son had recently died, Baum could never forget. The boy had been rescued from drowning but had been so weakened that he lived only a few days. While he lay in bed, he called for stories about Oz. The father bought all he could get in the town where they lived and borrowed others from friends. Day and night, as the child grew weaker, the parents and nurses took turns reading to him. His last words were "princess of Oz." On another occasion, following an infantile paralysis epidemic in New York, a surgeon wrote Baum: "All the doctors connected with this hospital feel you have done as much as anyone during this siege, for when little bodies are pain racked, arms and legs had to be stretched, and the children were told if they did their best a nurse would read an Oz book to them. An Oz book was as much a part of our nurses's equipment as a thermometer."*

Hundreds of children seemed puzzled as to why so many fairy tales begin with "Once upon a time—" and they asked Baum for an explanation. He had an answer that seemed to satisfy his young readers so well that he printed it in *The Life and Adventures of Santa Claus,* published in 1902. "When this world was young," he told them, "there were no autos, no airplanes to make a child wonder, nor were there railway trains. There were no telephones

* This was before the Kenny treatment was discovered, and the mistaken therapy was to stretch out limbs deformed by muscle spasm.

or mechanical inventions to keep people keyed up to a high pitch of excitement. Men and women lived quietly and simply. They were Nature's children and breathed clean air into their lungs instead of smoke and coal gas. They tramped through green meadows and deep forests instead of riding on streetcars and buses. They went to bed when the sun set and got up when it rose.

"The fairies felt sorry for the simple people of those times and helped them to look after their simple wants. Sometimes the fairies even showed themselves to those persons they had befriended. But today the fairies are shy because man's inventions are more wonderful than the wonders of fairyland. For that reason, fairy stories have to go back to the days when boys and girls and even older folk saw the fairies more often than they do today. And that is why such stories often start with 'Once upon a time.'"

A letter from a college professor, inquiring "for readers of what age are your books intended," caused Baum to reread some of the letters he had received, in the hope that he would find an answer there. He found a letter that read: "I am a little boy, just five years old and I just love your Oz stories. My sister who is writing this for me, reads me the Oz books but I wish that I could read them myself." Another read: "I am a great girl, thirteen years old, so you'll be surprised when I tell you I'm not yet too old for the Oz stories." Still another said: "Since I was a young girl I've never missed getting a Baum book for Christmas. I'm married now, but am as eager to get and read the Oz stories as ever." Finally was this one: "My good wife and I, both more than seventy years of age, believe that we find more real enjoyment in your fairy tales than in any books we have read." After pondering the story told by these letters, Baum replied to the professor: "My books are intended for all those whose hearts are young, no matter what their ages may be."

As *The Wizard of Oz* has lived on into its second half century with undiminished vigor, it is evident that his reply was not the braggadocio that it might easily seem. Instead, it recognized that so long as the young in heart exist, there will be a market for imagination, humor, fanciful characters, and a whimsical, happy story.

XI

NEW WORLDS

As THE new century lengthened into its second year, the success of *The Wonderful Wizard of Oz* guided Baum toward his destined career—the writing of books for children. He began to think of disposing of his *Show Window* magazine and began creating a whole new galaxy of magic worlds. At this time Baum had no thought of following up the popularity of Oz by writing a sequel. Indeed, he admits in the preface of his next book, *Dot and Tot of Merryland,* "the success achieved last year by *The Wonderful Wizard of Oz*—a book that not only ran through many large editions but brought to the author hundreds of letters from interested little folk—has induced me to follow that tale with another, herein presented."

Accordingly, in the next few years he issued a variety of stories. Some were among his most original and striking creations, highly imaginative and written at the peak of his powers. Nevertheless, they have been obscured by the sheer bulk of the stories about Oz.

Baum had aimed at creating modern American fairy tales in which the heartaches and blood-curdling incidents of the European models would be eliminated. This posed severe problems, the chief one being the invention of novel and exciting incident to replace the terror and conflict of the traditional forms. For example, in such a story as "Hansel and Gretel," the cunning and cruelty of the witch and the happy escape of the two innocents created a typical dramatic structure which kept the interest of children. But Baum's story telling ability had to rest on mastery of whimsical and comic characters, and on a plot structure which would achieve suspense without horror. In *Dot and Tot of Merryland,* his principal story for 1901, he was just coming to grips with the problem and was far from the fluent solutions he found later. Nevertheless it is a worthy companion piece to its more famous predecessor, *The Wonderful Wizard of Oz. Dot and Tot of Merryland* is a sunny book, unperplexed and quietly charming where *The Wonderful Wizard of Oz* is stormy and urgent. Though now a forgotten book, *Dot and Tot of Merryland* is one of Baum's most personal pieces of writing, for it reflects his own natural happiness and joy in life and recalls happy moments from his past. He seems always close to the reader in this carefree tale of drifting from one pleasant place to the next. *Dot and Tot of Merryland* was identical in size with *The Wonderful Wizard of Oz.* It was bound in yellow cloth with the figure of the Queen of Merryland, golden hair and all, on the front cover. Jointly copyrighted by Baum and Denslow, it was the last book in which they collaborated. It was also the last Baum book published by the Hill company. Bobbs-Merrill issued an undated edition in 1903, and another edition carries the Donohue imprint.

Denslow poured his decorative talent into the illustra-

tions and the text drawings. The character of the story
allowed him particular opportunity to parade rows of figures across the pages like comic friezes, but with each tiny
figure amusingly individualized by some feature or item
of costume. Vermilion and cocoa brown splash the pages
with barbaric gayety. In his preface Baum paid a grace-
ful tribute to his collaborator, saying: "Mr. Denslow's
quaint and merry pictures, which, I think, in this book
excel all his previous work, will be sure to induce happiness in the heart of every beholder."

The first chapter is sheer autobiography. The little
heroine, Dot, is living at Roselawn, a country estate whose
very name is that of Baum's childhood home near Syracuse. He describes it lovingly:

> The cool but sun-kissed mansion seemed delightful
> after the stuffy formal city house. It was built in a quaint,
> but pretty fashion, and with many wings and gables and
> broad verandas on every side. Before it were acres and
> acres of velvety green lawns, sprinkled with shrubbery and
> dotted with beds of bright flowers. In every direction were
> winding paths covered with white gravel, which led to all
> parts of the grounds, looking for all the world like a map.

Dot, the banker's daughter, and Tot, the gardener's son,
go on a picnic together. They discover a boat on the river
that flows by Roselawn, climb into it, drift from shore and
through a tunnel into Merryland, an enchanted country
made up of seven valleys. The first is inhabited by clowns
who are delighted to have Dot and Tot as visitors because heretofore they have never had an audience for
their tricks. The second valley—the Valley of Bonbons—
is the home of the candy people, plump from their high
calorie diet, and also very perishable. The third is the

valley where baby blossoms fall from the sky, unfold their petals and disclose a sleeping baby. The babies are cared for by storks until they are ready to be flown by their winged nurses into the world. The fourth valley is the realm of the Queen of Merryland, a lovely wax doll who reigns over other dolls and toys which she brings to life for a few hours every day. In her company, Dot and Tot— now Princess and Prince of Merryland—visit the last three valleys; those of the cats, wind-up toys and lost things. The wind-up toys are kept running by a schizophrenic, two-part man known as Mr. Split, and in the valley of lost things is the final resting place of shoes, gloves, toys, and other misplaced possessions of childhood. But the seven-fold allure of Merryland and even the glamor of royal titles are not enough to make Dot and Tot forget Rose-lawn; so the Queen of Merryland allows them to drift back home.

Many pages of *Dot and Tot of Merryland* deserve something better than a place in the valley of forgotten things. The chapter on the Valley of Babies is poetic and tenderly imaginative. It is a lullaby written by a man who loved children. Merryland is filled with the themes Baum knew were close to the hearts of children—candy and clowns, kittens and dainty dolls. The Valley of Lost Things with its piles of overshoes, boy's caps and broken toys certainly grew out of the experience of a father of four sons. Most memorable of all is Mr. Split, the wind-up man, who has so much business and so much territory to cover that he unhooks himself down the middle—an arm and a leg to each half of him—and goes about, his own double, at the chores of keeping the toys running.

Dot and Tot of Merryland is placid, poetic and gay, but

it was too delicate to survive in the rough world of children's books. From it Baum learned that spine tingling action is required to set the cash registers tinkling. He was finding his way as a story teller, and he now knew he must include excitement. Far from discarding the time tested formula of the folk tale, he was actually stretching it in two directions. One was toward the American and the familiar—Dorothy and Kansas, Tot and Roselawn, instead of Hans and the Black Forest. The other he extended beyond the merely quaint into a realm peopled with fantastic folk born of his teeming imagination: queens, gnomes and other traditional residents of fairyland jostle animal, vegetable, and mineral people, as all rush at the headlong pace set for them by their creator. Such a fanciful realm must be ruled by a firm master. Baum ruled it well so long as he had a sound story to tell. Little fault can be found with the full length tales he wrote before Oz began to monopolize his attention, nor with the earlier Oz stories. But when his facility for fantastic invention ran riot, either through sheer exuberance or through deliberate effort to conceal the poverty of the plot, the pitfalls to which his story telling way was exposed became apparent. Usually, however, he succeeded in keeping his young readers wide-eyed to the last page.

Just at this critical time of decision as a writer, Baum had the misfortune to lose not only his publisher, Hill, but also Denslow, the collaborator of the exciting days of *Father Goose* and *The Wonderful Wizard of Oz*. Details were never brought into the open, but the separation of Baum and Denslow appears to have arisen from more than one cause. First of all, no close bonds of personal friendship held the two men. Their primary association had been through business. They had different friends, different habits, and different ways of living. Denslow was quixotic and extroverted. A friend of his Roycroft days said he had the voice of a second mate in a storm—a voice like a foghorn, and that his sense of humor was upside down. He would carp and complain and grumble until he had suitably irritated his audience, then laugh uproariously at his success. The bohemian atmosphere of his studio, where his cronies gathered, was the center of his life. Baum, on the other hand, was quiet and spent most of his evenings at home.

In the second place, during the negotiations over the stage production of *The Wizard of Oz,* Denslow, as half owner of the copyright on the book, insisted on a share of the royalties from the dramatization, although he had had no part in preparing the story for the stage. To avoid a threatened lawsuit, Baum finally agreed. The diary of Paul Tietjens records some of the acrimony with which he and Baum resisted Denslow's demands. Finally, the failure of their publisher, Hill, at this time provided author and artist with a convenient occasion to part company.

In the fall of 1903 Denslow and his wife, Ann Waters, were divorced. Both had found new partners; for Denslow married again and went to live in New York, while his former wife became the bride of Lawrence Mazzanovich, a young painter of considerable talent who had been living with the Denslows before their divorce. She had first met "Mazzy" at the Roycroft Shops. Elbert Hubbard II recalls that "Denslow was a pretty gruff old fellow, and I can well understand that a soft talking, nice guy like Mazzy didn't have too much trouble in winning her away." He long survived her, dying in May, 1959.

Denslow's new wife was reputed to have wealth, and he had the income from books he had illustrated and from *The Wizard of Oz,* which had been the stage hit of the year in New York. In New York Denslow organized an advertising and design service and continued to illustrate books. Later, George W. Ogilvie, in Chicago, issued twenty-two of his color plates from *The Wonderful Wizard of Oz* as a pamphlet. In his flush New York days, Denslow bought an island in the Bermudas, still known by his name, and set himself up there as an absolute monarch, with Archie, an ancient boatman, as admiral of his fleet, and his Japanese cook as prime minister. In his last years in New York, however, he was down in his luck, doing art work for agencies, and pawning a cheap copy of *Hudibras* with a book dealer friend whenever he needed a dollar. One day a stranger brought the book in and announced that Denslow was dead. He died on March 27, 1915, and left his small estate to a friend, Dorothy Federlein, who cared for him in his last shabby days.

Of the three books which Baum published in 1901, the most readable is *American Fairy Tales,* a collection of short stories which were serialized in the juvenile sections of several newspapers between March 2 and May 19, 1901. Among these papers were the Chicago *Chronicle,* Cincinnati *Enquirer,* Pittsburgh *Dispatch,* Boston *Post,* and St. Louis *Republican. American Fairy Tales* is a small volume of two hundred twenty-four pages, bound in cloth and stamped in three colors. It was published by the Hill Company on the same day as *Dot and Tot of Merryland,* October 19, 1901, and was illustrated by three Chicago artists, Ike Morgan, Harry Kennedy and N. P. Hall. The text was printed within elaborate William Morris-style borders drawn by Ralph Fletcher Seymour, and the book sold for seventy-five cents.

The tales are not all American, nor are they all fairy tales. However, they are nearly the last deliberate attempt Baum made to keep his fancy in a native setting. Henceforth he would dwell in lands of his own creating. What makes the tales distinctive is that Baum went beyond his fairy tale formula into a new kind of fantasy. The *American Fairy Tales* have a tautness, an unexpected streak of irony, a sharpness of style and a maturity of imagination that is somewhat more piquant than the pablum usually provided for children. Some are peopled with mischievous folk whom the author dubbed "knooks and ryls"—sprites that he would call back into his service the following year in *The Life and Adventures of Santa Claus*. But most of the stories exist on an earthly level until some unearthly twist takes them into the realm of fantasy.

Typical is the first story, "The Box of Robbers." Nosy little Martha, who lives in Prairie Avenue in Chicago, unlocks a chest left in the garret long ago by her uncle. As she raises the lid, out step three Italian banditti—knife-in-teeth comic opera types—who boast of their wickedness and propose to show it by robbing the people of Chicago. When Martha timidly suggests that "I think they have all been robbed already," they plunder Martha's house instead. Just then the postman comes to the door and they rush back into their chest. Martha turns the key on them, and the moral—if it can be called a moral—is that if Martha had not been so nosy she would not have had to carry all the plunder down stairs again.

"The Glass Dog" recalls George Ade's *Fables in Slang*, which had been published in Chicago in the previous year.

Both point the finger of fun at the manners of contemporary society. The hero of "The Glass Dog" is a glass-blower who possesses one drop of a magic elixir. With it he saves the life of a young heiress. She goes back, however, on her promise to marry him until another magic potion makes him handsome. Then they are married and live unhappily ever after. In "The Queen of Quok," a prince is about to be married off to the rich and elderly Mary Ann Brodjinsky de la Porkus, (a meat packing heiress, of course) to save his kingdom from bankruptcy. Instead, he is able to save himself and the kingdom by means of a magic purse that is never empty. The tale's scale of values is as worldly as its plot is ingenious. Among the other stories, "The Laughing Hippo," a tale of the Congo with an O. Henry twist, and "The Wonderful Pump," a morality with a somber, Hawthorne-like atmosphere, are notably different from Baum's previous writing. Even though *The Wonderful Wizard of Oz* contained an occasional hint that Baum had a sharp eye for the foibles of mankind, these short stories are his first considerable venture into satire on social behavior.

American Fairy Tales was republished in 1908 by the Bobbs-Merrill Company in a larger format as *Baum's American Fairy Tales* and with the addition of three stories—"The Witchcraft of Mary-Marie," "The Strange Adventures of an Egg," and "The Ryl"—which added nothing to the quality of the collection. George Kerr's amusing full page illustrations were the most attractive new feature.

While he was completing the *American Fairy Tales* for Hill, the Bowen-Merrill Company approached Baum with an offer to publish a full length story from his pen. Because he was unwilling to compete on the bookstands with

his own forthcoming *Dot and Tot of Merryland,* Baum
accepted the Bowen-Merrill contract on the condition that
he would write a different kind of fairy story. The result
was *The Master Key,* the third of Baum's books published
in 1901. It is early day science fiction, the time-tested formula of the fairy tale freshened up with the magic and
wonder of electricity, as new and exciting then to a boy's
imagination as atomic power and guided missiles are today. In a prophetic mood, Baum described his book, in the
preface, as "a fairy tale founded upon the wonders of electricity and written for children of this generation. Yet
when my readers shall have become men and women my
story may not seem to their children like a fairy tale at all."
On the fly leaf of the copy of *The Master Key* that Baum
presented to his second son, Robert, he wrote: "This book,
dedicated to Robert, is due in its inception to his love of
electrical toys. For his workshop first gave me the idea of
an electrical story and 'The Electrical Demon' was a natural sequence. The book has been so well received that I
am sorry, now, I did not end it differently and leave an
opening for a sequel." Previously, in a letter to his brother,
Baum had mentioned that "Rob fills the house with electrical batteries and such truck and we are prepared to hear
a bell ring whenever we open a door or step on a stair."

Appropriately enough, the hero of *The Master Key* is
an American boy named Rob. While experimenting with
electricity, Rob by chance completes some hitherto undis-
covered circuit. This instantly calls before him the Demon,
or Genius of Electricity, who presents the boy with six
marvelous electrical inventions, including an "automatic
record of events" machine, which is essentially a super-
television set that shows not only contemporaneous events

but also events that have occurred throughout the world within the preceding twenty-four hours. With this set, a ray gun, tablet food, a wrist watch flying device, a protective suit and a pair of character-revealing spectacles, the boy sets out to see the world, and soon becomes involved in a series of melodramatic adventures. He learns, however, that possession of such inventions carries with it the power to do evil as well as good. Convinced that no man is good or wise enough to make proper use of them, he summons the Demon again and returns to him the electrical marvels, bidding him to keep them hidden until the Demon is convinced that mankind is ready for them.

Baum, of course, had been interested in invention from the time of his "Our Landlady" columns in the Dakota newspaper. In spite of his prophetic view of the dangers of some of science's discoveries, he had a serious respect for the kind of imagination that leads a boy to experiment and try to understand the nature of things. Scientific imagination had brought mankind out of the Dark Ages, and through the power of invention, into the age of the steam engine, talking machine and automobile, he wrote in the preface to *The Lost Princess of Oz:* "For these things had to be dreamed of before they became realities," he went on. "So I believe that dreams—day dreams, you know, with your eyes wide open and your brain machinery whirring—are likely to lead to the betterment of the world. The imaginative child will become the imaginative man or woman most apt to create, invent, and therefore to foster civilization. A prominent educator tells us that fairy tales are of untold value in developing imagination to the young. I believe it." The small volume of two hundred forty-five pages was bound in drab green cloth stamped in gold—a binding so ugly that even the excellent color plates and text drawings by Fanny Cory* did not make it any more alluring to a child's eye. *The Master Key* is significant in Baum's career as his first association with the publisher to whom he turned for help when the Hill company failed. Undoubtedly this association played its part in bringing him to the attention of Bowen-Merrill and alerted that company to the opportunity to get more Baum titles on its list from Hill's receiver.

For his next book, Baum returned to the scheme of his first, *Mother Goose in Prose,* which had clothed with imaginative detail traditional jingles attributed to that sage. In much the same way, *The Life and Adventures of Santa Claus* fills out the meager legend of childhood's beloved saint. In Baum's pages, Santa Claus is born, finds his life work, and attains immortality. The whole story is there, told in sweet, stately prose, just as the children would have it. The book was published in 1902 by the Bowen-Merrill Company with illustrations by Mary Cowles Clark. It had originally been advertised in January, 1902, for publication by the George N. Hill Company, only a few weeks before that firm went into bankruptcy. It became available to the Bowen-Merrill Company when the Baum-Denslow titles were taken over from Hill.

Because of his innate love of children, Baum knew that they were curious and that the legend of jolly, bearded Santa, as it is told in Clement Clark Moore's poem, for instance, is not enough to satisfy young, eager minds. He understood they could not help wondering whether Santa

---

* The illustrator of a number of books for Bobbs-Merrill Company, Miss Cory is the wife of Fred Cooney and lives in Canyon Ferry, Montana.

was once young like themselves, and why he brought toys
to children. Almost entirely disregarding the stock Santa
Claus legend, Baum wrote of a great forest peopled with
fairies, knooks, ryls, and nymphs, a rustic paradise of the
immortals, where man's civilization was unknown. Among
them was Necile, a nymph who found an abandoned baby
at the edge of the forest. She reared him as her own, calling him Neclaus, which in the language of the immortals,
meant "Necile's little one."

As Neclaus grew to manhood, he dedicated his life to
bringing happiness into the lives of the babies of mankind,
and in the Laughing Valley of Hohaho he built a hut
where, in idle moments, he amused himself by whittling
out little figures. Presently children began coming to the
hut to beg for them; for until this time toys had been unknown. Neclaus made more toys and carried them in his
pack to the cities so that the children there might also be
happy. Then he made a sled, drawn by a deer, so that he
could visit more distant cities in a trip. Because the houses
were locked at night, he had to enter with his gifts down
the broad chimneys.

As the years passed and his unselfish devotion to children became known, he could scarcely keep up with the
demand for toys. So he built a fine new sleigh, drawn by
ten reindeer, with which he could visit the whole world
in one night. Besides toys, he left fir trees to be decorated.
But Neclaus was mortal. He grew old. His beard was snowy
and his hands were too feeble to hold the tools that had
made the world's children happy. The immortals held a
great council, and as Neclaus lay dying they placed over
him the mantle of immortality. Although he kept the appearance of age, he had gained eternal youth. Once again

he could make toys and take them to the world's firesides. This he will always do because he believes that "in all the world there is nothing so beautiful as a happy child."

Santa Claus was not merely folklore in the Baum household, for the four boys had plenty of evidence that their father was familiar with the old saint and shared his spirit. Every Christmas, while they were young, Baum would bring home a fir tree and hide it. After the boys were in bed on Christmas Eve he would carry it into the living room, and he and Maud would spend hours decorating it with glass ornaments, tinsel, strings of popcorn and tin clamp-on holders for the candles. Then, on Christmas morning, while Maud kept the children at the breakfast table, he would slip out the back door and in through the front to light the candles. After that he would rush in through the back door ringing a string of sleighbells as the boys ran into the living room to see the tree and the presents piled underneath it.

As the years passed and the two older boys became more sophisticated about such things, the tree was brought in and decorated during the late afternoon and the sleighbells were rung as supper was finished on Christmas Eve. To Baum these things were essential and important, for they symbolized the affection with which parents cherish their children and the love that binds families together. In the lean years he and Maud would limit themselves on food and clothing so that their sons would not be disappointed by what they found under the tree.

Staging and production of *The Wizard of Oz* extravaganza in 1902 took up so much of Baum's time that his literary output was small that year and the next. The only entirely new book published in 1903 was *The Enchanted*

Island of Yew, issued by The Bobbs-Merrill Company. In the same year that company's first edition of *The Wizard of Oz* appeared, as well as *The Surprising Adventures of the Magical Monarch of Mo,* which was the Bobbs-Merrill title for a slightly revised version of *A New Wonderland* of 1900.

The Enchanted Island of Yew was issued in gray cloth decorated with a full length illustration. It was Baum's second book illustrated by Miss Cory. Once again the author created a magic dream world—a round island divided like a mince pie into four wedge-shaped kingdoms, with a fifth, Spor, in the center. The eastern kingdom is Dawna; the one where the sun goes down is Auriel; the fertile southland, Plenta; the northern land of the barons, Heg. The magic island is peopled by immortals, and one of these, whose sunny nature, energy, and whimsical humor forecast the character Baum would create later in Polychrome, the Rainbow's daughter, persuades the daughter of one of these barons to transform her into a young man for a year. Taking the name of Prince Marvel, the disguised immortal sets off on a white charger in quest of adventure. At the court of King Terribus of Spor, who is so sensitive about his repulsive appearance that he has become a cruel tyrant, Prince Marvel reforms the despot by making him handsome. The next, and best, of the adventures is in the Land of Twi, where all the people and things are double and the light is dim because, of course, it is Twilight. After turning this twin-centric land topsy-turvy the Prince vanquishes a phony sorcerer and Red Rogue, a giant who knows a good trick with magic mirrors. At the end of the year, Prince Marvel returns from his adventures, gives up his silver armor, and abandons his magic disguise—having stored up enough excitement to make endurable the next few centuries of uneventful immortality.

The Enchanted Island of Yew is fantasy by a now practiced hand. Yew is a long way from America, but Baum had learned how to fill his narrative with rapid fire action so that the young reader did not miss the conventional excitements of the European type fairy tale. The adventures at the court of King Terribus and those in the Land of Twi are highly original, yet not so fantastic that they are beyond the capacity of the child to believe and enjoy.

If *The Wizard of Oz* is Baum's greatest book (and the enthusiasm of millions seems to have established that), what is the one most worthy to stand beside it?

Certainly the author was at the peak of his story-telling ability when he penned *Queen Zixi of Ix,* published by the Century Company on October 1, 1905. The story appeared serially in *St. Nicholas* from November, 1904 through October 1905. The book was bound in green cloth stamped in red and green and illustrated by Frederick Richardson, noted artist and cartoonist of the *Chicago Daily News.* A London edition appeared in the next year.

The gossamer plot of *Queen Zixi of Ix* is woven around the magic wrought by a cloak which the fairies loomed to beguile an idle hour. The Man in the Moon advised them to give it to the first unhappy person they meet in the Kingdom of Noland. By this chance it falls to Margaret, a little girl who, with her brother Bud, is being taken by their stern aunt Rivette to live in the capital city, Nole, after the death of their parents. The King of Noland has just died, and an old law decrees that his successor shall be the forty-seventh person who enters the gates of the city. This chance makes Bud the new king, and he, accompanied by Margaret with her magic cloak that grants one wish to anyone who possesses it, goes to live in the royal palace.

The cloak does strange things to the old king's five fat councilors and his lean valet, Jikki, who make idle wishes while ignorant of its powers. But Queen Zixi, of the nearby kingdom of Ix, covets the cloak. Although by her own magic arts she makes herself appear eternally young and beautiful to human eyes, her own mirror is not deceived. It betrays her true appearance to herself, and her wounded vanity cries for the cloak's help. One wish and she will appear young to herself, too. Through war and trickery Queen Zixi gets the magic cloak, but the fairies had decreed when it was enchanted that it would be powerless in the hands of one who had stolen it. Finding it cannot help her, Queen Zixi throws the cloak away.

Meanwhile, Noland is being invaded by the Roly-Rogues, tough, basketball shaped savages who bounce down from the nearby high mountains. Bud and Margaret with their aunt, to whom the magic cloak has given wings, flee to Queen Zixi's kingdom. The Queen has now repented of her vain ambition and has become a wise ruler. Bud and Margaret, with Zixi's help, put the Roly-Rogues to sleep and roll them into the ocean. After this they try to regain the magic cloak, which had been cut up and made into a crazy quilt. The queen of the fairies who wove it comes to claim the pieces and to cancel the foolish wishes. Queen Zixi pleads for consideration, but the fairy queen tells her that the fairies will not give countenance to vanity and will not help her.

Though lacking the wonderfully earthy vigor of *The*

Wizard of Oz, Queen Zixi of Ix glistens with the golden luster of superb story telling. It is the most classical of Baum's stories. Margaret is Cinderella, Noland is Utopia, and the vain wishes recall the plight of the unhappy personage in the old fairy tale who wished the sausages on the end of his nose. The rebuke of vanity, exemplified by Queen Zixi, is a theme as old as mythology itself, and Aunt Rivette is the sharp-tempered foster mother known to all literature. The Roly-Rogues, though, are pure Baum; one of those strenuous tribes of "meanies" which become almost a convention in the later Oz books. But rarely have all these elements been put together so skillfully, with such unique humor, such a light touch of pathos, such unoffending morality, and so wistfully satisfying an ending. As Dr. Wagenknecht has said in his *Utopia Americana, Queen Zixi of Ix* is "certainly one of the best fairy tales in the world." And on the flyleaf of the copy which Baum presented to his oldest son, Frank, he wrote: "You are the last of my boys to have one of my books dedicated to you, but it was your own wish, and in waiting for this story perhaps you have not been unwise. In some ways *Queen Zixi* is my best effort, and nearer to the 'old-fashioned' fairy tale than anything I have yet accomplished."

An entirely different type was the last of the full length stories with which Baum attempted to escape from confinement in the Land of Oz. *John Dough and the Cherub,* published in 1906, is a romp—a magnificent farce that somehow escaped its proper place on the musical comedy stage. It was illustrated by John R. Neill, who would illustrate all of Baum's Oz books except the first, and published by Reilly and Britton, who published all except two of the subsequent Baum titles. John Dough is a ginger-bread man who comes alive by having been accidentally mixed with a mysterious Arabian elixir. Life in a ginger-bread-hungry world is hard for John. He has to avoid rain that might melt him and the Arab who wants to eat him to get the benefit of the elixir. On the island of Phreex John meets Chick the Cherub, an Incubator Baby, and a full roster of the characters whom Baum's imagination would naturally find in such a place. One, who is in disgrace because he is successful, invents an airplane in which John and the Cherub escape to several other islands. The Wright brothers had flown the first heavier than air machine in 1903, and Baum was not slow to exploit the interest of his young readers in man-made wings. John and the Cherub have more brushes with the elixir-hungry Arab and also encounter the mean little Mifkits who have heads like coconuts and bodies shaped like pears, until at last they find peace and a throne in the twin kingdom of Hiland and Loland.

Baum's humor was unrestrained when he wrote *John Dough and the Cherub*. His weakness for puns makes him describe John as "a delicatessen: a friend in knead, I might say, a Pan-American," whose pride is "bread in the bone." Spoonerisms abound, such as the name of Sir Austed Alfrin, Poet Laureate to the Kinglet of Phreex. Inasmuch as Sir Alfred Austin was Poet Laureate to King Edward VII at that time, the humor is topical. So is the name of a fluffy-haired musician, Tietjamus Toips, who is made supremely happy when told that his compositions are discordant and incomprehensible. Paul Tietjens, of course, had been Baum's musical collaborator in *The Wizard of Oz*.

John Dough and the Cherub is full of marvels—a tube that repels rain and keeps the wearer dry in a storm until the power runs out, a television set with which the King of the Beavers watches events from his cave under the waterfall, and an airplane that flaps its wings.

After *John Dough and the Cherub,* Baum's fantasy was pretty much confined to the Land of Oz and its environs. In the first six years of the new century he had created a half dozen magic worlds for the children. Since 1900 he had published close to a score of titles under his own name. One had become internationally known and had been the substance of a highly successful play. Baum could look back and say that he had found his place in the world after a half century of searching. And after this the way would be plain even though it would not always be smooth. For Baum the Gilded Age was over and the Age of Gold was at hand.

XII

A PLACE IN THE SUN

IN HIS YOUTH Baum had developed habits of industry;
necessity strengthened these habits in middle life, and he
kept his days and nights filled with many projects even
after success had come. Not only did he continue his magazine, *The Show Window*, until 1902, but he devoted many
months to the production of *The Wizard of Oz*. Later, despite a steady stream of books under half a dozen names,
he never allowed his interest in the theater to lapse. He
completed and staged two of half a dozen dramatic projects
as well as carrying out his *Radio Plays* tour and his venture in motion pictures.

In spite of such activity he had more time than in the
lean years to be with Maud and his four sons, who by this
time were young men. A few years later he told an interviewer: "I've got twenty-four feet, four-and-a-half inches
of boys myself. Four of them, and every one over six feet."
Royalties from *Father Goose* and *The Wonderful Wizard
of Oz* made possible more comforts and luxuries. Each of
the four sons, for example, owned a new Columbia Safety
bicycle, and he and Maud bought a tandem, but soon gave
it up for separate bicycles.

On a pleasant summer Sunday afternoon the six Baums would mount their six bicycles and pedal to nearby Humboldt Park. After a basket picnic they would lie on the grass or stroll around and talk with their neighbors while they listened to the music from the bandstand. In those days, when the phonograph was still an expensive novelty and radio was undreamed of, such music as the average American heard was made by park bands, church choirs, theater orchestras, or cafe musicians. In winter Baum would take his family to the North Side Turnverein Hall. An orchestra of forty to fifty German musicians played on a stage at one end of the large room, while dozens of families sat around the big tables listening to the music, drank coffee or beer and munched on hearty meat sandwiches or sausages and strong cheese. On such outings the head of the household frequently smoked a pipe instead of his usual cigar, stoking it with a fragrant mixture he himself blended with black Louisiana Perique, whose strength and pungency, plus Baum's almost incessant cigars, may have had something to do with the ulcer which later developed on his jaw. As a precaution against cancer it finally became necessary to remove a small part of the bone.

At home in the evenings when the supper dishes had been cleared away, Baum would often sing popular songs and accompany himself on the old square piano while the boys and Maud joined in with violin and mandolins. He could play both the piano and guitar and had an excellent singing voice. At his urging, each of his sons learned to play some instrument, even though none ever became more than a fair performer. For an hour or more the family orchestra would play while Baum sang such favorites as "The Bowery," "The Bullfrog and the Coon," "The Sunshine of Paradise Alley," "The Man Who Broke the Bank at Monte Carlo," "My Sweetheart's the Man in the Moon," and "Swim Out O'Grady." Parents and sons made light work of the music, laughing and joking as they played, until it was time for the boys to go to bed and for their father to get back to his writing and Maud to her mending.

In the golden retrospect of fifty years, Harry Baum testified that no family ever had a happier home life. Still preserved is an invitation to a reception on the occasion of the Baums' silver wedding anniversary. They could report as achievements of that period that they had "Borned and raised four (4) boys—smart as the average; quarrels, just a few; wife in tears three times (cat died, bonnet spoiled, sore toe); husband swore 1187 times, at wife 0; broke occasionally, bent often; future prospects good."

In 1903 the Baums moved from the West Side to a more fashionable address at 3726 Forest Avenue, now Giles Avenue, on the South Side. This was a large three story house with a basement, one of a row of identical dwellings. They lived there until 1907.

After 1902, when Baum sold his magazine, he was no longer tied to an editorial desk or to regular responsibilities. With new income and leisure he was able to spend some part of the winters in California, or in foreign travel. For escape from the city's heat, the family summered at Macatawa Park, in Michigan. He had heard of this lake resort from friends at the Chicago Athletic Club, which he had recently joined and where he regularly attended swimming meets, boxing matches, and other athletic

events. Macatawa Park was reached from Chicago by
overnight excursion steamer that ran daily during the
summer months. Advertisements for Macatawa Park had
appeared in Baum's *The Show Window* magazine, and in
the August 1899 issue he wrote an article about the resort,
with four illustrations, indicating that he made his first
trip there that summer.

The Baums were charmed with the natural beauties of
the place. The resort lay at the entrance to Black Lake,
an inlet of Lake Michigan. At the head of the lake, some
six miles distant, was the city of Holland. Thirty miles
northeast was Grand Rapids. Macatawa Park, on the south
side of the small lake, provided excellent fishing, boating,
and swimming. Along the shore trees covered the slopes
of the hills and grew down to the water's edge. Summer
cottages nestled among the trees and extended along Lake
Michigan for half a mile. From the board walk along the
lake shore, paths ran up into the hills to cottages half hidden in the foliage. Some of the cottages had electric lights,
but this was before the days of the electric range, and
cooking was done on kerosene stoves. For the first two
seasons, Baum rented a cottage at Macatawa Park. Shortly
before going over there, he had seen the skeleton of a
bottle-nosed whale in the Field Museum. Enchanted with
its scientific name, he made a sign, like the other cottagers,
but instead of Kum-Inn or some other summer resort
banality, he labeled the cottage "Hyperoodon rostratus"
after the whale. Great was the amazement of the tourists
and staid cottagers.

He and the family were so pleased with the natural
loveliness of Macatawa Park and the congeniality of the
fellow cottagers that in 1902 he bought a cottage overlook-

ing Lake Michigan. Because part of the purchase price
was paid with royalties from *Father Goose,* Baum named
this house "The Sign of the Goose." From the front porch
he hung a sign, which he had made, bearing a white, cut-
out goose (copied from Denslow's drawing of the goose
on the front cover of the book) inside a golden circle upon
which the name of the cottage was lettered in black. For
ten years the Baum family packed as soon as school was out
and moved to Macatawa Park, returning to Chicago just
in time to get ready for the opening of school in September.

For recreation on the water and fishing, Baum kept a
motor boat in his boathouse on Black Lake, and a pre-
model T Ford for short trips about the country and an
occasional jaunt to Grand Rapids. This early Ford was
strictly a hand-crafted model. It had brass carriage lamps
attached to each side of the dashboard, two heavy leather
straps angled down from the front of the top to brackets
fastened to the frame on each side of the radiator, and
the engine had been carefully selected by Baum's son,
Robert, who was attending a military academy at Orchard
Lake near Pontiac. On week-end leave he would visit the
new Ford factory at Detroit and watch progress on the
building of the motor which he had selected when his
father placed the order. The era of the Model T, the
assembly line, and mass production lay far ahead. This
Ford, like all cars of the period, was started by cranking
the engine. One had to be careful that the spark lever was
not too far advanced or the engine would suddenly kick
back on the crank and break an arm. In the morning Baum
would put gasoline in the brass petcocks on the cylinder
heads to prime the engine before it would start, and during the severe Chicago winters the radiator and carburetor

had to be thawed out with kettles of boiling water carried from the kitchen.

The "Sign of the Goose" cottage was furnished with oak furniture hand-made by the owner. One year Baum had suffered an attack of Bell's palsy. This resulted in a slight paralysis of the left side of his mouth from which he never entirely recovered, although the effects gradually wore off. His doctor recommended that he give up writing for some months and try light manual work as a hobby. Baum chose woodworking because he was naturally adept in the use of carpenter's tools. For the cottage living room he fashioned two large rocking chairs. The sides were outlines of geese painted in white enamel. The framework of the chairs was painted green, and Baum upholstered them in tan leather fastened with decorative nails that had brass geese as heads. These had been designed and cast for him by Harrison H. Rountree, president of the Turner brass foundry in Chicago, and an ardent admirer of *Father Goose*. Baum had become friendly with Rountree through Chauncey Williams, Baum's first publisher and associate in *The Show Window* magazine. Rountree was married to Williams' sister, Lillian.

Furnishings of the living room also included hand-made tables, stools, and a couch upholstered in tan leather and ornamented with the gooseheaded nails. The author commissioned a stained glass window for the room, with a large white goose in the center on a green background. He stenciled a broad frieze of green geese around the white walls near the ceiling from a pattern designed, drawn and cut out by himself. For the hall Baum built a grandfather's clock with panels depicting figures from the book.

While the Tietjens—Paul and Eunice, who had been

married recently—were visiting the Baums at Macatawa
in the summer of 1903, so that Tietjens and Baum could
work on a musical comedy idea,* Eunice recorded that
Baum's expedients to while away the time included one
that particularly amused her. "Last of all," she wrote later
in her autobiography,† "because all this had not yet rested
his brain enough, he had made an elaborate piano arrangement of Paul's music for *The Wizard of Oz*—though he was
no musician it was pretty good—had then figured out the
system by which pianola records were made and had cut
a full length record of this arrangement out of wrapping
paper. This seems to have done the trick, and he was presently back at work."

All the Baums went swimming daily in Lake Michigan
during the summer. Like other women at the resort, Maud
wore a dark blue serge bathing suit made with a full skirt
and bloomers with a blouse piped in white. Long black
stockings covered her legs, and she wore canvas shoes and
a floppy brim hat to protect her face from the sun.

Baum had developed a routine for entering the water.
Wearing a battered straw hat to keep off the sun's hot rays,
and puffing a large black cigar, he would slowly wade out
until he stood about waist deep. There he remained, often
as long as twenty minutes to a half hour, teetering back
and forth on toes and heels until his cigar was nearly
finished. Then he would slowly stoop until his shoulders
were under water and start swimming a leisurely breast
stroke. Unless the lake was unusually calm, within a few
minutes his head would be submerged by a wave. Momen-

* The idea never developed and was finally abandoned.

† *The World at My Shoulder*, Macmillan, 1938.

tarily he would disappear from sight to reappear seconds later, the straw hat floating near by and the water-soaked cigar butt clamped tightly in his teeth under his dripping mustache. Slowly shaking the water from his hair and face he would reach for his straw hat and calmly wade ashore. He had completed his day's swim.

With one or more of the boys Baum would take a day off to go fishing in Black Lake where bass abounded. He had been known to pull in twenty to thirty within a few hours. On such occasions the family enjoyed a hearty fish dinner, and their friends and neighbors shared in the catch. At other times Baum would take his motor boat through the narrow channel from Black Lake into Lake Michigan and fish for the small but delicious lake perch.

Maud, of course, was scarcely as footloose. She had to run the cottage and watch over the boys. One day Robert was detected sliding down the porch roof into the sand. His punishment was a spanking with a hairbrush. A few hours later Harry tried the forbidden stunt. He was caught, too, and the same punishment, even the same number of licks, was decreed. But in the meantime the hairbrush used to spank Robert had disappeared. Maud, in her strict, meticulously just way, decided that the sentence could not be carried out unless she had the identical hairbrush. So Harry got off Scot free.

The center of the resort's social life was the Macatawa Hotel, where the young people danced nightly while their elders played whist, pedro, and euchre at tables adjoining the dance floor, meanwhile keeping a watchful eye on their progeny. Baum also enjoyed a quiet game of cards at the cottage, and when friends dropped in he would make a welsh rarebit to top off the evening. One summer he had a one hundred pound wheel of cheddar cheese sent over from Chicago for a series of these rarebit parties.

But the big event of the resort season was Regatta Week, which Baum promoted. The spectacle, held in August, was sponsored by the Macatawa Yacht Club, of which he was an active member. The Club, on Black Lake, about a half mile from Macatawa Park, held boat races daily, and the men's bar, off the reception room on the lower floor, and the card room and dance hall on the second floor, were filled with merrymakers and aglow with lights. The crowning event of Regatta Week was Venetian Night. For this occasion the bay was outlined with Japanese lanterns hung in designs along the shore. The Yacht Club, the hotels at Macatawa Park and at Ottawa Beach across the channel, as well as other buildings facing the shore, were decorated with Japanese lanterns and bunting. Even the sailboats swinging at anchor displayed a like splendor. Bands played on the ferries crossing the lake, and bonfires flared from the tops of the hills. Just after sundown colored lights and oriental lanterns were illuminated on the motor boats. At a signal from the Yacht Club they moved in slow procession around the lake while, above them, rockets and Roman candles, fired from shore, burst in the sky.

The first Venetian Night was such a success that it became an annual affair. Boat owners vied with each other to create beautiful effects. Crowds came each year from nearby communities, and many even came on the overnight boat from Chicago to line the shores of Black Lake and applaud the spectacle. The celebration finished with a great ball at the Macatawa Club at which prizes were awarded to the owners of the best decorated boats.

Baum not only amused his neighbors with celebrations

of this sort, but he also entertained them with a slightly scandalous novel with the anagrammatic title of *Tamawaca Folks, a Summer Comedy,* written under the pseudonym, John Estes Cooke.* On the flyleaf of a copy he wrote: "Nobody knows who wrote this book but me—and I wish I didn't." The little volume of one hundred eighty-six pages, bound in green cloth with a sailboat stamped on the front cover, appeared in 1907 and was privately printed. Although in his foreword the author "begs his readers not to attempt to fit any of the fictitious characters to living persons," it is apparent that the main plot, which has to do with sharp dealing by resort realty operators, and the sub plot, which put social life in a resort in no favorable light, have their roots in Macatawa incidents.

The summer of 1910 was the last which the Baum family spent at Macatawa before moving to California. The cottage and boat were sold before the next season to a family named Todd. It and a number of beach cottages burned in 1927, and a few years later, the raging waters of a winter storm on Lake Michigan cut deeply into the land and washed the site of "The Sign of the Goose" into the lake. Just as a tornado carried Dorothy and her cottage into the Land of Oz, so perhaps by fire and storm the cottage where several of the Oz stories were born found its safe haven in the same enchanted realm.

---

* The close similarity to the name of John Esten Cooke, prolific, romantic and flowery Virginia novelist and historian, who died in 1886, is a bibliographical puzzle.

XIII

THE LAND OF OZ

ALTHOUGH *The Wonderful Wizard of Oz* is the keystone, it is only one stone in Baum's real monument—the Land of Oz itself. As Roland Baughman* has written: "It is entirely fitting that the name of L. Frank Baum came to represent Oz and only Oz to a whole generation of children, to be identified with a particular type of fantasy, and to become the hallmark of an unique humor and a wise and convincing philosophy."

Sharply envisioned by the author, Oz is bounded, peopled, and defined in more than a dozen books. It is more real and substantial in the minds of several generations of readers than the countries in their school geographies—and more unchanging.

"The Fairyland of Oz . . . is one of the happiest harbors in the whole great sea of ink," wrote Ruth Plumly Thompson, "a truly American fairyland with a geography as real as our own and a population characteristically and whimsically American.

---

* From "L. Frank Baum and the 'Oz' Books," p. 17, in *Columbia Library Columns*, May, 1955. Mr. Baughman is head of special collections in the Columbia University Library.

" 'When I look at the sky,' writes a little girl, 'I sometimes think Oz must be back of the bright clouds there.'
And who shall say it is not?—a gay, warmhearted kingdom
of adventure on the other side of the sunset?"

Oz is Utopia—Noland—the Never-Never Land of enchantment and magic. Where is it? Certainly Oz is not of
the earth. It is somewhere in the minds and hearts of its
readers. Baum once mapped it—a roughly rectangular
kingdom, divided into four countries of approximately the
same size. On the west live the Winkies, whose favorite
color is yellow. They are ruled by the Tin Woodman. On
the east is the Munchkin County where Dorothy dropped
into Oz on the wings of the cyclone. To the north is the
Gillikin Country, a purple land with mountains where
magic brews. And in the south is the Country of the Quadlings, the red land ruled over by Glinda, the Good Sorceress.

In the center of Oz lies a small district dominated by
the glittering towers of the Emerald City where Princess
Ozma reigns. We are told that her capital is thickly popu-
lated by precisely 57,318 people. The farms and fields,
forests and mountains of the rest of the country are "full
of pretty and comfortable farmhouses," except of course
in the strange forests and mountains occupied by such
peculiar people as the friendly live Teddy bears, or the
malevolent Li-Mon-Eags, who are one-third lion, one-third
monkey, and one-third eagle.

How big is Oz? The Royal Historian never says, but
Dorothy, the Scarecrow and the Tin Woodman—none of
them athletes—walked half way across it in six days. Thus,
in 1900, when first described in *The Wonderful Wizard of
Oz*, Oz may have been from one hundred to one hundred

and fifty miles across. But, as some punster among Oz enthusiasts has said: "Oz grows on one." The later books are
so peopled with odd tribes from Baum's imagination that
it must have become much larger. Indeed, in *The Emerald
City of Oz,* Baum states that more than half a million live
in Oz.

All around the Land of Oz is a belt of impassable country—called the Deadly Desert along the edge of the Winkie
Country, the Great Sandy Waste beside the Quadling
Country, the Shifting Sands bordering the Munchkin
Land, and the Impassable Desert along the rim of the Gillikin Country. By this means Oz is protected from foreign
peoples—many of them far from amiable.

In *The Tin Woodman of Oz* (1918), one of the last
Baum wrote, he summed up in a few paragraphs the history and the magic character of his story land:

Oz was not always a fairyland, I am told. Once it was
much like other lands, except that it was shut in by a dread-
ful desert of sandy wastes that lay all around it, thus pre-
venting its people from all contact with the rest of the
world. Seeing this isolation, the fairy band of Queen Lurline, passing over Oz while on a journey, enchanted the
country and so made it a Fairyland. And Queen Lurline
left one of her fairies to rule this enchanted Land of Oz,
and then passed on and forgot all about it.
From that moment no one in Oz ever died. Those who
were old, remained old; those who were young and strong
did not change as the years passed by; the children remained children always, and played and romped to their
hearts' content, while all the babies lived in their cradles
and were tenderly cared for and never grew up. So people
of Oz stopped counting how old they were in years, for
years made no difference in their appearance and could
not alter their station. They did not get sick, so there were
no doctors among them. Accidents might happen to some,
on rare occasions, it is true, and while no one could die

naturally as other people do, it was possible that one might be totally destroyed. Such incidents, however, were very unusual, and so seldom was there anything to worry over that the people of Oz were as happy and contented as could be.

Another strange thing about this fairyland of Oz was that whoever managed to enter it from the outside came under the magic spell of the place and did not change in appearance as long as they lived there. So Dorothy, who now lives with Ozma, seemed just the same sweet little girl she had been when first she came to this delightful fairyland.

Perhaps all parts of Oz may not be called truly delightful, but it was surely delightful in the neighborhood of the Emerald City, where Ozma reigned. Her loving influence was felt for many miles around, but there were places in the mountains of the Gillikin country, and in the forests of the Quadling country, and perhaps in far away parts of the Munchkin and Winkie countries, where the inhabitants were somewhat rude and uncivilized and had not yet come under the spell of Ozma's wise and kindly rule. Also, when Oz first became a fairyland, it harbored several witches and magicians and sorcerers and necromancers who were scattered in various parts, but most of these had been deprived of their magic powers, and Ozma had issued a royal edict forbidding anyone in her domains to work magic, except Glinda the Good and the Wizard of Oz. Ozma herself, being a real fairy, knew a lot of magic, but she only used it to benefit her subjects.

Dorothy, as a Princess and an inhabitant of Oz, became an immortal, like the rest of the fortunate people. This "prevented her from being killed or suffering any great bodily harm as long as she lived there . . . but she might be buried underground or 'destroyed' in other ways by evil magicians, were she not properly protected." Incidentally, many of the episodes in the Oz books are built around Ozma's determination to suppress such workers in the black arts.

The Land of Oz is a benevolent autocracy and a very pleasant place to dwell. "There is no other country so beautiful as the Land of·Oz. There are no other people so happy and contented and prosperous as the Oz people. They have all they desire; they love and admire their beautiful girl ruler, Ozma of Oz, and they mix work and play so justly that both are delightful and satisfying and no one has any reason to complain." Gold is so abundant that it is valueless; gems are as common as stones. The Emerald City is built of them. Money is unknown. In explaining this idealistic paradise to the Shaggy Man, the Tin Woodman said:

> If we used money to buy things with, instead of love and kindness and the desire to please one another, then we should be no better than the rest of the world. Fortunately, money is not known in the Land of Oz at all; we have no rich and no poor; for what one wishes, the others all try to give him in order to make him happy, and no one in all Oz cares to have more than he can use.
>
> To be sure, they (the citizens) work. . . . But no one works more than half his time and the people of Oz enjoy their labors as much as they do their play.

But even in paradise discipline is occasionally necessary, as the Shaggy Man discovered after he went there to live:

> "In this country," he remarked, "people live wherever our Ruler tells them to. It wouldn't do to have everyone live in Emerald City, you know, for some must plow the land and raise grains and fruits and vegetables. while others chop wood in the forest, or fish in the rivers, or herd the sheep and cattle."

Oz, then, is a place where Ozma reigns as the personification of benevolence. She is beloved, and her people are happy and busy. Evil exists in Oz, but Ozma's power gives the good people most of the trumps, although they occasionally have to struggle. Ozma has a Magic Picture, a super-television that can be focused on any person or place she wishes to see. She also has at her disposal Glinda's Great Book of Records, a sort of super-newspaper which reports all that goes on in Oz and elsewhere. War does not exist in Oz, and the army has only one soldier, who eventually gives up because of the lack of martial activity. For those who stubbornly persevere in wickedness, Ozma has in her palace grounds the Fountain of Oblivion. Evildoers who drink of its waters forget their plots and black stratagems.

Daily life in the Land of Oz is simple. The people live in cottages. There are roads, along which they walk, for there is no other way to get about. They wear quaint, rustic costumes. But in Ozma's palace are vast suites of rooms, flowing robes and great banquets. Ozma's court was once small—only Dorothy and her companions—but as the books multiplied Ozma had to put one leaf after another in the royal banquet table to accommodate all the court that the Royal Historian provided for her. And what a strange and fascinating crew!—Dorothy and two other little mortal girls, some boys, the Wizard, and such whimsical characters as Jack Pumpkinhead carved out of wood and wearing a Jack O'Lantern for a head, the Scarecrow and his friend the Tin Woodman, the Patchwork Girl made of an old patchwork quilt, a Clockwork Man, the Cowardly Lion and Hungry Tiger who guard Ozma's throne, the animated wooden Sawhorse who is Ozma's favorite steed, the Woggle-Bug, a live glass cat, Dorothy's dog Toto, and Billina, her pet hen. All of them can talk, and all of them do.

Oz is a fairyland, a land created to beguile young readers—not to be taken too literally. Nevertheless, it seems almost to exist; it possesses an aura of reality. It seems that on this troubled globe some such place should exist, where life is simple and happy and even the emeralds are flawless. Yet if Baum had had his way, Ozma and most of her companions would never have been heard of. They do not appear in *The Wonderful Wizard of Oz,* and Baum never intended to become a Royal Historian of Oz in fourteen books.

"My husband," Maud Baum once said, "liked the Oz books but he got tired of writing them as he had other stories to tell. But the children demanded them, so he kept on."

Generations to whom Christmas meant a new Oz book under the tree were delighted that Baum did keep on, even though he was slow in getting started. Not until four years after *The Wonderful Wizard of Oz* appeared in 1900 did a second Oz title reach the stores. In the meantime Baum had been turning out the other tales which teemed in his imagination. But irresistibly he was drawn back to Oz. How this came about is detailed in the preface to the second of the series, *The Marvelous Land of Oz,* which is almost the equal of its predecessor in vigor and quality of invention:

After the publication of *The Wonderful Wizard of Oz,* I began to receive letters from children, telling me of their pleasure in reading the story and asking me to 'write something more' about the Scarecrow and the Tin Woodman. . . . Finally I promised one little girl, who made a long journey to see me and proffer her request—and she is a Dorothy, by the way—that when a thousand little girls had written me a thousand little letters asking for another story of the Scarecrow and the Tin Woodman, I would write the book. Either little Dorothy was a fairy in disguise, and waved her magic wand, or the success of the stage production of *The Wizard of Oz* made new friends for the story, for the thousand letters reached their destination long since and many more followed them.

And now, although pleading guilty to a long delay, I have kept my promise in this book.

The Marvelous Land of Oz, later shortened to *The Land of Oz,* is an action-packed, exciting and skillfully plotted account of a boy named Tip and how he escapes from the humiliating guardianship of an old witch named Mombi. He whittles out Jack Pumpkinhead and sets him up as a dummy beside the road to frighten her. But Mombi, returning from a visit to another magician with an untried Magic Powder, tests it on Tip's dummy, and Jack Pumpkinhead comes to life. Soon after, Jack and Tip escape together from Mombi's house, and to ease their journey to the Emerald City they bring to life a wooden sawhorse as a steed to carry Jack's fragile wooden limbs. Of course, the way to the Emerald City is beset with dangers and adventures, until at last Tip's true identity as the Princess Ozma, who had been transformed into a boy by the witch's magic arts, is disclosed.

The preface mentions only two of the characters, the Scarecrow and the Tin Woodman, indicative of the first title considered for the book—*The Further Adventures of the Scarecrow and the Tin Woodman.* As late of May 14, 1904, the book was advertised under that title in *Publisher's Weekly,* and salesmen's dummies were being prepared when it was decided to change the title, which no one liked. Baum stopped in a bookstore one day and asked the owner what he thought of the title. "Terrible," was the reply. "You are making a great mistake not using Oz in the title." So that noon, while Baum was having luncheon with his publishers, he wrote a new title on a slip of paper and passed it around. It read *The Marvelous Land of Oz*. Some objected to the adjective, either preferring to eliminate it or to substitute some other word, but finally the title was accepted. In this way the long series of books, all having Oz in the title, got its start.

Dorothy does not appear in *The Marvelous Land of Oz*, but the greatest of Baum's comic characters, Professor H. M. Woggle-Bug T.E., made his debut in its pages. The Woggle-Bug is an insect that had escaped from a stereopticon screen in a class room while in a "highly magnified" (H.M.) condition. Consequently he is about as tall as a man, and because of the erudite atmosphere in which he had lived in a crack in the school room, he has given himself the degree of "Thoroughly Educated" (T.E.). No incident better illustrates Baum's imagination at work and his whimsical turn of mind than the one which gave birth to the Woggle-Bug. One summer day Baum was strolling along the beach at Macatawa Park. Absorbed in working out details of the plot of his next fairy tale, he almost tripped over a four-year-old girl, a friend of his who was playing alone on the beach. She had dug a hole in the sand and was busily catching such sea and shore life as the waves brought her. Just as Baum stopped to avoid stepping on her, the child thrust her hand into the hole and seized one of the squirming creatures in her fingers. As she held it up for closer scrutiny she became aware of Baum standing beside her.

"Oh, what is it?" she demanded of him.

"A woggle-bug," he replied without stopping to think,

using the first descriptive word that entered his mind.

The little girl squealed with delight. Jumping to her feet, she ran to where her parents were sitting a short distance away, waving the little creature, and cried:

"See what I got! It's a woggle-bug! Mr. Baum just told me. A woggle-bug!"

"Go put that thing back before it bites you," commanded the child's mother, shuddering at the squirming creature.

"It won't hurt me," cried the excited child. "It's only a woggle-bug!"

Hearing the child repeat the words so many times made Baum realize that for some reason they held a fascination for her young mind. He jotted them down on an old envelope, thinking he might use them sometime in one of his stories.

After publication of *The Marvelous Land of Oz,* the Woggle-Bug's popularity won him top billing in a large, thin picture book, *The Woggle-Bug Book,* published in 1905 by Reilly and Britton with full page drawings by Ike Morgan. Both the story and the illustrations are reminiscent of newspaper comic pages of that day. The insect even reached the stage in a musical version of *The Land of Oz,* called *The Woggle-Bug,* which was produced in Chicago on June 19, 1905.

Typical of the aggressive promotion which Baum's publishers gave *The Marvelous Land of Oz* is a newspaper contest and series of stories syndicated by the *Philadelphia North American* which appeared in the *Chicago Record-Herald* and a number of other newspapers in the larger cities. These serialized stories, published under the title of *Queer Visitors From the Marvelous Land of Oz,* were written by Baum and illustrated in comic page style by Walt McDougall. They started September 4, 1904 and appeared weekly for sixteen weeks in the childrens' and comic sections with illustrations in color. Each episode ended with a question to which the Woggle-Bug whispered the answer into the ear of one of his companions. Large four-column promotional advertisements, shouting "What Did the Woggle-Bug Say?," aroused interest in the series, and the newsboys wore yellow celluloid buttons with the same message as they hawked their papers. Reilly and Britton gave away five hundred thousand badges to advertise the contest and the book. A prize of five hundred dollars a month was offered for the correct answers to the questions.

Baum's story brings the Scarecrow, Tin Woodman, Woggle-Bug, Sawhorse, Gump, and Jack Pumpkinhead to the United States, which they find as marvelous as an American would find the Land of Oz. "Americans do by inventions what we do by magic," comments one of the visitors. These tales were put into book form and published in 1960 as *The Visitors From Oz*.

Nine somewhat longer stories followed the puzzle contest. They are worldly, tartly ironic commentaries on the manners and motivations of people, rich and poor. In spirit they belong with Baum's *American Fairy Tales*.

Another sign of the promotional acumen of the new publishers was the end papers in *The Marvelous Land of Oz* combining photographs of Montgomery and Stone as they appeared in the stage version of *The Wizard of Oz*, (which was still at the height of its long run), with drawings of the new characters in the new book.

Baum managed to put off his next Oz story for three years. Then he published *Ozma of Oz*. By that time he had devised a way to eat his cake and have it too, so far as fairy tale writing was concerned. *Ozma of Oz* has only the slenderest claim to being an Oz book at all, even though it is one of his best. Dorothy is the heroine, but she is really the heroine of one of those tales Baum wanted to tell about a land outside Oz. At the end he brings her back to the familiar country. Once again Baum's preface is the best account of his own feelings and of the forces that shaped his story:

> My friends, the children, are responsible for this new "Oz Book," as they were for the last one. . . . Their sweet little letters plead to know "more about Dorothy" and they ask: "What became of the Cowardly Lion?" and "What did Ozma do afterward?" . . .
> One little friend who read this story before it was printed said to me: "Billina is *real Ozzy*, Mr. Baum, and so are Tik-Tok and the Hungry Tiger."

Dorothy, so runs the story of *Ozma of Oz,* had been absent in Kansas while Ozma was regaining her throne. On a steamer trip to Australia with her Uncle Henry, Dorothy falls overboard in a storm and drifts ashore with Billina, a hen. They discover Tik-Tok, "that frighteningly contemporary piece of clockwork," as David Dempsey called him in a *New York Times* article, "that can do only what it is wound up to do." The locale of Dorothy's shipwreck is the Kingdom of Ev, ruled by Princess Langwidere, whose name is one of Baum's better puns, and whose singular habits make her one of his best satires. For unlike ladies who must wear the same face all the time and can only get variety by changing their gowns, the princess changes her head whenever she fancies and always wears the same costume. She has cabinets full of live heads of all complexions and humors, and no sooner does she lay eyes on the shipwrecked travellers than she covets Dorothy's head for her collection. So Dorothy is clapped into prison because she objects to parting with her own head and accepting one of Princess Langwidere's cast-offs in its place.

Ozma and the army of Oz arrive just in time to free Dorothy, and they proceed together to the domain of the Nome King,* who is holding the royal family of Ev captive. The crafty Nome King almost gets the best of Ozma and her followers until Billina, the hen, outwits him. Dorothy then breaks the Nome's power by gaining possession of his magic belt. With it to protect them, they return Ev's royal family to their palace and ride a magic carpet back to the Emerald City.

Both *The Marvelous Land of Oz* and *Ozma of Oz* were written in Baum's study on the back porch of the summer cottage at Macatawa Park. But he and Maud spent the winter of 1907-8 at Coronado Beach, across the bay from San Diego, California, and *Dorothy and the Wizard of Oz,* next in the series, reflects the influence of the new environment, for it is the first with a California setting.

Dorothy and the Wizard of Oz, which was published in 1908, is the harshest, the somberest, the farthest removed from Baum's kindly philosophy, of all the Oz books. Although it brings back that lovable hum-bug, the Wizard, it does not bring back his spirit to the plot. Dorothy and the Wizard drop through a rift in the ground caused by a California earthquake and meet in a glass city, the abode of a people who grow like vegetables. But the vegetable people prove to be quick-tempered and deadly. After es-

* Baum rejected the classical spelling, "gnome," because he felt no child should be asked to spell that way.

caping from them, Dorothy and the Wizard face the dangers of a land where everyone, including a race of maneating bears, is invisible. Having run the gauntlet of its perils, they encounter the flying wooden Gargoyles, equally unpleasant, and are rescued at the end of the tale from the interior of a dragon-infested mountain by Ozma's magic powers. In Oz they find safety and rest from the incessant activity of their adventures.

Baum explained this melange of incidents in his preface:

> They (the children) have flooded me with thousands of suggestions, and I have honestly tried to adopt as many of these suggestions as could be fitted into one story. . . . The children won't let me stop telling tales of the Land of Oz. I know lots of other stories, and I hope to tell them sometime or another, but just now my loving tyrants won't let me.

In spite of its gloomy, even savage, atmosphere, *Dorothy and The Wizard of Oz* has always had enough partisans to make it one of the most popular of the series. The next, however, *The Road to Oz,* which appeared in 1909, has been described as the poorest of the first six Oz books, even though it introduces several characters who became fixtures in the Baum dramatis personae. Like *The Wonderful Wizard of Oz*, it is the story of a pilgrimage for a purpose to the Emerald City, but, despite the title, it is mostly road and very little Oz.

The story begins when Dorothy tries to help a tramp called the Shaggy Man to find his road. Presently she and her dog Toto and the Shaggy Man are hopelessly bewildered by a multiplicity of roads. They take the seventh, as good story book characters should, and the adventures begin. Along the way they pick up a little boy, Button-Bright, and Polychrome, the Rainbow's daughter, a shimmering creature garbed fittingly in robes of many colors. Together they brave somewhat unexciting adventures along the way, until they arrive at last at the Emerald City just in time for a sumptuous birthday party for Ozma. To this party come all the Oz people, as well as John Dough, Queen Zixi, Santa Claus, the Queen of Merryland, and many others from Baum's earlier stories.

The readers of the first edition of *The Road to Oz* were treated to the novelty of a change in color of the pages as the travelers progressed through the various districts to Oz. Neill, the illustrator, had his little joke when he portrayed Dorothy and Toto stopping to look at the tin statues of themselves in the castle of the Tin Woodman. The statues, of course, are as Denslow drew them for *The Wonderful Wizard of Oz,* complete to "Den's" seahorse signature on the pedestal.

Ten years after his publishers had refused to publish a book with the name of a jewel in the title, Baum overcame their reluctance. He named his 1910 Oz book *The Emerald City of Oz.* This was the title he had originally planned to use for *The Wonderful Wizard of Oz.* It was written while he was wintering at Coronado Beach.

"I am merely an editor or private secretary for a host of youngsters whose ideas I am requested to weave into the thread of my stories," he wrote in his preface. "My readers have told me what to do with Dorothy and Aunt Em and Uncle Henry, and I have obeyed their mandate."

Baum allowed his fancy to roam freely in *The Emerald City of Oz* while he assembled a nightmare crew of allies for the greedy and envious Nome King's nefarious plot to

View of cottages along the shore at Macatawa Park as it appeared in 1905. The Baum cottage is at right center with flag flying from the roof.

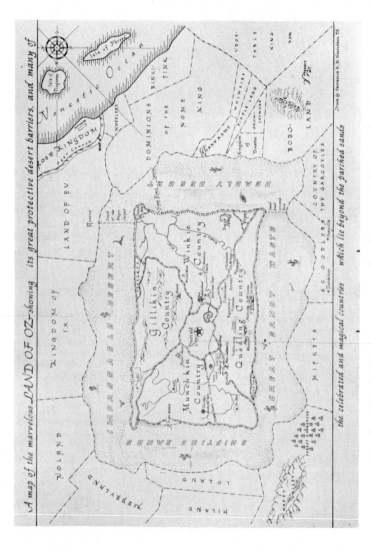

Drawing of the land of Oz and surrounding deserts and other countries, like
that used as end papers in *Tik-Tok of Oz*.

Only known surviving view of the Oz Film Manufacturing Company lot, taken in 1914, soon after the first full length movie was made there.

Crowded Houses — Playing to Standing Room only—at the Strand Theatre, New York City. Be sure you book the

Patchwork Girl of Oz

Released Through Paramount Program

Now Ready! Another Big Winner—A Wonderful Feature

The Magic Cloak of Oz

Produced under the personal direction of the author, L. FRANK BAUM. Five reels of pathos, comedy, magnificent scenes and brilliant photography. Write or wire for bookings at once.

His Majesty, the Scarecrow of Oz

The most spectacular and entertaining photo extravaganza yet produced. Just completed. Arrange your bookings.

The Last Egyptian

Now being produced. A wonderfully dramatic story, full of thrills love and adventure! Don't miss it.

"The Oz Film Company has made a debut which places it in a decidedly strategic position on the motion picture map," says the N. Y. Morning Telegraph.

IF YOU HAVE NOT YET BOOKED OZ FEATURES DO SO AT ONCE!

The Oz Film Manufacturing Co.

Studios and Laboratories: Santa Monica Blvd., Gower to Lodi Sts.

Los Angeles, California

Advertisement in *Moving Picture World* promoting four of the full length movies made by the Oz Film Manufacturing Company.

Scene from *The Patchwork Girl of Oz* as it appeared on the cover of the October 3, 1914, *Moving Picture World.*

Maud Baum and her four sons in 1900 and in 1945. The sons, left to right in both pictures, are: Robert, Harry, Kenneth and Frank J. Baum.

L. Frank Baum in his celebrated garden at Ozcot, about 1914, one of the few informal pictures ever taken of him (above). Ozcot, the home of Frank and Maud Baum in Hollywood, California (below).

L. Frank Baum in picture taken in 1910 by a photographer named Green. As he took the picture Baum wrote: "There are several greens in the world, the bottle green, the green gage and the green apple colic—but"

destroy and plunder Oz. The Nome King's invasion succeeds, but his purpose is frustrated by crafty tactics that spring from the needle-sharp brains of the Scarecrow and the peace-loving disposition of Ozma.

The Emerald City of Oz is remarkable for two reasons. First of all, Neill ornamented it with illustrations of great beauty, touched gently with an iridescent green ink. Second, it was Baum's first full scale use of a story-telling device which he was to employ again and again. In *The Marvelous Land of Oz* he had first experimented with a double barreled plot, in which the separate threads are brought together to form the climax. In *The Emerald City of Oz,* while the Nome King is plotting conquest and all manner of evil against Oz, Dorothy is guiding her unsophisticated aunt and uncle on a grand tour of Ozma's kingdom. The aunt and uncle have come to Oz, incidentally, as refugees from a sheriff's sale of their mortgaged Kansas farm. Dorothy's party returns to the Emerald City just as the Nome King and his allies are launching their attack.

Having written six books about Oz, Baum availed himself of Ozma's narrow escape from the Nome King to invent a device for his own protection against having to compose more Oz stories. He has Glinda work a spell and Oz becomes invisible. In the last chapter Dorothy writes: "You will never hear anything more about Oz because we are now cut off forever from all the rest of the world." Baum was tired of Oz and thought this device would convince his little readers that it would be impossible to write another book about it. His imagination was bursting with ideas, and he was resolved to forget the Land of Oz and introduce his young friends to other lands. Therefore, as

Royal Historian of Oz, he commented, "This seems to me
too bad, at first, for Oz is a very interesting fairyland. Still,
we have no right to feel grieved, for we have had enough
of the history of the Land of Oz to fill six story books."

Having burst his bonds Baum now turned to those other
fairy tales he wished to tell. The first of these was *The Sea
Fairies* (1911), followed by *Sky Island* (1912). Both are
charming stories in which the discerning reader will de-
tect a certain "Ozzy" flavor.

"I hope my readers who have so long followed Dorothy's
adventures in the Land of Oz," he wrote, "will be interested in Trot's equally strange adventures." Trot is a
California style Dorothy, with Pacific beach sand in her
shoes instead of Kansas dust.

The story of *The Sea Fairies* suggested itself to Baum
while he was walking along the beach at Coronado. Trot
and her companion, a salty, peglegged old sailor, Cap'n
Bill, take a boat ride on the Pacific and turn into a cave.
The author had in mind the caves along the shore of La
Jolla, just north of San Diego, where, at high tide, visitors
enter by long stairways from the ground above, and enjoy
the sight of sea life in its natural habitat. Trot and Cap'n
Bill find mermaids in the cave and are persuaded by them
to visit the world under water and meet the Queen of the
Mermaids. In company with the Queen they make a grand
tour of the shimmering depths, fall into the toils of an evil
magician, Zog, and are rescued by the great sea serpent
who rules that realm. *The Sea Fairies* is one of Baum's
most delicate, most imaginative tales; it is also one of his
most somber.

Having explored the sea beneath, it was natural to take
Trot and Cap'n Bill aloft in *Sky Island* the following year.

Button-Bright, who first appeared in *The Road to Oz,* drops down on the California beach with a magic umbrella, reminiscent of the machine given Rob by the Demon of Electricity in *The Master Key.* The flying magic umbrella will take its possessor soaring through the air wherever he commands it to go. Cap'n Bill rigs up a harness so he and Trot can go along with Button-Bright, and all three start for an island off the coast. But by mistake they land on an island in the sky where the Blue and Pink people live, separated by a sticky, damp Fog Bank. Trot and her friends fall into the clutches of the tyrant who has seized power over the Blue people. They escape, without their magic umbrella, into the land of the Pink people, whose gracious hospitality does not keep them from dooming the intruders to a deadly exit into space over the edge of the island. But Polychrome, another old friend from *The Road to Oz,* saves them by a shrewd argument; Trot becomes queen of the Pink people, and leads them to battle against the Blues. The tyrant is ousted, the umbrella recovered, and the adventurers fly back to California.

Baum confessed to his readers that *Sky Island* is one of his stories that "wrote itself," and he mentioned in his preface that it had astonished him considerably.

"The sky country is certainly a remarkable land," he said. "After reading about it I am sure you will agree that our old Mother Earth is a good place to live on."

With characteristic economy Trot and Cap'n Bill were integrated into the Oz series in *The Scarecrow of Oz.*

Although in the preface to *Sky Island* Baum reported that *The Sea Fairies* was "received with much approval by my former readers, many of whom have written me they like Trot 'almost as well as Dorothy,'" nevertheless, his youthful correspondents clamored for more about Oz. Just why Trot did not replace Dorothy in their affections is no doubt attributable to the innate conservatism of children. They are loyal to what is familiar. Either that, or there was something really magical about the magic of Oz.

By 1913 Baum surrendered and restored communication with Ozma's realm. *The Patchwork Girl of Oz* was the result. This came about, so Baum confessed in his preface, through one of his juvenile collaborators:

"One of the children inquired why we couldn't hear from the Princess Dorothy by wireless. . . . So the Historian rigged up a high tower in his back yard . . . and then began to call 'Princess Dorothy of Oz' by sending messages into the air."

When Glinda learned of the messages through her Great Book of Records, Baum reported, Ozma appointed the Shaggy Man to tap out the story of what had been going on in Oz behind the curtain of invisibility.*

The Patchwork Girl of Oz is notable chiefly for its heroine, a crazy-quilt creature of patches sewed together in the form of a girl. Scraps, as she is called, was intended to be a servant and was endowed with brains and life by means of the Magic Powder. She is a saucy, independent, flouncy creature with a personality as individual as her patchwork exterior—all "glad rags" and without a single "cross patch." Naturally, this maiden of gingham and

---

* Perhaps it is more than coincidence that the vigil kept at The National Radio Astronomy laboratory, Green Bank, W. Va., for possible signals from intelligent beings in outer space is known as Project OZMA.

cotton makes the heart of the similarly fashioned Scarecrow beat with love.

The children welcomed the return of their favorite Christmas readings so warmly that henceforth, so long as he lived, Baum came up with a new Oz book each year. They are *Tik-Tok of Oz* (1914), *The Scarecrow of Oz* (1915), *Rinkitink in Oz*, (1916), *The Lost Princess of Oz* (1917), *The Tin Woodman of Oz* (1918), *The Magic of Oz* (1919) and *Glinda of Oz* (1920).

Tik-Tok of Oz, a veritable slumgullion of Ozzy tidbits, had as end papers in the first edition two maps attributable to the Royal Historian. A book dealer first suggested the printing of a map of Oz. Baum was enthusiastic about the idea. After dinner of the day on which it was broached, he took a piece of white cardboard and drew a "Map of the Countries near to the Land of Oz." It was printed in colors and used as the back end paper of *Tik-Tok of Oz.* The front end paper was a "Map of the Marvelous Land of Oz," a larger scale drawing of Oz itself, and by the same hand.

On the first map Baum placed the Land of Oz with the Emerald City in the center and the four countries of the Munchkins, Quadlings, Winkies and Gillikins as quarterings of the area around the capital city. Outside Oz lay the Deadly Desert, the Great Sandy Waste, the Impassable Desert and the Shifting Sands. Beyond the deserts stretched lands made familiar by his other tales—Noland, Ev, Merryland, Hiland and Loland, and the Forest of Burzee, as well as others. By this device he made plain that all his tales belonged together as a chronicle of one continent of the imagination.

But even the best informed minds can err. On the map

their creator put the Munchkins, who live in eastern Oz, in the west. They had traded places with the Winkies. But in Oz, of course, anything is possible; so the east and west directions on the map were reversed to compensate for the Royal Historian's forgetfulness!

Noteworthy among the later Oz stories are *Rinkitink in Oz,* the only one with a boy hero since *The Marvelous Land of Oz,* and *The Magic of Oz,* unique for its young scalawag and for the sharp worldly tones which Baum's voice takes in telling his story.

Rinkitink in Oz had spent many years in manuscript before it was published; for Baum had written it under the title of *Rinkitink,* probably sometime around 1905, without thought of making it part of his Oz series. Nearly a decade later he fitted it out with a last chapter of festivity in Ozma's capital. Otherwise the tale is closer in spirit to *Queen Zixi of Ix* than to anything else that Baum had done. It is the story of Prince Inga, whose parents, peaceful rulers of the prosperous island of Pingaree, are carried away into captivity and their fair kingdom is laid waste. But Inga and the Falstaffian Rinkitink, a playboy king who is on vacation from his imperial responsibilities, avoid capture, and, with the aid of three magic pearls, Inga frees his parents and people. All crown their success by enjoying a banquet at Ozma's table in the Emerald City.

In *The Magic of Oz,* Ruggedo, the rascal who had been deposed as Nome King, and a young scamp named Kiki Aru, who has literally stumbled on a magic word that gives him the power of transformation, plot the conquest of Ozma's kingdom. With the word, *Pyrzqxgl,* which he alone knows how to pronounce, Kiki Aru and his companion give Dorothy and the Wizard and the Cowardly Lion a bad time. Disguised as monkeys with the wings of eagles and the heads of lions, they have things pretty much their own way until the Wizard disenchants himself and subdues them by their own trick. Meanwhile, the quest for a birthday present for Ozma involves some of the others of her retinue in a nasty adventure with a magic flower. Besides being an exciting story, *The Magic of Oz* draws vitality from Baum's deft characterization of Kiki Aru, surely the most realistic, the most believable young man he ever created.

With fourteen books, Baum won the undying allegiance of children to the Land of Oz. How was he able to capture the imaginations of his young readers so completely that years have not dimmed the charm of his stories? It is useless to speculate, because only in the books themselves lies the evidence of the magic which keeps them fresh and alive. Fundamentally, of course, the vitality of the Oz stories springs from their author's narrative skill. Forthright, always lively, crammed with unexpected turns and exciting incidents, and marching to a logical but unforeseen climax, they hold the child's attention with "fine, free-wheeling fantasy, rich in imagination, humor and inventiveness"—the pure gold of story telling. Baum always relied primarily on action in his tales. Description is rarely present for its own sake; Baum used it only to augment his plot. The pastoral landscapes, the gloomy caverns, and the bejeweled cities form stage settings against which the rapid movement takes place. Even the people of Oz, good and bad alike, are subordinated to the events in which they play their parts. Nonetheless, they are full of vitality and character—the wooden wisdom of the Sawhorse; the high spirits of the Patchwork Girl; the needle sharp clev-

erness of the Scarecrow; the tenderness of the Tin Woodman's pure silk heart; the sweet dignity of Ozma, every
child's dream-mother, and the sharp common sense of
Billina, the farmyard hen who has the power to terrify the
ill-tempered Nomes, for they are vulnerable to only one
weapon, a strictly fresh egg.

Without writing down to his sub-teen audience, Baum
made communication easy by simple, short sentences and
by casting his episodes into fast-moving dialogue. The plot
may soar into fantasy, but the telling is always down to
earth. "Everything in life is unusual until you get accustomed to it," remarked the Scarecrow. Baum helped his
readers get "accustomed" to Oz by carefully expressing its
wonders in terms of the daily life of an American boy or
girl. For instance, when the Scarecrow, Jack Pumpkinhead, and Tip escaped from the Emerald City on the Sawhorse, they were tied on its back with a piece of clothesline.
It was not a magic spell that held them on, but an humble
household cord that any child is familiar with. And the
Tin Woodman! Is he silver-plated? No, nickel-plated like
the coffee pot in the kitchen. Tik-Tok's discoverers lose
their fright when they see that the mechanical man "is only
made out of copper like the old kettle in the barnyard at
home."

The Gump, that overstuffed, plush flying machine that
rescues Tip and his cronies in *The Marvelous Land of Oz*,
was made of two sofas tied face to face, a mounted animal's
head in front, a broom in back for a tail, and palm leaves
for wings—all brought to life by a magic powder. This is
typically American fantasy of the familiar and humor of
the incongruous which has been a favorite device of Amer-

ican humorists from the *Knickerbocker Tales,* through
Mark Twain and Will Rogers, right up to today.

The Oz stories, however, also rest on a solid foundation
of tradition. Baum stands on the shoulders of those who
throughout the ages created the very form of the fairy tale.
From this endless treasury come Baum's giants and nomes,
witches and spells, and the whole world of princesses and
palaces, caverns and gems. Such things are eternal pass-
ports to a child's affection. But Baum's primary task, foreshadowed in *The Wonderful Wizard of Oz,* was to build
a new world more splendid than the traditional fairylands
he had inherited. Only there, in a place of rainbow colors,
shimmering with emeralds and gleaming with gold, would
the shiny Tin Woodman, the gaudy Patchwork Girl, and
the blinding raiment of the Woggle-Bug seem at home.

As a stage for his actors, Baum created a utopia where
most of the confusions and frustrations and petty cares of
earthly life are swept out of the way of the story. For the
model of his happy land, Baum probably was influenced
by two of the serious utopians of the day—William Morris
and Edward Bellamy.

Oz is city-centered and oligarchial like Bellamy's imaginary society, but in other respects it is far more akin to
the rustic, medieval, handcraft way of life extolled in
News from Nowhere, which Morris had published in 1891
to correct "the mechanical picture of the future" drawn
in Bellamy's *Looking Backward.* Like Oz, Morris's England is an uncomplicated land of small farms and villages.
How close they are to the spirit of Oz appears in an incident in *News from Nowhere* which might have come right
out of Ozma's kingdom:

The road menders have piled their good clothing, woven of gold and silver thread, beside the highway as they work. Now and then they stop to laugh and chat with several young women gathered at the roadside. Just then a cart drives up. The foreman sings out: "Spell, ho, mates! Here are neighbors want to get past," and all the workers drop their tools to help shoulder the cart over a rough spot in the road.

Bellamy, Morris, and Baum dispensed with money in their never-never lands, supplying society's needs from public warehouses. Bellamy's warehouses were stocked with the products of labor-saving machinery; Morris extolled the creative satisfactions of making things by hand; Baum's people are rarely seen at toil. Bellamy's setting is the city; the citizens of Oz and of Morris's England live in cottages. For all, the hours of labor are short; life is easy, free of compulsions, and conducive to happiness. Unlike the other utopias, however, with their somewhat socialist implications, Oz is a monarchy. Kings and queens and princesses are the stuff of romance, and on them Baum depended for atmosphere and story.

The compromises of daily living and the moral and ethical confusions of earth have been skillfully simplified in Oz. Oz is a place where love conquers all, whether it be as kindliness, friendliness, happiness, or merely gracious manners. The Shaggy Man's Love Magnet hangs over the gates of the Emerald City, a talisman of the pleasures of dwelling together in amity, and the Tin Woodman expresses the creed of Oz when he says that "happiness is the best thing in the world." Dorothy is the embodiment of love, which carries her through seeming adversity with winning confidence. Of her Baum wrote: "She had accomplished all these wonders not because she was a fairy, or had any magical powers whatsoever, but because she was a simple and sweet little girl who was honest to herself and to all whom she met. In this world in which we live simplicity and kindliness are the only magic wands that work wonders."

Aggressiveness, ambition, rudeness, and bad temper are the cardinal sins in Oz, and the sinners expiate them by the penance of unhappiness and impotence. The terrible tempered Nome King, even though he has justification for his rages, loses his throne; Ugu the Shoemaker; Zog, the evil magician of *The Sea Fairies;* and the King of the Blue People crumble away because they did not build good lives. Evoldo, who sold his queen and ten children into slavery, drowns himself. It is better to be a "poor and humble man who lives unnoticed and unknown," asserts Nikobob, the charcoal burner of *Rinkitink in Oz,* in a station where one can "appreciate the joy of living" than to suffer such worldly troubles as envy, scorn and loss of possessions.

In an order of life in which love is normal and evil abnormal, all things should work toward good. This belief, rooted in the nineteenth century confidence in progress, contributes to the feeling that Oz is akin to the Garden of Eden, still fresh and perpetually innocent, but, like the Garden, it is a place where disobedience of the law of love can happen. Thus the Shaggy Man says: "That wall . . . is what is called an optical illusion. . . . It is the same with any other evils in life; they seem to exist and yet it's all seeming." This is the Shaggy Man speaking his own character, and not as Baum's spokesman; for, though Baum was a man of his time, he was not a woolly-minded visionary. The cruel invisible bears and the unfeeling wooden

Gargoyles who pursued Dorothy and the Wizard are evidence that Baum acknowledged the presence of evil in the world, though even in his magic countries it does not triumph.

The child reader senses that Oz is not the "real world" with its problems; that very difference is the charm of that magic land. In Oz evil is the exception; for it to succeed is unthinkable. Oz is a gentle land, and even its justice respects the feelings of the law breaker. When Ojo, in *The Patchwork Girl of Oz*, breaks the law by picking a six-leaved clover, which he needs for a magic formula to release two persons turned to stone by a magician's blunder, he is arrested and imprisoned for trial in the Emerald City. But his imprisonment is not an unpleasant experience. The food is good, the quarters comfortable, and he enjoys all the amenities of an honored guest. When he expresses astonishment, his jailer, a woman, explains:

> We consider a prisoner unfortunate . . . because he has done something wrong and because he is deprived of his liberty. Therefore we should treat him kindly. . . . Ozma thinks that one who has committed a fault did so because he was not strong and brave. . . . You see, it is kindness that makes one strong and brave; and so we are kind to our prisoners.

Among the threads of traditional story telling and the golden strands of his own imagination, Baum not infrequently wove inconspicuous patterns of his own tastes and prejudices. Perhaps the most obvious of these is the ridicule he pours on soldiers and armies. Ozma's armies, the feminine phalanx with which Jinjur dethroned the Scarecrow, and Queen Ann Soforth's cohorts that set out to overthrow the Nome King resemble in no way the martial array of older folklore and myth. Armies in the Land of Oz are composed mostly of officers, with perhaps one private to do the fighting. For officers are gentlemen, and gentlemen don't fight, because "fighting is unkind and liable to be injurious to others."

When Ozma's capital lay at the mercy of the invading Nome King and his allies, Ozma found other than military means to save it. After declaring that she would stay and share her people's fate, she said, "I do not wish to fight. No one has the right to destroy any living creatures, however evil they may be, or hurt them or make them unhappy. I will not fight, even to save my kingdom."

When asked why he made fun of military forces, Baum replied that this idiosyncrasy probably went back to the miserable experiences he had while a student at the Peekskill Military Academy under instructors whose cadets regarded them as unsympathetic martinets. Some of Baum's most genuinely comic pages describe the antics of his fighting men and women. In the fighting women, of course, he was also mocking the ultra-feminist "women's righters" of his time, of whom his mother-in-law had been one.

Baum found pretentiousness, especially pedantry, equally ridiculous. The Woggle-Bug, who is "thoroughly educated," is the most obvious example of this. This insect is principal of a school, apparently the only educational enterprise in the Land of Oz, where the students get their learning in capsule form.

"You see," said the Woggle-Bug, "until these school pills were invented, we wasted a lot of time in study that may now be better employed in practicing athletics. . . . Our boys . . . are never obliged to interrupt their game for the lesser branches of learning."

In *The Emerald City of Oz,* Dorothy and her entourage visit the city of the Rigmaroles, who are long-winded, tedious people. It is a sort of penal colony for bores. After hearing them talk, Omby Amby, the green-whiskered captain general of Oz, comments:

"If those people wrote books it would take a whole library to say the cow jumped over the moon."
"Perhaps some of them do write books," asserted the Little Wizard. "I've read a few rigmaroles that might have come from this very town."
"Some of the college lecturers and ministers are certainly related to these people," observed the Shaggy Man, "and it seems to me the Land of Oz is a little ahead of the United States in some of its laws. For here, if one can't talk clearly and straight to the point, they send him to Rigmarole Town, while Uncle Sam lets them roam wild and free, to torture innocent people."*

Some of Baum's satiric passages have been regarded as evidence of anti-intellectualism, but generally it is not intelligence but pseudo-intellectuals who are mocked in the Oz stories. Wisdom, as in the character of Glinda, the wise sorceress, is taken seriously in Oz. Glinda, Ozma, and the Wizard (who has "studied" magic) all embody wisdom. But the pretentions of people who claim to know more than they do are heartily laughed at. For example, Baum lived in an era when opera was becoming fashionable in the United States. People who knew little about music were vying to hear imported performers and sitting solemnly under an avalanche of sound which as yet meant little or nothing to them. Perhaps apropos of this, in *The*

* "Bores of society," Morris calls pedantic people in *News From Nowhere.*

Patchwork Girl Baum makes a phonograph that has come
to life say:

It is classical music and considered the best and most
puzzling ever manufactured. You're supposed to like it,
whether you do or not, and if you don't, the proper thing
is to look as if you did.

Baum sometimes hints that pretentiousness and false
standards extend into all aspects of life, as when he makes
the King of Foxes in *The Road to Oz* say:

To become civilized means to dress as elaborately and
prettily as possible, and to make a show of your clothes
so your neighbor will envy you.

The Woggle-Bug is the embodiment of false-intellectual-
ism, but he has a saving grace—the love of puns. This
weakness, it might be added, his creator shared in full
measure. The Woggle-Bug, of course, has to put this ad-
diction on a sound academic basis, which he expressed in
a delightful paragraph from *The Land of Oz:*

Our language contains many words having a double
meaning, and . . . to pronounce a joke that allows both
meanings of a certain word proves the joker a person of
culture and refinement, who has, moreover, a thorough
command of the language. . . . I myself am thoroughly
educated, and I say that puns display genius. For instance,
were I to ride upon this Sawhorse, he would not only be
an animal, he would become an equipage. For he would
then be a horse-and-buggy.

The Woggle-Bug has his greatest opportunity as punster
in the thin, large fragile book that bears his name. His eye
has been taken by a gaudy dress in a shop window, and

he needs money to get it out of the shop so that he can give
it to some girl where it will be appreciated in its full glory.
To earn the price, he gets a job digging ditches.

"He seized two spades and began working so rapidly," so
the story goes, "with his four arms that the foreman said:
'You must have been forewarned.' 'Why?' asked the insect.
'Because there is a saying that to be forewarned is to be
forearmed,' replied the other. 'That is nonsense,' said the
Woggle-Bug, digging with all his might, 'for they call you
a foreman, and yet I see only one of you.' "

To dissect a story is to take away the spirit that gives it
life. Whatever they are made of, and however they are
fashioned, the fourteen Oz books have demonstrated that
they have a life of their own that time has not been able
to take away. They pleased readers one and two generations ago, and they please readers today. This is the unique
fact about them, besides which all else is unimportant.
Nevertheless, it is still proper to inquire whether these
tales conform to the somewhat restrictive program which
Baum set for himself in the preface to *The Wonderful
Wizard of Oz,* even though at that time he did not know
that he would be so prolific. Are these American fairy
tales? Are the heartaches and nightmares left out? In the
larger sense, Baum remained faithful to these ideals, perhaps because they grew out of his own outlook and personality. The United States is the starting point for reach-
ing the Land of Oz, and the standard of comparison by
which its wonders are made evident. The big nightmares
are left out, but enough narrow escapes and tense moments
remain to please the children, as James Thurber pointed
out in an essay about Oz in the *New Republic* in 1934.

"I know that I went through excruciatingly lovely
nightmares and heartaches when the Scarecrow lost his

straw," Thurber wrote; "when the Tin Woodman was taken apart, when the Sawhorse broke his wooden leg it hurt me, even if it didn't Mr. Baum."

The true importance of the fourteen Oz books lies in the evidence they give of the creative skill with which Baum modernized the fairy tale, discovered a new and contemporary fairyland that never grows old, peopled it with the Scarecrow and Tin Woodman and all the others who through Baum's alchemy have won the loyalty of generations of American children, and realized Baum's ambition to write books which would do "a bit to brighten up a few lives," as he modestly expressed it in a letter written toward the end of his life. The sincerity of this purpose is well expressed in the preface to *Dorothy and the Wizard in Oz,* where he wrote to the children:

I believe, my dears, that I am the proudest story-teller that ever lived. . . . To have pleased you, to have interested you, to have won your friendship, and perhaps your love, through my stories, is to my mind as great an achievement as to become President of the United States.

Louis Sullivan, the famous Chicago architect of the Auditorium and other buildings, who was born in the same year as Baum and flourished with him in the same burst of creative energy that distinguished Chicago around the turn of the century, wrote in his *Autobiography of an Idea* (1924), words that could be applied to his contemporary:

For where lives the man who does not firmly believe in magic and in fairy tales; who does not worship something with a child-like faith; who does not dream his dreams, however sordid or destructive, however high, however nobly altruistic?

XIV

BOOKS AND THE MEN

———————————————————————

AN AGGRESSIVE young publishing company and an illustrator whose imagination could keep pace with the Royal Historian of Oz were collaborators in Baum's later success.

Unlike the George M. Hill Company, which had been cautious in its relations with Baum and conservative in promoting the sale of his books, the new publisher, the Reilly and Britton Company, filled its list with his books and promoted them to the hilt. After three changes of name and fifty-nine years of publishing, it is still active as Reilly and Lee.

In 1902 when the Hill Company went bankrupt, Frank Kennicott Reilly and Sumner S. Britton were out of jobs. Reilly had been production manager, and Britton head salesman. They took desk space in a building on Madison Street and formed the Madison Book Company as jobber for dictionaries, home medical books, and the like which had formerly been a part of the Hill stock. Both Reilly and Britton had grown up with printer's ink on their fingers. Reilly was born at the Grove, a suburb of Chicago, March 19, 1863, the son of Dr. Frank W.

Reilly, former managing editor of the *Chicago Morning News*. Dr. Reilly was also secretary of the Chicago Board of Health and, later, assistant health commissioner. Young Frank was an employee of the Chicago and North Western Railroad from 1878 to 1885, then went into the lumber business. In 1895 he became a department manager for the Werner Book Company. Just before the turn of the century, he joined the Hill Company. Britton, three years younger than Reilly, had his first taste of Chicago life as a representative of the *Kansas City Star* at the World's Columbian Exposition in 1893. He returned to Chicago to live on July 1, 1894 and later became a salesman for Hill.

The Reillys and the Brittons were personal friends of the Baums, although Mrs. Reilly was an invalid and frequently unable to share in their social life.

Both men were ambitious to expand their little jobbing concern into a publishing firm. Therefore on March 1, 1904 they organized the Reilly and Britton Company, with Britton as president and Reilly as secretary-treasurer. Their Madison Book Company was kept alive for several years but was finally absorbed into the growing publishing enterprise.

In 1913 Reilly became president, and William F. Lee, who had made a reputation as a Bible salesman for the A. J. Holman Company, became vice-president and salesman. In 1916 Britton sold his interest in the company to Lee and moved to New York. On January 11, 1919, Lee became a partner and the title of the firm was changed to its present name of Reilly and Lee. For a number of years the offices were on South Michigan Avenue, then they were moved to 536 Lake Shore Drive. After nearly thirty

years at 325 West Huron Street on the city's Near North
Side, the company moved back to the central business district in May, 1959, when it became affiliated with the
Henry Regnery Company. Lee, the aggressive salesman
and promoter, died in 1924 at the age of fifty-seven, just
a few years after a young salesman, Frank O'Donnell, had
been employed. O'Donnell acquired stock in the corporation and after Frank Reilly's death became president.

Baum had a satisfactory publisher in 1903, but when his
friends Reilly and Britton came to him just as he was
leaving for the summer at Macatawa Park and appealed
to him for a book-length children's story they could feature
on their first trade list for the 1904 season, he agreed. The
new firm needed the glamor of an established author, and
Baum realized that it would give greater attention to
promoting sales of his books than he could expect from
a company with a longer list.

The Marvelous Land of Oz was the result. It stood at
the top of the first page in the modest catalog issued by
Reilly and Britton in the spring of 1904. Twelve more
Oz books by Baum were to follow it on the firm's lists, as
well as such book-length fantasies as *Sky Island*, *The Sea
Fairies*, and *John Dough and The Cherub*, together with
dozens of other titles written under Baum's many pen
names.

One of the first ingenious promotions of Reilly and
Britton was the series of short newspaper stories in connection with the Woggle-Bug Contest which many years
later, in 1960, was to be issued as the book, *The Visitors
From Oz*. The newspaper series, together with *The Woggle-Bug Book*, and the play staged in 1905, helped bring
the title and characters from *The Marvelous Land of Oz*

before the juvenile public. Another successful promotion
of that year was issuance of a small newspaper, *The Ozmopolitan*. A million copies were given away in book stores.
From the style of a copy reproduced in *Publisher's Weekly*
for October 21, 1905, it is a good guess that the items were
written by Baum himself. These short humorous bits advertise several current Baum books from the Reilly and
Britton press. A good sample of the brash style of the little
sheet is the headline article:

EXTRA! EXTRA!
60,000 KILLED?

No! Almost. Our reporter made a slight error.
It was 60,000 sold.

A reporter for *The Ozmopolitan* was riding home in a
wireless trolley car last night when he overheard a conversation between two strap hangers in which he heard
the words, sixty thousand. Of course he thought it had to
do with war or an accident, and accordingly telephoned
the office. We at once set our headline writer (employed at
$500 a week) to work on this extra.

It turned out that one of the strap hangers is in the
book business and was telling of the wonderful sale—60,000
copies—of *The Christmas Stocking Series*—six little books
for children, published by the Reilly and Britton Company of Chicago. . . .*

The Ozmopolitan was revived in 1928 to promote the
organization of Ozite Clubs complete with pin and magazine "for fun and to tell all the Oz news that happens in
between books." The second number reported a circulation of sixty-five thousand. It also noted that Professor

---

* Baum wrote an introduction, explaining the Christmas stocking custom, for these miniature books, which reprinted well
known stories. The set was issued in a tiny wooden book case.

Woggle-Bug had found his pupils tiring of their history, geography and arithmetic pills "so that he had now compressed the necessary knowledge into crackers which he calls 'Wise Crackers.' " The writer and editor of the later *Ozmopolitan* was Ted MacDonald.

One of the most entertaining promotions in the early days of the firm was the Cherub contest. When *John Dough and The Cherub* was being printed, Reilly and Britton asked Baum whether the Cherub was a boy or a girl.

"Surely I told in the story," was Baum's disingenuous reply; for he had been careful to use no pronoun except "it" in referring to the Cherub.

"No, the child you call Chick, the Cherub, might be either a boy or a girl so far as we can see."

Baum smiled and said nothing.

"Well, what are you going to do about it?" demanded his publishers.

Baum smiled again and left the office. But the question continued to bother the publishers. The next time Baum came in, Reilly told him that he could not leave the story that way because children demanded detailed information about characters they liked.

"I wrote the story as I felt it," Baum replied after some moments in thought. "I can't remember that Chick the Cherub impressed me as other than a joyous, sweet, venturesome and lovable child. Who cares whether the Cherub is a boy or girl?"

Reilly put it up to his manuscript readers and even the office staff to decide the matter. Some stated positively the Cherub must be a boy and others were equally positive she was a girl. They backed their opinions by citing traits

of character, phrases used by the Cherub and certain mannerisms, such as the way the Cherub's coat was buttoned.

Baum was called in for consultation and an opinion.
After some discussion he suggested that the decision be
left to the children who read the book, and the last line
of the story was made to say that the records do not state
whether Chick was man or woman. A green ballot was
bound into the front of the book, so that the reader might
express his opinion and the reason for it in twenty-five
words or less. Prizes were offered for the best answers with
the top prize of one hundred dollars in gold. Newspapers
in a number of cities conducted regional contests for a
ten dollar gold prize.

The booming prosperity of the 1920s and the depression
that made the next decade a challenge to Reilly and Lee's
salesmen stimulated them to a series of ingenious promotions. One, so successful that it was repeated over a number
of years, consisted of a series of playlets designed to be
put on by children. These were still being acted long after
Baum's death, and were successful as promotion for the
continuing Oz series. Each play put the principal Oz characters on the stage, and each worked its way through puns
and chitchat to a climactic mention of the Oz book of the
year.

The Land of Oz, first of these scripts by Ruth Plumly
Thompson, who was also the author of Oz books published
after Baum died, is typical of them all. The script for the
forty minute presentation and directions for making costumes for the six characters—Ozma, Dorothy, the Patchwork Girl, the Scarecrow, the Tin Woodman and the Cowardly Lion—were supplied by the Reilly and Lee Company. Leading department stores, such as Hudson's in

Detroit and Marshall Field's in Chicago, provided publicity and the auditorium. Casts were chosen by the schools
or, in a few cases, amateur acting groups, and arrangements were made to let pupils attend the performances.

The playet shown in 1925 through 1927, *A Day in Oz,*
also known as *A Trip to Oz,* was so popular that it was
taken to twenty-four cities, including Los Angeles and
Seattle. The Meier and Frank Company of Portland, Ore-
gon, reported that two thousand children crowded in for
the performances, and that they bought more than one
hundred Oz books in a single day. Elsewhere store after
store had "greater attendance than our accommodations
could take care of." The youngsters enjoyed the show because they saw the Oz characters come to life, they saw
their school mates on the stage, and they could laugh at
such repartee as this:

Professor Woggle-Bug: Did you ever see a board walk?
Scarecrow: No, but I have seen a stone step.
Cowardly Lion: And I have felt a window pain. I am
afraid to go into the woods. I am afraid of the dogwood
bark.
Professor Woggle-Bug (sarcastically): Perhaps since you
are all so clever, you can tell me when a dog's tale is not
a dog's tale.
Scarecrow: I know. When it's a waggin'.

As late as the spring of 1933, the May Company in Cleve-
land was sponsor of an elaborated version of the playlet,
acted by students from a school of expression.

The promotions appeared so fast that it almost seemed
as though Professor Woggle-Bug was thinking them up.
Oz books were the prizes in a map coloring contest that

closed on August 1, 1927. Presumably it was designed to draw the youngsters to book stores to get their outline maps of Oz, which they were supposed to decorate appropriately, as well as locate places mentioned in their books. More sophisticated was the promotion built around Miss Thompson's unfinished story, "The Enchanted Tree of Oz," which involved the four comrades of *The Wonderful Wizard of Oz* in a perilous adventure, which the young contestants presumably resolved to a happy conclusion.

Another scheme to keep the Oz books before the eyes of the juvenile public was a small folder, three by five inches, entitled "The Scarecrow of Oz Answers Questions by Radio." Inside was a dial carrying a concealed magnet and marked with various questions about the Oz books. When one of these was centered below an arrow and the folder was closed, a small steel hand swung to the answer on the cover. This toy was given as an advertisement.

Reilly and Lee also arranged for publicity and bookings through book dealers for the Jean Gros puppet show, *The Magical Land of Oz,* by Miss Thompson. Starting in 1927, the show toured the United States with considerable success for several years.

The depression spawned a newspaper cartoon strip. *The Wonderland of Oz,* which ran in 1932 and 1933 in nearly a dozen American and Canadian dailies. The strip, drawn by Walt Spouse, was reprinted in 1938-9 in *The Funnies* comic books. Reilly and Lee produced for these newspapers a scrapbook to be sold or given away to children wishing to preserve the strips.

Baum not only started the Reilly and Britton Company auspiciously on its long and successful career, but he remained a mainstay on its list as long as he lived. Besides publishing at least one major fairy tale a year under his own name, he wrote under half a dozen pseudonyms. In this guise he was the author of several of the series for boys and girls which made up a good part of the Reilly and Britton list.

Baum used pen names primarily because he wished to be known to the American reading public as the author of fairy tales. Both he and Reilly and Britton felt that parents would buy only one Baum book at Christmas, so they limited that choice but satisfied the demand for other types of children's books by such series as *Aunt Jane's Nieces* and *The Boy Fortune Hunters,* which Baum wrote under other names.

In his various pen personalities, Baum poured out a flood of stories within his two creative decades. Even though most have dropped out of sight in the dusty yesterday of old bookshelves and yellowed magazine files, they must be dusted off and inspected briefly to give a full view of their author's work. The variety of saleable fiction that he turned out in a relatively few years is surprising; so is the ingenuity with which he sent some of his more popular pieces to market time and again.

One whose notions about Baum have been formed only by the Oz books will be most astonished among the lesser known writings to find a number of short stories that exhibit another and very different facet of Baum's talents. Sometimes sentimental, sometimes comic, sometimes merely fashionable, they at times also speak in unfamiliar, harsh, even savage tones, completely alien to the sunny climate of Ozma's realm.

First in point of time among them is "The Suicide of Kiaros" from the September, 1897 *White Elephant.* Well contrived although conventional, its moral chaos violates all the Baum canons. According to the story, a young business man is about to marry his boss's daughter and become a partner in the firm. But examination of the books for drawing up the papers will disclose that he has been embezzling. In this emergency he secretly calls on Kiaros, a Greek money lender, stabs him to death, disguises the crime as suicide, steals $12,500, covers his tracks cleverly, restores the embezzled money, is married and prospers. No retribution, no fantasy—just cold-blooded horror.

Baum tried this mode only once. His next story, however, marked the way he would go. "The Mating Day" (September, 1898 *Short Stories*) with its bloody, elemental struggle to the death between two champions for the chief's daughter and power, foreshadows the grimness of many of his animal stories, while its sentimental climax, in which the hero chooses his mate for love, not power, belongs in the gentler mood of others. One of these is "Aunt Hulda's Good Time" (October 26, 1899 *Youth's Companion*), a tenderly homely tale of a young wayfarer who treats a farm wife to the Cinderella delights of a night at the circus. With minor changes, the story appeared under the title "Aunt Phroney's Boy" in the December, 1912, *St. Nicholas*.

"The Loveridge Burglary" (January, 1900 *Short Stories*) treats as farce an amateur detective's wager that he can engineer a "perfect" housebreaking, only to have the joke turn on him. It is O. Henryish, a vein which Baum did not find congenial.

"Jack Burgitt's Honor" (August, 1905 *Novelettes*) revives the mood of sentimental melodrama that brought Baum his first success in *The Maid of Arran* a quarter century before. Jack, an unsuccessful gold miner, steels himself to commit murder to gain possession of a rich California claim, but loses his resolution when his intended victim trusts him with a big bag of gold dust. After Jack delivers the gold to the bank, the rich miner makes him a partner, saying: "Jack Burgitt, an honest man is scarcer in these diggings than gold itself," while Jack declaims: "Mother allus said that a man as kep' honest would prosper better in the long run."

"A Kidnapped Santa Claus" (December, 1904 *Delineator*) reads like a chapter from the allegorical life of that saint which Baum had only recently published. The Daemons of Envy, Selfishness, Hatred, Malice and Repentance, angry because Santa has left them so little to do, lasso him from his sleigh as he is starting out for the long night of delivering his presents to the children on Christmas Eve. The daemons chain Santa in a cave, hoping that the children will be angry and hateful when they find no presents under the tree next morning. But Santa has four of his helpers in the sleigh, and they make the rounds. Defeated, the daemons free Santa as an army of Immortals comes to rescue him.

In January, 1905, the *Delineator* published the first of the nine *Animal Fairy Tales*. Like *Queen Zixi of Ix*, which was being serialized in *St. Nicholas* at the same time, these stories belong to Baum's "classical" period; for they conform in general to the conventions of the age-old beast fable. With *Queen Zixi of Ix* they made 1905 one of the high points of Baum's career.

The mood of the *Animal Fairy Tales* is winsomely set in the Prologue:

Once I had a friend who was a gray squirrel. I used to lie flat upon the grass in the orchard while my little friend sat near me.

He could talk, this gray squirrel, and chattered very prettily in his quaint tongue. But I could not understand the words because I was ignorant of his language.

To pass away the time I told him fairy tales, and he listened earnestly, and in return gave me a perfect flood of chatter, which I believed to be fairy tales also, and grieved not to comprehend. Yet, when I looked into his bright eyes, dark brown and velvety, I thought I could read therein what the words could not convey—the Fairy Legends of the Animals.

They were wonderful stories, it seemed to me; so I wrote them down, that my comrades, the children, might enjoy them with me. For why should not the animals have their fairies, as well as mortals? And why should their tales not interest us as those concerning the Fairies of our own?

So here are the gray squirrel's stories, which I read in his dark eyes.

"The Story of Jaglon," first of the animal fables, sets the pattern of revenge and rough justice found in many of the other stories. Jaglon, a royal tiger of noble character reared under the care of the tiger fairies, redeems the name of his kind by destroying an usurping lion and becoming king of the beasts. Two other of the stories, "The Enchanted Buffalo" and "The Jolly Giraffe of Jomb," exemplify the same stern moral of vengeance by fang and claw on the usurper and the trickster.

Two stories, "The Discontented Gopher" and "The Transformation of Bayal the Porcupine," teach that whether in the Dakota prairie or in the jungle, contentment with one's lot is better than the wounds and woes that the desire for riches and power brings.

Finally, four of the fables are comic in the worldly,

ironic spirit that Baum had first exploited in the *American Fairy Tales,* and notably in such a story as "The Laughing Hippopotamus." Baum alternated these in the *Delineator* series with the more didactic tales. "The Forest Oracle," in which an artful young ape displaces his elder as the voice of wisdom to the other animals, and "The Pea Green Poodle," which tells how a canine David tumbles a St. Bernard Goliath from his throne, are the most memorable of the comic tales.

The *Animal Fairy Tales* inevitably invite comparison, and most obviously with Kipling's *Jungle Books,* which had appeared about a decade before. There are resemblances, because both men were writing within the limits of a traditional form, but each had his style as a master story teller, and they were worlds apart in experience.

A tint of allegory heightens the realism of Mowgli's ambivalent life between the worlds of his wolf brothers and his human kind. The genius of these stories, however, does not lie in allegory but in Kipling's ability to recreate the heat and lushness of Indian jungle, village and camp. Baum's Bayal the porcupine, like Mowgli, learns to accept his place in the scheme of things, for such is the law of the jungle. But the fairies, not the forces of tropical nature, guide Bayal's education, and his fable teaches a truth of life rather than portraying a way of life.

Without pressing too hard for a comparison, the spirit and form of the *Animal Fairy Tales* comes closer to that of Joel Chandler Harris's Uncle Remus fables than to the Kipling stories. Chip-Cheloogoo Chimpanzee, the irreverent ape who becomes the forest oracle, is brother to the artful Brer Fox. Neither Baum nor Harris had the unique background to personify the struggle of good and evil in such an exotic creature as Rikki-Tikki-Tavi, Kipling's mongoose who rids his master's home of cobras.

Two unpublished stories in manuscript belong in spirit and subject with the *Animal Fairy Tales*. Perhaps "The Tiger's Eye" was too strong meat for the taste of its day. It narrates a mad, sadistic, savage history of a magic maker's eye which passes from him to a baby tiger, then to a jungle boy, then to a deer, imbuing each with its indomitable killer spirit. This is Baum speaking in accents never heard in the Land of Oz. The other story brings a rattlesnake under the Mosaic law; for it kills the man who killed its mate, but learns that a life for a life is vengeance enough.*

"Juggerjook," (December, 1910 *St. Nicholas*) is the tale of Peter Rabbit with a moral twist that takes it out of the primary grade. Mortals sometimes will recognize their own better nature mirrored in the behavior of animals and can then feel the pity to spare them, as they would another person, Baum's fable teaches. It is one of the most skillful as well as one of the sweetest stories that Baum ever wrote about animals.

Three Baum stories have recently come to light in the 1910 and 1911 *Ladies World*. Two of them are conventionally sentimental and do not require mention, but the third, "Bessie's Fairy Tale," is worthy of record in Baum's short-story writing career. It has charm, tenderness, wit, and humor in its story of a little girl who confused a cow

---

* Two other stories of minor interest exist in manuscript: "The Littlest Giant," which recounts the mischief done by a boy giant who surrenders his father's talisman of power for mince pies; and "Chrome Yellow," probably written in 1916, a story of revenge in the orange groves of California.

with a cat, and in the theme that "if you're ign'rant an' call things by their wrong names you're sure to get all mixed up."

The Land of Oz was a world of Baum's own fashioning, though one to which he set very definite emotional and narrative limits, as well as geographical barriers; but in the diversity of the short stories, with their overtones of worldliness, of Mosaic morality, of jungle vengeance, and for contrast, a fairly restrained sentimentality, may appear the unsophisticated measure of Baum's talents as writer and his traits as human being. Like the dualism of night and day, the Oz chronicle and the *Animal Fairy Tales* fit together to form a coherent literary personality.

Baum's first novel for adults, *The Fate of a Crown*, was published in 1905, under the pen name of Schuyler Staunton. The following inscription in his handwriting appears on the flyleaf of a copy:

This book I wrote under an assumed pen name because I did not think it wise to produce a novel to compete with my fairy tales, which occupy a field of their own. The name Schuyler Staunton is taken from that of my mother's brother, the modern "Stanton" having been formerly written "Staunton." As Uncle Schuyler is long since dead I took the liberty of perpetuating his name in this way. As I write this the book is well received and going into a second edition.

L. Frank Baum

The novel's Graustarkian adventures take a young American to Brazil and involve him in a melodramatic revolution. Hidden vaults, hairbreadth escapes and a romantic heroine keep the plot moving along at the pace which, no doubt, won it considerable success.

The winter of 1905-6 Maud and Baum spent abroad, traveling for five months on the Continent and in Egypt. Despite this holiday, 1906 was a banner year. It was marked by publication of a second Schuyler Staunton novel for adults, *Daughters of Destiny,* a melodrama of the struggle for the throne of far-off Baluchistan in which a group of Americans seeking a railroad concession become involved. Murder, harem intrigue, false identities and marvelous coincidences keep the plot galloping like the Arabian horses ridden by the heroes.

Baum also published the first of his many novels for teen-age girls. *Annabel* was written under the name of Suzanne Metcalf. Its unabashed exploitation of the threadbare "rags to riches" plot was popular enough to encourage Reilly and Britton to ask Baum to follow up its success with similar books. The result was a long series, the *Aunt Jane's Nieces* books, published under the name of Edith Van Dyne.

The first of these, *Aunt Jane's Nieces,* resembles in no way the usual fare for young girl readers. Covetousness, bitterness, and hypocrisy rule the three young girls who are brought to the estate of their rich aunt Jane so that she may decide which shall inherit her property. Louise is greedy and false-hearted, Beth is needy and embittered, and Patsy's soul has been seared by her aunt's neglect of Patsy's mother. Aunt Jane has brutalized her rightful heir, Kenneth Forbes, and a supposedly poor relation, Uncle John, also turns up at Elmhurst, which in physical respects resembles the estate where Baum himself grew up. Uncle John washes away all the bitterness with a flood of money to bring the book to a properly happy ending.

Aunt Jane's Nieces and its sequel, *Aunt Jane's Nieces*

Abroad, which also appeared in 1906, stand far above their successors in characterization, narrative interest and realism. *Aunt Jane's Nieces Abroad* describes vividly the Naples area, an eruption of Vesuvius, and Sicily, which Baum had recently visited. Uncle John is kidnapped for ransom while in Sicily with his three nieces. They rescue him through a not too improbable series of adventures. The novel is notable for the freshness of the descriptions and for the sharply ironic twist at the end of the story that saves it from sentimentality.

In that same year, Baum published *Sam Steele's Adventures on Land and Sea,* using the name of Captain Hugh Fitzgerald. Along with it he issued the *Twinkle Tales,* six small books for a younger audience, illustrated by Maginel Wright Enright, and published under the name of Laura Bancroft. The six stories—"Mr. Woodchuck," "Bandit Jim Crow," "Prairie Dog Town," "Prince Mud Turtle," "Twinkle's Enchantment," and "Sugar-Loaf Mountain"— discern with a magic eye the presence of a fairy prince, an enchanted valley and a fabulous city in the Dakota prairie. In such company it is astonishing to come across the savagely moralistic tale of Jim Crow, who refuses to live by the law of the wild and is made to pay for it.

Sam Steele's Adventures on Land and Sea, first of a series of books for boys, is a very creditable example of Baum's writing for a teen-age audience. Sam is a sea captain's son, presumably left an orphan in the care of a grasping woman who drives him out. He falls into the hands of a nautical uncle and with him shares the adventures of a trip to an uncharted Alaskan island where Sam is captured by gold seekers, then periled by mutineers among the prospectors, but finally profits greatly from his courage and loyalty.

On the 1907 list were *Sam Steele's Adventures in Panama,* and *Father Goose's Year Book,* which had the subtitle "Quaint Quacks and Feathered Shafts for Mature Children," published under Baum's own name. This was a sort of almanac and engagement blank book, containing an appropriate original poem and an illustration by Walter J. Enright at the beginning of each month. Aphorisms and topical remarks appeared on the left hand pages while the right hand ones were blank. Typical is this Baumism: "The man who does things by halves may expect no quarter. There's some sense in this."

One of the livelier poems is this one for the July 4 holiday:

> Hurrah! Hurroo! Hip, hip, hooray!
> The 4th is Independence Day
> The small boy is now much elated;
> The population's decimated;
> Toes, fingers, eye-balls scattered wide
> Proclaim this day our nation's pride.

On the same list was a story for the very young, *Policeman Bluejay,* detailing the adventures of two children, Twinkle and Chubbins, who are transformed for a while into birds; speak and understand the bird language, and live with the forest creatures. It was written under the name of Laura Bancroft.

Another event of the year was Baum's compilation of a series of letters written by his wife describing their trip abroad. *In Other Lands Than Ours* was privately printed and illustrated with photographs taken by Baum. Some of Maud Baum's passages were amusing or memorable. At Shepheard's Hotel in Cairo she wrote: "A Hungarian gypsy band . . . saluted our entrance (to the dining room) with selections from 'The Wizard of Oz.' "

At this same hotel Baum saw a little girl reading *The Wizard of Oz*. When he asked her how she liked it, the child's mother told him that the family had traveled to Cairo from the interior of Algeria on camel back and the child had been able to bring only one doll and one book. *The Wizard of Oz* had been her selection. Baum surprised them both by disclosing his authorship and autographing the precious volume.

At the Great Pyramid, Maud observes tartly in one of her letters: "L. F. did not venture to climb the pyramid with me. . . . Few women, and those mostly Americans, undertake the feat." And as they steamed up the Nile she recorded: "Today is Washington's birthday and at dinner L. F. made a neat speech in which he asked all Americans present in this land of tombs to rise and drink a toast to that simple tomb at Mount Vernon so sacred to us all. Every American was on his feet in a minute, and the speech made quite a hit."

At Taormina, Sicily, March, 1906, she records dryly: "We plan to stay here three weeks as L. F. must finish a book in order to save the publishers the expense of a cable every few days demanding the manuscript." This may have been *Aunt Jane's Nieces Abroad,* which has most of its action in Taormina. There Baum wrote a letter while sitting on a terrace from which he could see Mount Etna. "It smoked almost as much as I do," he observed.

In her last letter from the boat returning to the United States, Maud wrote: "L. F. said the Statue of Liberty in New York harbor was the most beautiful sight he had seen since he left home. He thinks too much of his comforts, for Europe is not very comfortable. We live better and more sensibly in America."

Baum drew on his experiences of the trip abroad for *The Last Egyptian,* an adult novel described in the sub-title as a romance of the Nile. It was illustrated by Francis P. Wightman and published in 1908 by Edward Stern of Philadelphia. The Baums had become acquainted with Stern on their trip together up the Nile. He begged Baum for a book manuscript, and after *The Last Egyptian* had been offered to the Century Company it was given to Stern, who published it anonymously. The book grew out of Baum's interest in the subject, as he made clear in a letter written in November, 1906. He mentions that he is writing a novel "based upon material I picked up in Egypt. . . . It will have to be published under a pen name . . . because I cannot interfere with my children's books by posing as a novelist. But I wanted to write this Egyptian tale."

The last Egyptian is a young Nile dweller of the royal blood of the ancient Pharaohs, living with his grand-mother in a filthy hut. In her dying moments she discloses to him the hiding place of the treasures of ancient Egypt, concealed thousands of years ago by their ancestors. She swears him to revenge her own betrayal years before by an English lord. Prince Kara, as the young man now styles himself, uses some of the treasure to set himself up as a member of Cairo society so that he can ruin the two men left of the English family. But love for a young woman of the family betrays him, and in the end he is buried alive in the treasure house of his ancestors. The first part of the novel is as exciting as anything written by H. Rider Haggard, but in the later part the revenge plot and the love affair become so entangled that the reader is bewildered.

In 1908 the two Sam Steele books were reissued under new titles as *The Boy Fortune Hunters in Alaska* and *The Boy Fortune Hunters in Panama*. They became the first of a new series. With them appeared another which was, naturally, *The Boy Fortune Hunters in Egypt*. For this series Baum used the name of Floyd Akers. That same year he published *Aunt Jane's Nieces at Millville*.

Next year brought along *Aunt Jane's Nieces at Work* and *The Boy Fortune Hunters in China*, and there were corresponding titles, *Aunt Jane's Nieces in Society* and *The Boy Fortune Hunters in Yucatan*, on the Reilly and Britton list for 1910. Baum's principal book that year was *The Emerald City of Oz*, but *L. Frank Baum's Juvenile Speaker* was popular. It contained an original two-act play-let, "Prince Marvel," together with instructions for making the costumes and scenery for a home performance, as well as other readings and selections in prose and verse from Baum's published books. The preface pointed out that the popularity of the Oz books had created a demand for this type of material for use in schools.

The Daring Twins, one of two novels for older children which Baum wrote under his own name, came out in 1911. It was illustrated by Pauline W. Batchelder. With it appeared *The Flying Girl*, first of a new series under the Edith Van Dyne pen name, illustrated by Joseph Pierre Nuyttens. In an advertisement, Reilly and Britton printed a view of Baum's home and gardens at Hollywood, with the explanation that "in the center of the pergola is the little sheltered garden house where Edith Van Dyne, a guest of Mrs. Baum, wrote *The Flying Girl*."

Other books of that year were *Aunt Jane's Nieces and Uncle John, The Boy Fortune Hunters in the South Seas,*

a reissue of the 1906 *Twinkle Tales* in one volume under
the title *Twinkle and Chubbins,* and a reissue of the 1907
Policeman Bluejay under the title of *Babes in Birdland.*
The latter was published with a new preface and Baum's
name on the title page in 1917.

The year 1912 brought along *Phoebe Daring,* second of
the Daring books; *The Flying Girl and Her Chum,* second
of that series; *Aunt Jane's Nieces on Vacation;* a reissue
of the 1910 *L. Frank Baum's Juvenile Speaker* under the
title, *Baum's Own Book for Children,* and a new edition
of the 1906 *Annabel. Phoebe Daring,* like its companion
volume, is a mystery story. A young crippled law clerk is
accused of stealing, and the authorities, although aware
that he is blameless, prefer to "railroad" him rather than
to involve the prominent family guilty of the theft.
Phoebe, one of the twins, unravels the twisted threads of
the plot against the clerk, his name is cleared and his fortune is made. Horatio Alger could do no better for his
heroes.

The year 1913 saw publication of the six small volumes
of *The Little Wizard* series, illustrated by John R. Neill,
stories about Oz for young readers, and *Aunt Jane's Nieces
on the Ranch.* The Little Wizard stories were reissued in
one volume in 1914 as *The Little Wizard Stories of Oz.*
Eighteen years later, Reilly and Lee printed a total of a
million copies of four of the stories for the manufacturers
of Jello, who gave them away in connection with a radio
program. These were printed from the original plates with
the addition of some advertising matter. At the same time,
Reilly and Lee ran off an edition of paperback copies of
the same stories and combined them with jigsaw puzzles
made from the colored center spread pages into two boxed

sets known as the Little Oz sets. Each contained two of the booklets and two corresponding puzzles. Also on the 1914 list was *Aunt Jane's Nieces Out West*. The last of that long series, *Aunt Jane's Nieces in the Red Cross*, reached the bookstores in 1915.

These stories, a total of ten volumes, were written for girls before the days of movies, radio and television. The books became so popular that an eastern publisher wrote to Miss Edith Van Dyne, their supposed author, in care of Reilly and Britton, telling her the publisher wished to send a representative to call with a view to having her write for him. Since it seemed inadvisable to let the publisher know that the name had been assumed by Baum of Oz fame, Reilly and Britton suggested that the publisher's representative meet Miss Van Dyne at tea at a hotel in Syracuse, New York, her supposed home. Baum was visiting relatives there at the time. A woman author on the Reilly and Britton list posed as Miss Van Dyne after reading all of the *Aunt Jane's Nieces* series. Under assumed names, Baum and his wife attended the tea. The publisher's representative was charmed with Miss Van Dyne but was unsuccessful in winning her services for his company.

In 1916 and 1917, Baum published *The Snuggle Tales,* six thin volumes of selections from his writings, with illustrations by Neill. *Jack Pumpkinhead,* one of the six, reprinted the opening chapters of *The Marvelous Land of Oz,* using the original plates except for changes in the last part to bring the story to an end. Similarly *The Gingerbread Man* repeats the story of the making of that worthy as told in *John Dough and the Cherub. The Magic Cloak* includes the opening chapter of *Queen Zixi of Ix* together with some jingles from *Father Goose. The Yellow Hen* is made up of the first chapter of *Ozma of Oz* with more short poems; *Little Bun Rabbit* is the story of that name from *Mother Goose in Prose* with shorter selections, and *Once Upon a Time* is a collection of jingles and short pieces. The material of the last four, which were the first published, was drawn from the 1910 Baum's *Juvenile Speaker.*

As a successor to the *Aunt Jane's Nieces* series, Baum started the *Mary Louise* books under the Edith Van Dyne pseudonym. Mary Louise was the name of his favorite sister, Mrs. Brewster. Two titles, *Mary Louise* and *Mary Louise in the Country,* were issued in 1916. Starting in 1917, three more titles were added, one each year—*Mary Louise Solves a Mystery, Mary Louise and the Liberty Girls,* and *Mary Louise Adopts a Soldier*—titles keyed to the interests of girls living in World War I days. After Baum's death in 1919 this series was carried on for a number of years under the Edith Van Dyne name by Emma Sampson, who was employed by the publishers.

Among titles that appeared posthumously were *Oz-Man Tales,* a reissue of the 1916 *Snuggle Tales,* and *Jaglon and the Tiger Fairies,* a reprint in 1953 in book form of the first of the animal fairy tales from the January, 1905 *Delineator.* Illustrations were by Dale Ulrey.

In 1939, Rand McNally and Company, under license from Reilly and Lee, capitalized on the interest aroused by the M-G-M movie, *The Wizard of Oz,* by publishing a junior edition which included the durable *Little Wizard of Oz* stories doubled up into three volumes, and abridged versions of six of the Oz books—*The Land of Oz, The Road to Oz, The Emerald City of Oz, The Patchwork Girl of Oz, The Lost Princess of Oz,* and *Rinkitink in Oz*—with the Neill illustrations.

The Oz books continued to sell despite the distractions

of World War I and increased in the first year following it. If 1919 was a normal year, it appears that the older titles had settled down to a sale of about 6,000 copies each, and that the new Oz book of the year was certain of sales of more than 25,000. Following are the figures:

	1918	1919
The Land of Oz	3,914	7,387
Ozma of Oz	3,138	6,398
Dorothy and the Wizard in Oz	3,360	6,323
The Road to Oz	2,657	5,584
The Emerald City of Oz	2,811	5,721
The Patchwork Girl of Oz	2,839	6,205
Tik-Tok of Oz	2,774	5,564
The Scarecrow of Oz	2,926	6,071
Rinkitink in Oz	2,731	5,821
The Lost Princess of Oz	4,139	6,622
The Tin Woodman of Oz	18,600	7,439
The Magic of Oz		26,219

John Dough rolled up 1,562 in 1919, *The Sea Fairies* 611, and the *Little Wizard Stories* 767, and the *Mary Louise* and *Aunt Jane's Nieces* series were good for an average of about 1,500 for each title in the series.

Besides an aggressive publisher, Baum had the good fortune to have a young and imaginative illustrator, John R. Neill. Neill was twenty-five when he made his first appearance as Royal Iconographer with *The Marvelous Land of Oz*. Neill was born in Philadelphia November 12, 1877, studied at the Pennsylvania Academy of Fine Arts, and left there to get practical experience by working for Philadelphia and New York newspapers and various magazines. Some of his illustrations in *The Saturday Evening Post* brought him to the attention of Reilly and Britton. In *The Marvelous Land of Oz* and all the other Oz books he illustrated, Neill had the double responsibility of adhering faithfully to Denslow's conception of the original characters from *The Wonderful Wizard of Oz,* and of creating his own representations of the new characters as they mushroomed in number and variety with each new Oz book. A better draughtsman than Denslow, Neill pictured a winsome and childlike Dorothy, while the Scarecrow and the Tin Woodman, the Cowardly Lion and the Wizard, went on their immortal way just about as Denslow had first imagined them. Neill was naturally influenced in his drawings by the standards of beauty of the time, and his willowy, long-limbed portrayals of Ozma and Glinda bring to mind the Gibson girls so fashionable in that day.

Neill's style, however, was far from static. In *The Marvelous Land of Oz* he drew with a solid, poster-like technique which was not too startling a transition from Denslow's. *Ozma of Oz* seems rather drab because the color plates were printed on the same paper as the text, and they lack the sparkle which results from coated paper. But in *Dorothy and the Wizard in Oz* and *The Emerald City of Oz* Neill hit his stride with a light, highly decorative style that seems natural to him and was admirably adapted in spirit to his subject. *The Sea Fairies* is the most purely decorative of all the books and is notable for the elaborate border printed in colors around the narrow panel illustrations, while *Sky Island* marked a transition to something like his final sketchy style of lines rather than heavy masses of color.

Neill and Baum met only a few times and had few social or other contacts. When Reilly and Britton received a new manuscript from Baum, in Chicago, Macatawa, Coronado, or Hollywood, they would send a copy of it to Neill at his home in Pennsylvania. He would read it, sketch out ideas for illustrations from the episodes he selected as having the best pictorial possibilities, and send them to the publisher for approval. Approved sketches would then be turned into finished illustrations, usually for the color plates in opaque or water color, and the black and white text drawings in pen and ink.

In his later years, Neill worked at his home just outside Flanders, New Jersey. He died on September 19, 1943.

Manuscripts of Baum's stories were returned to him by the publishers, and for many years they were preserved in a trunk in the attic of his house in Hollywood. One day Maud decided to clean out the attic, and she burned the contents of the trunk in the incinerator behind the house. Only the original longhand manuscripts of *The Magic of Oz*, in the possession of Mrs. Robert Baum, and of *Glinda of Oz*, now the property of Kenneth Baum's daughter, Ozma Baum Mantele, were preserved.

When the members of the family expostulated with her for destroying the manuscripts, Maud remarked that they had been published, the royalties were coming in, and she could see no point to cluttering up the attic with a lot of worthless paper.

XV

GREASE PAINT AND
KLEIG LIGHTS

PRODIGIOUS IS the fitting word for Frank Baum's seemingly endless flow of fairy tales, adventure stories and magazine fiction in the first decade after he published *The Wonderful Wizard of Oz*. In the single year of 1906 he published seven books and, in the next two years, six books each, a record which he equalled in 1911 and approached with five books in 1912.

But his first love, the forum where his first recognition had been won, was the stage. Apparently no amount of other activity could make him forget the lure of the footlights, and this had been strengthened by the acclaim won by *The Wizard of Oz* in 1902. In the golden afterglow of this success he undertook several dramatic collaborations, sketched out many more original extravaganzas and brought two of them into production. It seems almost incredible that he could have found the time and energy to superimpose so much writing for the stage on top of his growing pile of books. But as Eunice Tietjens, the gifted poet who was the wife of Baum's collaborator in *The Wizard of Oz*, put down in her autobiography,

Baum's "imagination and vitality constantly ran away with him." He also twice plunged into the problems and perils of the new dramatic medium, the movies, and managed to swim ashore, having lost his shirt in these adventures.

The first of the post-*Wizard* dramatizations to reach the public was *The Woggle-Bug,* which made its bow at the Garrick Theater in Chicago on June 18, 1905 after three shakedown performances in Milwaukee. *The Marvelous Land of Oz,* published the previous year, had shown signs of being a second *Wonderful Wizard of Oz* in its appeal to the public. Hoping to repeat his luck of a few years previously, Baum made a faithful adaptation of the new story for the stage, describing it in advertisements as a "fantastic fairy extravaganza for children between the ages of 6 and 60." The producer was Henry Raeder, owner of a stock company known as the Dearborn Amusement Company, which had control of the Garrick Theater. Raeder had enlarged his operations to produce such successful musical shows as *The Burgomaster* and *The Storks,* and had his greatest hit with *The Tenderfoot.* However, his next production—*The Forbidden Land*— had cost him the profits from his previous successes. He saw a chance to recoup with a play that might duplicate the financial success of *The Wizard of Oz.* Frederic Chapin, who had written the music for *The Storks* and *The Forbidden Land,* composed the songs for Baum's lyrics, while the scenery was created by the talented hands of Walter Burridge, who had painted the famous poppy field set and other scenes for *The Wizard of Oz.* Frank Smithson, a widely known theater man, was the stage manager.

Raeder and Baum had signed the contract for the show

in November, 1904, but by March 1, 1905, Baum had become dissatisfied and brought suit to break their contract, alleging that Raeder's Minerva Company did not have adequate financial resources to produce the play. Baum offered Raeder four thousand dollars to cancel the contract so that John A. Hamlin could produce it, but apparently Raeder raised the money to produce the play, and the suit was dropped.

Baum, Chapin and Raeder sounded confident in their publicity that they had another *Wizard of Oz*. Indeed, *The Woggle-Bug* had much in its favor, even though, in effect, Baum was competing with himself, because *The Wizard of Oz* was returning within a very few weeks for its third run in Chicago. A great deal of money—mostly Raeder's—had been invested in eight elaborate stage settings. A company of one hundred people was superbly costumed. Smithson had done an excellent job with the staging, although it soon became evident that the production was too elaborate for the small stage of the Garrick. Besides extensive newspaper promotion, giant papier-mâché figures of characters from the play were erected in an amusement park to attract the attention of children to the show at the Garrick.

The lighting effects were much admired, especially the use of animated projections on screens set on the stage to expand the Woggle-Bug to his highly magnified condition. There were several principals in the cast who had followings in Chicago, and the music, so said the *Tribune's* critic, was "rich in melodic beauty." It was described as "the best heard here since Victor Herbert's *Babes in Toyland* came to us."

But *The Woggle-Bug* was a failure from the start. The

critics were at no loss for reasons. James O'Donnell Bennett in the *Record-Herald* complained that "the stage pictures are rather pale imitations of the effects originated by Julian Mitchell in *The Wizard of Oz*." He went on to say that "it is *The Wizard of Oz* without Montgomery and Stone, with Jack Pumpkinhead in place of the Scarecrow and the Woggle-Bug in the place of the Tin Woodman." The *Inter-Ocean* in a postmortem paragraph said: "*The Woggle-Bug* was a childish affair and a flagrant imitation of what had gone before; but it was not so poor an entertainment that it was without promise. . . . But the novelty of characterization was not in the least novel (after *The Wizard of Oz*) and there was no Montgomery and Stone specialty."

The reflected glory of Baum's great stage success, which was still in the full tide of popularity on the road, dimmed the luster of his new script. As Burns Mantle wrote in the *Inter-Ocean:* "The Wizard is palpably the inspiration for the newer extravaganza. The chief difference is this: Someone took the book of the Wizard after Mr. Baum got through with it and did so many things to it that the original author could hardly recognize it, while with *The Woggle-Bug* the impression is strong that the original manuscript has been altered but little."

Baum had ignored the lesson taught him by Mitchell. In a signed article in the *Chicago Record-Herald,* printed on the very day of the play's opening, he had insisted that he had written an extravaganza, with "the dignity that clings ever to the real fairy tale, and which must carry with it its own quota of awe and wonderment," and not a musical comedy, which he described out of the side of his mouth as a "burlesque of grand opera, a jest." As a result, the show was damned by a critic as "an entertainment smothered in simplicity in which the child will revel, and before which the adult mind will nod."

Besides these handicaps, the pace of the show suffered from a long prologue in Mombi's cornfield, complete with a chorous of sprites going through illuminated evolutions, from what the critics described as an "unfortunate" rain of cats and dogs in the courtyard of the royal palace at the beginning of the second act, and from a tedious epilogue in the rose garden of a sorceress.

While some blamed Baum's book, others complained of the "audaciously unprepared" state in which the show was brought to Chicago and put the blame on the management. Baum at once began to rewrite the book, and by July 10 he had what amounted to a new script ready for the public. But the shot in the arm came too late. The cast refused to continue without pay. The outfitters and electricians descended on July 12 and seized costumes and other properties, forcing the show to close the next day after an embarrassing performance put on without those essentials.

"*The Woggle-Bug* has ceased to woggle," wrote the *Inter-Ocean* on July 14. "No more will the pretty chorus girls . . . disport before the admiring gaze of parquet occupants. The constables have taken their tights; they haven't been paid for three weeks, they say."

And the *Record-Herald* printed a mock obituary in its news columns, in this style:

H. M. Woggle-Bug, T.E., is Dead.
H. M. Woggle-Bug, T.E., died yesterday, at its residence, the Garrick Theater, after sev-

eral weeks prolonged illness from a complication of diseases arising from internal
injuries and financial embarrassment.

The *Tribune* commented briefly, summing up its opinion by saying: "It was heavy and tiresome, notwithstand-
ing the money that was melted into scenery and costumes."

Despite all this adverse comment, individual performers
in the show were treated generously by the critics. Fred
Mace,* as the Woggle-Bug, made a hit with such songs as
"Mr. H. M. Woggle-Bug, T.E." and "There's a Ladybug
a Waitin' for Me," even though it was acknowledged that
he was not a talented comedian. He was replaced later in
the run by Sidney Bracey. Hal Godfrey, an eccentric
dancer of the Montgomery and Stone type, in the role of
Jack Pumpkinhead sang one of the most popular songs
"Jack O'Lantern," but was otherwise undistinguished.

The men yielded honors to the women, especially to
Mable Hite† as Captain Prissy Ping, an aide to General
Jinjur, with her "ragtime feet" and their "syncopated
stepping in the Soldier's March." The *Inter-Ocean* objected that Miss Hite was "too Weber and Fields for such
as are drawn to a children's spectacle," but the *News* called
her "a marvelous little creature full of genius going to wild
and lamentable waste." Close behind her in popularity was
Blanche Deyo, "a sparkling creature who dances in a
winged fashion." Miss Deyo wore shorts, a frock coat and
Windsor tie in the part of Tip, until she was transformed

* Later a noted motion picture actor with the Mack Sennett
Company.

† Miss Hite made a name for herself on the stage, teamed in
vaudeville with her husband, Mike Donlin, New York Giants'
baseball star. She died of cancer when she was about thirty years
old.

into Ozma, and she won applause for her singing of "My Little Maid of Oz" and the duet, "Patty Cake, Patty Cake, Baker's Man." Phoebe Coyne, wife of the stage manager, was acclaimed for her portrayal of the witch with "zest, picturesqueness and musical weight." Most popular of the spectacles was the storming of the City of Jewels by the army of revolt under General Jinjur, which bombarded the walls with hundreds of toy balloons while performing an intricate military march. This spectacle closed the first act.

Not long before Baum became involved with *The Woggle-Bug,* he tried his hand at dramatic collaborations with two other Chicago authors. However, none of their three scripts ever got beyond the preliminary stage. Most elaborate of these efforts was a dramatization of a children's fantasy, *Prince Silverwings,* by Mrs. Carter Harrison, wife of the mayor of Chicago, and author of a half dozen books for the young. The title page of a scenario printed by Mc-Clurg and dated 1903 described this as a musical spectacle in three acts and eight scenes. Tietjens was chosen by the authors to write the music for their spectacle, but it was denied a chance to be born. According to a tradition in the Harrison family *Prince Silverwings* was being prepared as the opening feature of the new Iroquois Theater. It was not ready in time; the theater was destroyed by fire, and Mayor Harrison advised his wife and Baum to abandon the project.

The year 1903 also brought Baum into his first collaboration with Emerson Hough, destined for fame as a writer of novels about the West. Hough at that time was on the staff of a sports magazine. He and Baum became acquainted at the Press Club and their acquaintance ripened into friendship. Together they drew up the scenario of an oddly modern farce, *The Maid of Athens,* a story of parallel plots on a college campus and in ancient Greece. It is leaner, sharper and less crowded with stage business than anything Baum wrote in his later years for the stage. A printed copy of the scenario survives in the Library of Congress.

In 1905 Baum and Hough sketched an extravaganza as clotted and cluttered as *The Maid of Athens* had been lean. *The King of Gee-Whiz* is full of slapstick situations, but the authors were unable to interest a producer in their book. Baum then went ahead with *The Woggle-Bug,* and Hough thriftily employed the title for a children's book published in 1906.

These early days of the century have also left behind other proposals for dramatic efforts with which Baum's name is connected. He and Tietjens, for instance, talked about collaborating on an opera, *The Pagan Potentate,* and in July, 1904, Tietjens noted in his diary the improbable information that they were dramatizing *Father Goose* —a book of jingles.

When interviewed in 1909 by *The Theater,* Baum, who was at his house at Coronado Beach in California, admitted that his winter workshop was a busy place and went on to detail some of his dramatic projects.

"The new operas," he said, "will all be put out early in the season. The one that I may say is practically finished is *The Pipes of Pan.* Paul Tietjens is writing the score for this and it is true comic opera. . . . This opera will be presented by the Shuberts at the Lyric in New York early in the fall.

"I am not neglecting the musical comedy idea. An extravaganza that will go either by the name of *Ozma of Oz* or *The Rainbow's Daughter* will be put on the first week in October by Montgomery and Stone at the Studebaker Theater in Chicago. . . . You can tell that the mechanical effects will be remarkable, for we have working with us Arthur Voegtlin, who is without a doubt the greatest scenic painter in America. . . . The music for this play is being written by Manuel Klein, composer of *The Land of Nod.*

"I am particularly engaged just now, though, with an opera I am doing for Mr. Dillingham, that will be put on by Montgomery and Stone, succeeding *The Red Mill.* . . . The exact date of this production is not decided yet, and neither is the title, though we are thinking seriously of *Peter and Paul.* One of the big things in it is the music. Arthur Pryor has written it, and it is going to make a big hit."

The interviewer, who made Baum sound more positive about some of these projects than the author perhaps had intended, also noted Baum's interest in the possibility of building a theater in New York, near Carnegie Hall, for the production of fantasy plays for children. Besides weekend performances of dramatizations of the beloved stories of childhood, Baum had in mind organization of traveling companies to take the plays on the road. In later years such groups as the Goodman Theater of the Art Institute of Chicago have proved the worth of Baum's idea, which no producer was venturesome enough to back at that time. He also considered for a time the purchase of Pedloe Island, lying off the California coast, and converting it into a Land of Oz, with a palace complete with statues of the Scarecrow, the Tin Woodman, the Woggle-Bug, and their companions; and a Wizard's Point graced by a statue of Jack Pumpkinhead. Problems of transporting children to an island finally caused him to abandon an idea which in the last few years has been closely realized in the elaborate California promotion of Disneyland.

Of these ambitious schemes nothing remains except a typescript of *The Pipes O' Pan,* fairly complete with lyrics, stage directions and cast of characters. As its title indicates, the play draws on Greek mythology, although irreverently, in musical comedy fashion. Involved in the plot are a comic woodsman, King Midas and a gypsy girl he fancies after a single sight of her, and Pan and Apollo, whose musical contest with pipes and lyre Midas is forced to judge. Asses' ears are his reward for preferring Pan's skirling to Apollo's strumming. A fine Baum touch is the accompaniment played by mechanical woodpeckers on xylophones hidden in the trees. The lyrics, as they should be, are light and gay and unmemorable. George Scarborough collaborated on the script.*

Baum's restless genius had not been quiet more than three years after the failure of *The Woggle-Bug* when he was knocking on the stage doors again with an ambitious project which he called the *Radio Plays.*

William Nicholas Selig, one time circus magician and minstrel show performer, patented a motion picture machine in 1896 and formed the Selig Polyscope Company in Chicago to manufacture it. Later he built a studio in Chicago to produce movies, and he is reputed to have constructed the first set in the Los Angeles area. Selig financed expeditions which brought back wild animals which he used in making adventure films. After some preliminary attempts to make a picture based on the Oz characters, to be shown in the nickelodeons of the day, Baum prepared a two hour lecture about the Land of Oz and its

* *Maid of Athens, The King of Gee-Whiz,* and *Pipes o' Pan* scenarios are reprinted in *The Musical Fantasies of L. Frank Baum,* by Alla T. Ford and Dick Martin, Chicago 1958.

inhabitants and employed Selig to make a movie, hand tinted by Duval in Paris. Baum's aggressive publishers helped promote the scheme by sponsoring the lecture and by advertisements calling attention to Baum's forthcoming book, *Dorothy and the Wizard in Oz,* as well as preceding titles. Baum's friend, Harrison Rountree, lent him the money to pay for the movie, taking a note as security.

The movie, described as this "merry, whimsical and really wonderful Fairylogue and Radio Plays" consisted of two parts: *The Land of Oz* and *John Dough and the Cherub.* According to the advertisement, the first was adapted from *The Land of Oz* and *Ozma of Oz.* On a screen, framed in red plush, the audience saw a large book. Its pages were opened by a page boy, and the familiar characters stepped out one by one and were introduced by their creator. Following this prologue came fourteen scenes; they began in a cornfield in Oz, progressed to the two most popular episodes—the shipwreck of Dorothy and her hen, and the flight of the Gump—proceeded to the Nome King's underground realm, and reached their climax in the throne room of the Emerald City. This was followed by an intermission of "dissolving" scenes advertising *Dorothy and the Wizard in Oz.* Six scenes made up the second half of the program. These followed the story line of *John Dough and the Cherub* fairly closely, from John's coming to life in the bake shop, through his adventures on the Isle of Phreex, to his elevation to the rule of Hiland and Loland.

To rest the eyes of the audience, colored still pictures of the Oz characters, made from paintings by E. Pollock, were projected on the screen at intervals from a magic lantern.

Baum appeared in person with the *Radio-Plays* at Orchestra Hall in Chicago on October 1, 1908. For twenty-five cents to a dollar, patrons could see him attired in a tailor-made white frock coat with silk-faced lapels sporting a red carnation and trousers of white woolen broadcloth, while he narrated the story of the film's two-hour run to a musical accompaniment by part of the Theodore Thomas Orchestra.

A genial reviewer in the *Chicago Tribune* wrote of the first performance.

The Scarecrow, the Tin Woodman, Dorothy Gale of Kansas, and a number of other pleasantly familiar characters returned to Chicago Thursday evening under interesting circumstances.

In the first place, they brought with them their creator, L. Frank Baum, who wore a lovely frock coat and won the affections of a good-sized audience of children and grownups. In the second place, they added two perfectly good words—"fairylogue" and "radio-play"—to the vocabulary of our overworked press agents. . . .

For the benefit of grownups, who always have to have fairyland explained to them, it may be stated that a fairylogue is a travelogue that takes you to Oz instead of to China. A radio-play is a fairylogue with an orchestra at the left hand corner of the stage. . . . The idea is a new one, and with Mr. Baum's charming whimsicalities as its base, proved to be well worth while. . . . (The program) is a series of colored motion pictures interspersed with fanciful drawings and accompanied by incidental music from the orchestra.

Mr. Baum reveals himself as a trained public speaker of abilities unusual in a writer. His enunciation is clear and incisive, and his ability to hold a large audience's attention during two hours of tenuous entertainment was amply demonstrated. He has secured some motion pictures of real beauty, and, altogether his program is worth the attention of any youngster who can induce his parents to let him sit up until 11 P.M.

The *Inter-Ocean* was equally hospitable to the venture, asserting that "these tales by Mr. Baum are in a class by themselves as the only series of fairy romances that contribute new and original characters to the realm of childish fancy, and they are told in delightful fashion." The *Record-Herald* remarked that the *Radio Plays* "manifestly had cost a great deal of money."

After three night performances and a matinee in Orchestra Hall, the frock coated lecturer and his eldest son, who was the projectionist, took the *Radio Plays* on tour of several midwestern states. They returned to the Fine Arts Theater in Chicago on October 24 for a week of matinees, varied by two autographing parties, and a Thursday performance at which the Dorothy of the Radio Plays film, little Romola Remus, made a personal appearance in her red dotted dress and fluffy tulle bonnet. After this, the show went on the road again, closing just before Christmas at the Hudson Theater in New York City.

Audiences on the road tour were satisfactory, and even the counterattractions of the holiday season did not cut too heavily into the attendance in New York. But expenses were heavy. Besides rental of the theaters and salaries for musicians, Baum had to carry with him his own projection equipment and screen, as well as a heavy steel projection booth. This was bolted together and erected in the balcony to make the entertainment conform to municipal fire laws. Freight, drayage and labor ran up the costs. When Baum, who throughout his life ignored financial details, at last faced up to a profit and loss statement on his tour, he realized that he was losing money and closed the Radio Plays after the New York engagement.

He returned to Chicago for the last time. The Baums were then living in a second floor apartment at 5243 South

Michigan Avenue where they had moved in 1906. The family by this time was shrinking. Their son Frank, a military school graduate, had left in 1904 to begin his army career in the Philippines, and the other sons were also breaking their home ties.

Chicago had been Baum's realm of glory, but by 1910 the glory had tarnished. *The Woggle-Bug* and the *Radio Plays* had been losing ventures; Chicago had no business value any more to an established author, and Frank and Maud preferred California, where they had spent several of their winters, to the summers at Macatawa Park. The Royal Historian was at last footloose, he could begin a more leisurely life on the West Coast. The cottage at Macatawa Park was sold, and the Baum moved their possessions to a house in Los Angeles at 199 Magnolia Avenue. Their son Harry stayed behind in Chicago and was married there in 1910, but Robert and Kenneth went along to Hollywood and were married in the family home in 1914.

Not long after the Baums were settled in Los Angeles, Maud spent part of an inheritance from her mother's estate to buy a large corner lot at Cherokee Avenue and Yucca Street* in the sparsely settled suburb of Hollywood. Money was borrowed to build a two-story frame house on the lot. Baum christened it Ozcot. After Maud's death in 1953, the house was demolished and an apartment house built on the site.

Behind him in Chicago, Baum had left a small mountain of debt piled up since 1908, principally by the *Radio Plays* venture. He filed a petition in bankruptcy on June

---

* 1749 Cherokee Avenue.

3, 1911 in the Federal District Court in Los Angeles. Against debts of $12,600 he listed as assets two suits of clothing, "one in actual use and another kept in his room at 149 North Magnolia Avenue," eleven second-hand books and a five-year-old typewriter.

His principal creditors were Edmond W. Pottle of Los Angeles, whose successful suit for a judgment on notes for $3,157.50 a few weeks before in Los Angeles County Superior Court had apparently precipitated the bankruptcy plea; the Selig Polyscope Company of Chicago, two notes for $1,500; Leon Mandel of Chicago, a note for $500; the National Printing and Engraving Company of Chicago, note for $1,150.20, and the W. F. Hall Printing Company, $1,242.20, as well as bill posters and advertising media in several states. Presumably all these were borrowings and debts incurred to launch the *Radio Plays*.

Dozens of other unpaid bills, including $500 to Henry Berger and Company of Chicago, for merchandise, and $500 to Basil P. Finley of Kansas City, as well as smaller ones to department stores, groceries, doctors and dentists, a laundry, a jeweler, a livery company and even a private school, were mute evidence of hard times in the Baum household in 1908 and 1909. The petition was granted on the same day it was filed.

Not long after he had straightened out his financial affairs and settled his family in the new home, Baum joined the Los Angeles Athletic Club, whose membership included the leading business and professional men of Southern California. Among them was a young and progressive theatrical producer, Oliver Morosco. Morosco, whose real name was Mitchell, had made a great success of bringing hit shows from New York to California for production by his stock company. Later he was to win fame for himself as the producer of *Peg O' My Heart* and *Abie's Irish Rose,* to be four times married, to make fortunes, and to die penniless in 1945.

Morosco suggested that, in view of the success of *The Wizard of Oz* extravaganza more than a decade previously, the public might welcome a new musical comedy based upon the later Oz books. He introduced Baum to Louis F. Gottschalk, a composer and orchestra conductor, and the three of them agreed to collaborate. Baum was to write the book, Gottschalk the music and songs, while Morosco would take charge of bringing their work before the public. Baum had already given some thought to writing a musical show which he had tentatively called *The Girl from Oz* but found it unsuitable for the new venture and abandoned it. In his summer house in the garden at Ozcot, he put together a script based on several of the Oz books. He called it *The Tik-Tok Man of Oz.* The title character became the central figure of his Oz book in the following year.

James C. Morton and Frank F. Moore, an experienced vaudeville team, were engaged to play Tik-Tok and the Shaggy Man respectively. Charlotte Greenwood was Morosco's choice for the comedy role of Queen Ann Soforth, the girl with an army of fifteen officers and one private. Lenora Novasio, a brisk, petite beauty, was cast as Betsy Bobbin, the leading lady; Fred Woodward as her pet mule, Hank; Beatriz Michelina as Princess Ozma, and Dolly Castles, a blonde from Australia, as Polychrome, the Rainbow's daughter. Later, on tour, Josie Intropidi replaced Miss Greenwood.

Advertisements heralding *The Tik-Tok Man of Oz* as a

forty thousand dollar spectacle introduced its opening at the Majestic Theater in Los Angeles on March 31, 1913. After five weeks playing to standing room only, it moved to San Francisco for three weeks and then went to Cohan's Grand Opera House in Chicago for the summer. It closed there on August 23 for a tour which kept it on the road until it returned to the Majestic Theater in Los Angeles on January 18, 1914 for a final engagement of several weeks.

Patrons entering the theater were greeted by a musical tick-tock, and the curtain rose on a ship sinking in a storm at sea, and Betsy and her mule Hank adrift on a raft. Morosco described this as the most powerful first act he had ever seen. Cast ashore in the Rose Kingdom of the Land of Oz, Betsy and Hank fall in with the Shaggy Man, a droll comedian, who is searching for his long lost brother, Wiggie. Wiggie, they learn, has been hidden by the Metal Monarch in the Metal Forest.

Princess Ozma blossoms out of a rose as it becomes full blown and joins them. The flower garden was represented by chorus girls lying on their backs and moving their petal dressed legs in precision maneuvers. At a cross roads they meet Polychrome, who has been left on earth when she stepped off the end of her father's rainbow. Presently Betsy and Hank discover Tik-Tok in an old well. This copper man is rescued and wound up so that he can walk, talk, and think. The little party becomes a crowd when Queen Ann and her army arrive, and after several spectacles and songs they all enter the Underground Caverns of Ruggedo, the Metal Monarch. In Ruggedo's kingdom, devils, pounding on twenty-four anvils tuned like a xylophone, and shooting out sparks at every stroke, heralded Ruggedo's power, and the rescue of Wiggie was accomplished amid the maneuvers of well drilled choruses and spectacular transformation scenes made possible by electrical and mechanical effects for which Baum claimed copyright in the program.

The Tik-Tok Man of Oz was Baum's first stage success since *The Wizard of Oz*, principally because he had at last written an original show—not an adaptation—and it was a story which adults as well as children could enjoy. Morosco's skill in staging and casting the piece and Gottschalk's tuneful melodies and descriptive music could be favorably compared with the best Chicago had seen. The critics who had belabored *The Woggle-Bug* and the *Radio Plays* as fare for children accepted their successor as suitable for adults. Los Angeles critics such as Henry C. Warnack of the *Times* polished up their best adjectives. "Rich favorite," "such a maze of scenic effects and imagination that it pops and sizzles like a live wire," "the show effervesces with good looks and good lines" were some of the descriptive phrases.

But when *The Tik-Tok Man of Oz* reached Chicago, Baum again learned the bitter lesson that success is harder to live down than failure. *The Wizard of Oz* had played in the same Grand Opera House eleven years before, and the critics would not let their readers forget it. They seemed to be especially resentful that a worth-while musical comedy had been produced "out in the sticks" in Los Angeles.

"So put on your old gray bonnet with the wild rose on it and bask in fond recollection handsomely dolled up for 1913," wrote Amy Leslie in the *Daily News*. James O'Donnell Bennett in the *Record-Herald,* used the headline:

"Mr. Baum tries again in the same place," and wrote: "The entertainment from the far west which was disclosed at the Grand Opera House last evening is a harmless, if somewhat brazen, attempt to invoke the long vanished spell of *The Wizard of Oz.* Mr. L. Frank Baum, the Oz man, did not deny that intention, and in a speech he made to the audience after two hours of the gaudy glories had passed by he appeared to be satisfied with the fulfillment. . . . That statement of the case may satisfy Mr. Baum and Los Angeles, where his present skit was first presented and much liked, but it will hardly carry conviction to those who remember the old 'Wizard.' "

Percy Hammond of the *Tribune* also belabored the similarity to *The Wizard of Oz,* which he describes as "a previous fable by this Cook County Hans Christian Andersen." "Mr. James Morton," he wrote, "is not so funny as Mr. Fred Stone was, of course, but then his side partner, Mr. Frank Moore, is not so unfunny as Mr. Dave Montgomery. In fact, Mr. Moore is rather funny." Hammond then drew the parallel: Dorothy, the girl from Kansas, and Betsy, the girl from Oklahoma; Dorothy's cow and Betsy's mule; Dorothy's cyclone and Betsy's shipwreck in a storm at sea; the Scarecrow and the Tin Woodman; the Shaggy Man and Tik-Tok; the poppy field and the rose garden. But having this out of his system, Hammond's mood became more genial as he praised "the animated flowers and songs about flowers, things that 'light up' prettily, a comic mule (which makes the hit of the show), villainous monarchs, handsome girls in tights and rich dress, and scene after scene of attractive canvas splendor." He closed by saying that Baum spoke gravely after the first act "and thanked those who gave him assistance in the work of production. If he had talked all night, he could not have expressed his debt to Mr. Morosco for quite the handsomest presentation of extravaganza this generation of children has seen."

Charles Purcell, as Private Files, and Miss Michelena, as Ozma, sang a particularly effective duet in the hit song, "Ask the Flowers To Tell You." Purcell also scored with a ballad: "My Wonderful Dream Girl," and so did Moore as the Shaggy Man with "The Magnet of Love." Best of the chorus numbers was a swinging march: "The Army of Oogaboo."

In the last week of July *The Tik-Tok Man of Oz* had a gross of $8,500, which was splendid business at a top price of a dollar fifty. Both in Chicago and on the road, as well as back in California, the show played to good houses. But Morosco, who was deeply involved in organizing road shows of his great hit, *Peg O' My Heart,* closed the expensive Baum musical while it was still on the right side of the ledger.

The success of *The Tik-Tok Man of Oz* afforded Baum the satisfaction of seeing Oz again on the stage and of advertising its glories to a new generation of children. But the day of such spectacles was dying. Bennett acutely observed in his review:

Old style, tinsel extravaganza is dead. The smart, flexible "revue" killed it. People don't believe in these pink fairies on a pulley any more; they believe in Bert Williams and Henry Watson and Flo Ziegfeld with their rough and pungent jibes at the follies of the minute. The last pretentious experiment in old-fashioned extravaganza— "The Pearl and the Pumpkin"—sounded the death knell of this form of fooling. It costs too much and it doesn't mean anything.

Baum sensed the change in popular taste and moved with the times. He turned to the rising new medium—movies—which was beginning to bring his quiet little Hollywood village out of the obscurity of the orange groves into the glare of Kleig lights.

Not many months after the closing of *The Tik-Tok Man of Oz* a group of men who held good fellowship meetings weekly in the Blue Room of the Los Angeles Athletic Club asked Baum to draw up a proposal to form a club. The Lofty and Exalted Order of Uplifters was the result, and its platform gave Baum ample space to indulge his liking for puns. For example, the president was known as the Grand Muscle, "because the chief requisite in uplifting is muscle." His emblem was a clam, "because the clam is recognized as the finest mussel known to man." In the same spirit, the vice-president was known as the Elevator; the secretary as the Royal Hoister; the treasurer as the Lord High Raiser, and the board of governors as the Excelsiors, "because Excelsior means higher." The motto of the order was, of course, "Keep It Up."

Until his death, Baum was an Excelsior as well as poet-laureate. He also played the bass drum in the Uplifters' orchestra, which performed for the occasional parties. Poems and what passed for them were recited at these parties, and several collections, including parodies and occasional verse by Baum, were published.

Most of the members were business men whose dues supported the high jinks of the organization, but the membership also included a number of actors and artists who contributed their talents in lieu of money. At various times the Uplifters included in their ranks such celebrities as Will Rogers, George Arliss, Frederick Warde, Hal Roach,

Frank Borzage, Leo Carillo, Harold Lloyd, Sigmund Rom-
berg, Darryl F. Zanuck, Irvin S. Cobb and Paul G. Hoff-
man.

The Uplifters held their first annual outing in 1914.
For the second one in Santa Barbara in 1915, Baum wrote
a farce, *The Uplift of Lucifer, or Raising Hell,* with musical score by Gottschalk. Its cast included several nationally
known actors who were members. For the third outing at
Del Mar, Baum wrote *The Uplifters' Minstrels* with music
by Byron Gay. In 1917 the outing was at Coronado Beach,
and Baum's play was *The Orpheus Road Show,* again to
music by Gottschalk. These outings were abandoned when
war broke out, and Baum died before they were resumed.

Out of the Uplifters, however, came the inspiration for
organizing a motion picture company to produce Baum's
Oz fantasies for the screen. Hollywood's film industry was
just getting started, and the opportunity to promote the
fortunes of a fellow member looked bright. A corporation,
the Oz Film Manufacturing Company, was established and
a block of stock was issued to Baum for exclusive rights to
make movies from his stories. The full one hundred thousand dollars in capital stock was subscribed within ten days
by members of the Uplifters and the Athletic Club.

Baum was elected president, Gottschalk vice-president,
Clarence H. Rundel secretary, and Harry F. Haldeman
treasurer. A studio site was selected at the edge of Hollywood in a section known as Colegrove because it was part
of the estate of Senator Cole. The seven-acre lot, just south
of Hollywood proper, faced Santa Monica Boulevard,
across the street from the Universal Film Company, and
extended a full city block from Gower to Lodi streets. A
high board fence was built around it, and the new com-

pany erected an enclosed stage, sixty-five by one hundred feet, at that time one of the largest in the United States. Under the stage was a concrete tunnel, designed by Baum to make possible all sorts of magical effects and transformations. An army of men and girls, on horseback or afoot, could appear or disappear through trap doors opening into this tunnel from the stage floor. Alongside the tunnel was a large concrete tank and eight smaller ones which could be filled with water to create the illusion of ponds or rivers. Space was also provided to fabricate settings large enough to fill the entire stage, and to make papier-mâché properties and Oz character masks.

Production of the first picture, *The Patchwork Girl of Oz,* in five reels, was started early in July, 1914. Baum wrote the scenario. Although he had written and produced plays and extravaganzas, this was his first experience with turning out a script for a motion picture. The *Radio Plays* produced in 1908 had been merely an illustrated retelling of the stories from his books. Frank Moore and Fred Woodward, who had appeared in *The Tik-Tok Man of Oz,* were in the cast of *The Patchwork Girl of Oz.* The part of Ojo was taken by Violet MacMillan, and that of the Patchwork Girl by Pierre Couderc, making his first American appearance. An original musical score came from the pen of Louis Gottschalk.

The film was completed in a month and first shown privately in the gymnasium of the Los Angeles Athletic Club. But Oz Film Company's novice officials soon discovered that producing a motion picture was one thing; getting it released into the movie houses of the nation for showing to the public was quite another. Most of the motion picture theaters were tied up by the big producers, who had the firm intention of keeping them as exclusive outlets for their own pictures. Nevertheless, arrangements were finally made with Paramount Pictures for release of *The Patchwork Girl of Oz* on September 23, 1914. But about that time the Motion Picture Patents Company, which claimed to own Thomas A. Edison's patents on motion picture making equipment, filed suit for infringement against all independent motion picture companies. A long series of negotiations followed. The patent situation was finally settled and production at the studio was resumed.

The plot of *The Patchwork Girl of Oz* followed fairly closely that of the book of the same title, although, as a reviewer in the *Motion Picture World* indicated, the story was enlivened with "much good spectacular work in which the soldiers and the court of the Kingdom of Oz play a prominent part." W. Stephen Bush, this same critic, called the acting fair and found some fault with the photography but recommended the picture to exhibitors as "children's entertainment." Obviously, Baum had not kept in mind the lessons he should have learned from Julian Mitchell when the latter overhauled *The Wizard of Oz* to make it adult entertainment, nor had he absorbed the sharper lessons of *The Woggle-Bug* and the *Radio Plays*.

The lesson was not long in coming home, but it did not come soon enough. For in the meantime the Oz Film Company had started work on another five reel movie, *The Magic Cloak of Oz*, which Baum had adapted from one of his finest stories, *Queen Zixi of Ix*. When this new picture was completed it was offered to Paramount for release, but much to the chagrin of the directors of the company, Paramount declined to take it. Business on *The Patchwork*

Girl of Oz had not been good, the directors were told; everywhere it had been shown throughout the country, attendance had fallen off. Patrons resented a "kid story" when they expected to see adult entertainment, and some even wanted their money back. When the experience of the theaters with *The Patchwork Girl of Oz* became known, no releasing company would touch *The Magic Cloak of Oz*. With an unsaleable property on his hands, Baum cut the picture from five reels to two two-reelers and offered them on a "states' rights" basis as fillers. They found few takers.

In the meantime, however, the company had gone ahead with a third five reel movie, *His Majesty, the Scarecrow of Oz*, which introduced the Scarecrow and the Tin Woodman—characters which had been such a tremendous hit on the stage in *The Wizard of Oz*. Frank Moore played the Scarecrow, Couderc the Tin Woodman, and Miss MacMillan was Dorothy. The story itself was a melange of elements from *The Wizard of Oz*, *The Land of Oz*, and even *The Road to Oz*, with the love of the Scarecrow for an enchanted Princess Gloria (played by Vivian Reed), her love for a gardener's son, and the machinations of King Krewl and Old Mombi as the dramatic elements. He used portions of this plot in the book, *The Scarecrow of Oz*, published in 1915.

Most of the releasing firms were in New York; so the company attempted to get closer to them by opening an office at 220 West Forty-second Street. Little progress was made until October, when the Alliance Film Company agreed to distribute the picture if its name was changed to *The New Wizard of Oz*. Under that title it was offered as late as 1919 by Lyons-Royal Enterprises.

By this time Baum and the owners of the Oz Film Manufacturing Company realized that there was no profitable
market for the sort of films they had been making. In an
effort to continue in business by appealing to adult audiences, production was begun on a five reel dramatization
of Baum's anonymous novel, *The Last Egyptian*. Booking
firms were reluctant to accept this adult adventure picture, because of the industry's experience with the company's earlier films, but it was finally released on December
7, 1914, by the Alliance Company and was reasonably successful in the theaters.

After this, production was stopped while negotiations
went on with various releasing companies in New York.
The best terms that could be obtained required Baum's
company to get approval of a scenario before starting production, but did not bind the releasing company to accept
the finished picture until it was regarded as satisfactory.
On April 1, 1915, the studios were reopened to film the
story of a Roman Catholic sister who helped Allied soldiers
escape from behind the German lines. It was a good picture, well photographed and building up to a strong and
exciting climax. The subject matter was timely, for the
First World War was then raging in Europe. But rather
arbitrarily. so Baum and his associates felt, *The Gray
Nun of Belgium* was turned down by exchanges and exhibitors alike without their taking time to preview it.*

For several months after this the studio was rented to
other companies. This was unprofitable, and in the fall of
1915 the Oz Film Manufacturing Company surrendered

---

* The Oz Film Company also made four one-reel fairy tales
starring Violet MacMillan under the general title of *Violet's
Dreams*. One of them, *The Magic Bon-Bons*, apparently was
taken from Baum's story of the same name in *American Fairy
Tales*.

its charter. In exchange for the return of his stock, all motion picture rights to his stories were reconveyed to Baum, including those of the stories which had already been filmed. He had lost nothing in the collapse of the venture except the effort of many months. His pride suffered, however, even though he hid his disappointment from his family and associates. As for the films, unseen and unsung, they have long since disappeared.

Four times Baum had tried to repeat the great successes of *The Wizard of Oz* and *The Maid of Arran* before it. *The Tik-Tok Man of Oz* had been his best effort; for he had adapted his fantasy to the taste of mixed and adult audiences. Three times—with *The Woggle-Bug* of 1905, the *Radio-Plays* of 1908, and the Oz Film Manufacturing Company in 1914 and 1915—he had failed because he had not given the public what it wanted. Disappointment and financial loss had been the result.*

Yet Baum's repeated inability to look beyond his work and judge the entertainment demands of adults is understandable in one who had been most successful when he lost himself in the make-believe world so dear to children and wrote stories for them. Fortunately, he did not have to depend on the grownups.

"It isn't through opera that I hope to live, that I base any hope that I may have of seeing my name written in bronze," Baum remarked. "My important work I consider to be my fairy tales, not my plays."

After 1915, he was content to serve one master, the children who clamored for the Oz books.

* A television version of *The Land of Oz*, written without major violence to Baum's story by Frank Gabrielson, was successful enough to be repeated in 1961. It starred Shirley Temple, Sterling Halloway, and Agnes Moorehead.

XVI

THE ROYAL HISTORIAN DEPARTS

WHEN BAUM built Ozcot a block north of Hollywood Boulevard, Hollywood was a quiet, leisurely paced small town, reached by an interurban line from Los Angeles. He once told a friend that he could take a shotgun out in the boulevard at eight o'clock at night and fire it up and down the street without hitting a soul. By dark everyone was at home. There were no restaurants and very few stores.

Big estates sprawled along the boulevard and the nearby streets. They were built up with comfortable California type houses, half hidden behind wooden picket fences and huge flower gardens. The streets were shaded by giant pepper trees which in season were scarlet with berries.

Ozcot was arranged for comfortable living rather than architectural display. On the first floor was an immense living room, dominated by a fireplace in which the author kept large logs burning on cool nights. A solarium opened off the south side of the living room, and the remainder of the downstairs was taken up by a library with shelves on all four walls filled to the ceiling with books, a dining room of generous proportions, a kitchen fitted with a three-oven range with a breakfast nook at the side, and maid's quarters. On the second floor were four large bedrooms and a railed-in sun porch over the solarium. From this floor stairs led to an immense attic which covered the whole house and was lighted by dormer windows.

The center lighting fixture and four corner lights in the dining room were Baum's handiwork. He sketched the intricate design, traced it on large sheets of copper and cut it out with a jeweler's saw. He then formed and soldered the fixtures, after which he cut and fitted thick pieces of emerald glass behind the copper so that the light came through, softly tracing his design in green. These fixtures stayed in the dining room for forty years, until the house was torn down.

At Ozcot Baum for the first time in his life could fall into a congenial monotony of routine. He got up about eight o'clock and, after his usual hearty breakfast, went to his garden, changed there into work clothes and fertilized, cultivated, and otherwise cared for his flowers. A gardener did such heavy work as digging beds and weeding, but Baum did everything else. After lunch at one o'clock he went to his study upstairs—a bedroom which he had converted into a workshop. Here he revised and typed his penciled first drafts of the current Oz book or whatever story he had in hand. On days when he had no manuscript to revise, he would sit writing in the garden, with his papers on his knee. Occasionally he would get up, walk, or work with his flowers until he had worked out the next incident in the plot, then return to his chair. If the weather was bad, he would write in the solarium.

He enjoyed golf, and for several years he devoted occasional afternoons to playing at Griffith's Park in Los Angeles. He had first taken up golf when he wintered at Coronado, where he played a couple of hours every afternoon. Baum was always fastidious about his clothing, wearing tailor-made dark suits, white shirts with wing collars, an ascot tie with a gold nugget pin, and a gold headed cane. On the golf course he was as carefully arrayed in baggy knickerbockers buckled below the knee, wool hose, a red vest with a scarlet silk back, and a plaid cap with a long visor. An absent-minded player, he was vague about his score, and if someone inquired he would say, "Oh, I made it in about ninety-eight. Of course, that's for the first nine holes."

Often Baum was called from his writing to meet a group of juvenile admirers who had come all the way to Hollywood for enchanted moments at Ozcot with the Royal Historian of their favorite make-believe country. At such times Baum was at his genial best; for his love of children was genuine, and in their company he always felt at home. Soon he would have his little visitors laughing, and some would even muster up enough courage to climb into his lap. Guy Bogart, a fellow Californian whose son's interest in the Oz books led to the father's friendship with the Baums, recalls such a visit that he and his son, Bob made to Ozcot:

Bob was brought up on the Oz books. . . . Like all small children there were lots of problems he wanted orientation on. . . . When I could not answer him honestly, I so stated. He invariably said: "Well, I'll bet Frank Baum would know." . . . Finally, after many months of this phrase . . . I asked for a Saturday afternoon appointment. Winston Churchill disturbing Eleanor at the White House conferences with FDR would not have been received with more courtesy than Bob before L. Frank Baum. Here was the

greatest Creation in the world—a child—before the High
Priest of Childhood. The two were at home immediately
and every question was understood, solved and answered
to fullest satisfaction. . . . It might have been reminiscent
of Sinai except there was companionship instead of fear
and thunderings, sunshine instead of clouds, loving trust
instead of awe. . . . For here the atmosphere of Baum's
New Fairyland prevailed. Something new had come into
the world, a realm of love-in-adventure, and the Black
Forest horrors of ancient fairyland were replaced with the
laughter and sunshine of Oz. I had caught this note of the
new world in my reading of Oz, yet here at my feet, Baum
with my young son presenting the problems of childhood
curiosity and receiving the correct answers direct from the
Authorized Apostle of Love and Joy in a new world, my
understanding grew. . . . That is why the books of L. Frank
Baum are not ephemeral nor for a generation—they are a
part of the understanding gospel of childhood.

Most of the children came in groups, often accompanied
by a school teacher. From such a group Baum first learned
of the Oz Reading Clubs that had sprung up over the
United States. Some of these met in schools, but most
met after school in the homes of the children who shared
their Oz books and heard a favorite one read aloud.

After an afternoon of work on his stories or in audiences
with children, Baum was ready for dinner at six o'clock.
After dinner, he would start up the player piano or phonograph for Maud, and for their dog, a cocker named Toto,
who was the third member of the household after the last
of the sons was married in 1914. Many of the quiet family
evenings were passed over the chess board, however, with
one of the sons as opponent. Frequently the Baums entertained guests, for both enjoyed conversation and a game
of cards. After the guests had left and the family had gone
to bed, Baum would seat himself in a large leather-covered

club chair placed in a corner of the library and pencil the next series of episodes in his current story.

Although Maud is authority for the statement that "L.F.," as she called him, knew little about flower growing when they moved to Hollywood, she forgot his early years in the gardens of Roselawn. Baum soon made a name for himself as a grower and exhibitor of prize dahlias and chrysanthemums. His blooms won so many awards in strong competition in that land of flowers that he was often described as the champion amateur horticulturist of Southern California. Many of his twenty-one cups were won in shows held by the Hollywood Woman's Club and organizations in nearby Pasadena.

The garden at Ozcot, one hundred feet wide and one hundred twenty-five feet deep, was enclosed by a six foot fence of redwood. Behind the solarium, flower beds stretched to a goldfish pond in front of a chicken yard along the rear of the lot. In the center was a summer house with long pergola wings dividing the yard lengthwise. These were half hidden under grape vines. Parallel to the pergolas and summer house was another long row of flower beds, with a circular aviary almost twelve feet in diameter and containing a constantly running fountain, in which Baum kept several hundred song birds and brilliantly colored members of the feathered kingdom. These were the companions of his hours while he sat in the summer house penning a new story. At the far end of the lot, adjoining the chicken yard, was the garage for two cars. On the south side of the garden, parallel to the fence, Baum had an archery range. A target was kept handy on this range, and the bows and arrows were stored in the summer house for the many sunny afternoons when the author and his sons tried their skill.

Near the summer house stood a concrete pedestal on which was mounted a copper sun dial. Baum had calculated the proper positions for the hour markings at Hollywood, then etched them into the metal and filled the marks with color.

About half the flower beds were devoted to chrysanthemums and dahlias, especially the cactus variety of which he was extremely fond and which won him many of his silver trophies. Some of his show blooms were as much as a foot across. In memory of the formal gardens of his childhood home, he planted each of the other beds with a single variety of flowers—delphinium, iris, oriental poppy, shasta daisy, aster, columbine, marigold, snapdragon and sweet pea—creating a brilliant pattern of variegated colors painted in broad strokes.

One of the secrets of Baum's success with flowers was the painstaking study he devoted to the subject and the care he gave his blossoms. During part of the growing season he would cover his beds with cheese cloth fastened to six foot poles to temper the hot California sun to the tender plants. He also mixed his own fertilizer according to a formula which he did not disclose even to his own family.

Occasionally the pressure of outside events was bound to break into this idyllic life and take the master away from Ozcot, his books, his family, and his flowers. Personal appearances with the road company of *The Tik-Tok Man of Oz* required Baum to be away from home for many weeks, and he poured months of strenuous effort into the vain attempt to keep the Oz Film Manufacturing Company enterprise afloat.

The strain and disappointment of the motion picture venture ravaged Baum's far from robust health. Severe attacks of angina pectoris reminded him that he could never escape from the limitations on his activities set by the heart ailment from which he had suffered since childhood. On top of this painful disease was piled the excruciating pain of tic douloureux, which stabbed his face with almost unbearable attacks without warning. At times he would have to leave the dinner table, or give up work on a story, because of a seizure. After he had walked the floor for hours, because sitting or lying down only intensified the agony of the attacks, the pain would vanish as suddenly as it had come. At first, especially in 1914 when the facial attacks began, a physician would be called to give him morphine, but even this relief was denied him except in emergencies for fear of forming a narcotic habit. These attacks continued their unpredictable course as long as Baum lived. Through all his troubles Baum forced himself to work on the whimsical and humorous episodes of his children's stories. Although few traces of agony are detectable in his work, there were many times when tears would stream from his eyes and wet the paper as he wrote.

Perhaps the first note of concern about his health appeared in the preface to *Tik-Tok of Oz,* published in 1914, where he remarked almost casually: "If I am permitted to write another Oz book." Baum had grown used to living with a defective heart; tic douloureux was very painful but not dangerous; but he had been alarmed by several gall bladder attacks in recent months. At first a mustard plaster brought relief, but after completing *The Scarecrow of Oz* in 1915, Baum was in such distress from the gall bladder attacks that he had to give up writing for a time.

His doctor advised him to have his gall bladder removed, but like many of his generation, he felt confident that he could cure himself. He had grown up in an age before patent medicine advertising and the sale of cure-alls and nostrums were restrained by enactment of the pure food and drugs act. His vivid imagination feasted on the symptoms described in such advertising and "sold" him so completely he would hurry to the drug store for a bottle or a box, take a dose or two, then put the nostrum on the shelf where it was soon forgotten.

Three heavy meals a day, spiced with patent medicines, no doubt laid the ground work for Baum's gall bladder attacks and must have put considerable added strain on his heart. Such a diet was ill suited to his sedentary life. Despite his ailments, he continued to write in 1916 and 1917, but all the time he was at work on *The Lost Princess of Oz* he was in constant pain day and night.

By December, 1917, he was too sick to write and finally acknowledged an operation to remove his gall bladder could no longer be postponed. The operation was performed by Dr. Orville Weatherby, a fellow member of the Uplifters and of the Los Angeles Athletic Club, and a personal friend. At the same time Baum's badly inflamed appendix was removed. The surgery was successful, but it was soon apparent the strain of four hours on the operating table had further damaged his heart. After a few weeks in the hospital Baum was taken by ambulance to Ozcot and ordered to stay in bed for six weeks.

The convalescence period came and went, and Baum's heart was still alarmingly weak. He lay in his old fashioned brass bed, with its high headboard of elaborately bent tubing, unable to sit up. Gradually he adjusted himself to life as an invalid, and his restless mind turned over ideas for the next Oz book—*The Tin Woodman of Oz*.

The day arrived when he could be propped up in a

sitting position, with pillows at his back, and for a short time each day he was allowed to write. While he thought of Oz, the world seemed far away from that sick room. American soldiers were in battle in Europe and one of them was his eldest son. Perhaps Baum was putting up a good front; perhaps he was encouraged that he would once again write of his beloved Oz. In any event it is characteristic of his disposition that a letter written to his son in France at this time is sunny, optimistic, and confident of Divine Goodness and help. It follows:

Ozcot,
Sept. Second, 1918

My dear son:

Your last letter from "somewhere in France" was very welcome, for it let us know you were still in good health.

Your descriptive account of recent army activities is fascinating and vital—and gives an extremely vivid picture of what goes on around you. In descriptive writing you do a job far superior to anything I have ever done or am capable of doing.

We were sorry to learn of your great disappointment in certain phases of your military assignment. But do not be too downhearted, my boy, for I have lived long enough to learn that in life nothing adverse lasts very long. And it is true that as the years pass, and we look back on something which, at that time, seemed unbelievingly discouraging and unfair, we come to realize that, after all, God was at all times on our side. The eventual outcome was, we discover, by far the best solution for us, and what then we thought should have been to our best advantage, would in reality have been quite detrimental.

Continue to be self-confident, honest and faithful in performing your assigned duties to the best of your knowledge and ability as you have always been. Be loyal to your superior officers and ever vigilant of the lives and welfare of your soldiers. Through such actions God will ever be on your side, and as you put your reliance on Him and trust in His guidance, you can not fail to have a happy, complete and worthwhile life.

I have lately been much improved in health and trust that before many weeks the doctors will allow me to leave my bed and at least move about the house.

We all send you much love, and I continually pray for a speedy end to this terrible war and your safe return to our beloved country.

Your loving and devoted
Dad.

This same sturdy spirit carried over in *The Tin Woodman of Oz,* one of the most imaginative and broadly amusing of the later Oz books. *Publisher's Weekly* commented: "This year's chronicle from the Royal Historian is as joyous as ever." It was the last Baum book published by Reilly and Britton, which was shortly to become Reilly and Lee.

By late in 1918, working slowly, Baum had completed *The Magic of Oz.* It had been nearly a year since his operation, but there was no hope that he would ever leave his bed. In the preface to *The Magic of Oz* he merely mentioned the long illness that had kept him from answering letters from his "children." Baum's real feelings though, find expression deep within the story, where he had put into Cap'n Bill's mouth these words: "There's lots of things folks don't 'preciate. . . . When a person's well, he don't realize how jolly it is, but when he gets sick he 'members the time he was well, an' wishes that time could come back." Such words must have been wrung from the heart, for by this time Baum knew he would never again dig in his beloved garden, or sit there in the warm sunshine listening to his song birds while he dreamed of the Never-Never Land where no one was ever ill, where there were no wars, and where the days were always golden and never gray.

Making notes and writing *Glinda of Oz* whiled away the winter of 1918-19, but by early May his illness took a sudden turn for the worse. His heart action became erratic, his breathing difficult, and on May 5 he lapsed into unconsciousness. In the evening he opened his eyes and smiled at his wife, who was sitting at his bedside.

"What is it, Frank? Can I get you something?"

"No, dear, I just wanted to tell you that I'm going to slip away in a few hours. I feel this is my last farewell."

For a moment he struggled for breath and she begged him not to talk.

"I'm all right. There is little pain now. And there is something I want you to know—and remember. All my life, since I first met you and fell in love with you—I've been true to you. There has—never been—another woman in my life—or thoughts."

His breathing quieted a bit and he lay still with eyes closed. Maud thought for a time he had again lapsed into unconsciousness. But presently he opened his eyes and said:

"This is our house, Maud. I would like to think you are staying here where we have been so happy. The royalties will last for many years. You should have plenty to live on without worry."

"I shall stay here as long as I live," she replied.

He smiled faintly. His eyes closed. For a long time Maud stood by the bed watching his erratic breathing. At last she realized he had again slipped into a coma.

On the morning of May 6 the nurse realized the end was near. She called his wife to the bedside. For many minutes he lay motionless except for his labored breathing.

Suddenly his lips moved as if he desired to speak. Maud

leaned over the bed but could not distinguish any words.

"What is it, Frank?"

The nurse slowly shook her head. "He is still unconscious," she said.

Again Baum's lips moved. Softly he murmured some indistinct words. Then, slowly and clearly, he spoke:

"Now we can cross the Shifting Sands," and he was gone.

It was just ten days before his sixty-third birthday, and half a continent away the presses were pouring out copies of *The Magic of Oz*.

Funeral services were conducted in the Little Church of the Flowers at Forest Lawn Memorial Park in nearby Glendale by the Rev. E. P. Ryland, a personal friend. There Baum lies in the family lot which he had selected many years before. His grave is beside a tree-lined park driveway on those beautiful grounds with the simple inscription,

L. FRANK BAUM
1856—1919

Maud was placed there beside him, thirty-four years later. She died on March 6, 1953. Kenneth, the youngest son, suffered a fatal stroke on April 2, 1953, less than a month after his mother's death, and Robert, the second son, died April 21,1958. Both now rest beside their parents. And by chance, or fate, Fred Stone, whose career was so closely linked with that of the creator of *The Wizard of Oz*, was buried in the same cemetery after his death March 6, 1959 in Hollywood.*

* Frank Joslyn **Baum**, eldest of the four Baum sons, and co-author of this biography of his father, died December 2, 1958, and was buried with his parents and brothers.

XVII

OZ LIVES ON

Glinda of Oz was ready for the Christmas trade in 1920. Its preface contained only the simple note that: "In May, 1919, he went away to take his stories to the little child souls who had lived here too long ago to read the Oz stories for themselves."

Probate of Baum's will leaving his estate to Maud did not impose any unfamiliar burden on her. For years she had been her husband's business manager. In addition to being the owner of Ozcot, she had insisted that Baum assign to her his copyrights as they were issued. All royalties from his books and plays were paid into her hands except for a short time when Baum had assigned some copyrights to secure a loan. She deposited all checks in her personal account and paid all household expenses. Baum kept a small checking account under an arrangement with the bank that he was to be notified when it was overdrawn. When the account was depleted Maud would deposit enough money to keep her husband in funds for a while. This arrangement spared the author from having to keep any record of his checks or expenditures.

Baum's death was not only a personal loss to his family and friends, and to the thousands of children who loved his books, but it was also a serious business loss to the Reilly and Lee Company, his publishers. Reluctant to see the end of such a successful series as the Oz books, William F. Lee of the publishing firm invited Ruth Plumly Thompson, a young Philadelphian whose stories in *St. Nicholas* had caught his eye, to continue the series. Mrs. Baum at first refused to approve this arrangement but reluctantly gave her consent in return for a contract that guaranteed a fixed royalty for her and Baum's heirs on every Oz book, no matter who was the author. Details of the agreement were handled through the publishing firm, and neither Mrs. Baum nor any member of her family met the woman who was to carry on the stories of Oz.

Having been "handed the key to that wonderful kingdom," as she expressed it, Miss Thompson wrote *The Royal Book of Oz** in 1921, when she was twenty years old, and completed eighteen more titles before wearying of the annual chore. "As I had been brought up on the Oz books, this was not hard," she once remarked.

The third to take up the task was John R. Neill, illustrator of all except the first Oz book. He wrote three books: in 1940, 1941 and 1942. After Neill's death, the Oz series was continued in 1947 and 1949 by Jack Snow and in 1951 by Rachael R. Cosgrove.

Under the contract, the Baum heirs have continued to receive royalties on the Oz books by other hands, as well

* Published under Baum's name with a preface by Maud Baum asserting that the book was "made" by Miss Thompson from "some unfinished notes" by Baum. It appears certain, however, that *The Royal Book of Oz* was almost entirely Miss Thompson's work.

as on the fourteen written by Baum. Total sales of the
Baum titles, although they are older, have consistently
exceeded those of the later titles, reflecting the margin of
popularity that they have retained through succeeding
generations. Frank O'Donnell of Reilly and Lee estimated
that currently the Baum titles outsell the others about six
to one.

Comparison of these sequels makes vividly evident
Reilly and Lee's acumen in deciding to continue the Oz
series. It is remarkable that Miss Thompson was able to
fit herself so well into the highly personalized world of
Baum's imagination. She was another natural story teller;
her plots were good enough to hold the patronage of
Baum's juvenile following; she wrote with a light touch,
almost too romping at times; and she displayed decided
ability to create original characters that were true to the
Land of Oz and at the same time distinctly her own. But
Miss Thompson had inherited the Land of Oz, and like
most heirs, she could not resist the impulse to play with
her inheritance. Her books, for all their excellence, often
fail to carry the conviction that the author believes somewhere, somehow, there must be a Land of Oz—the essential, convincing ingredient that Baum was able to put into
all his stories.

Out of the long list of titles to Miss Thompson's credit,
a recent poll of a number of readers disclosed that *Ka-
bumpo in Oz,* (1922), *Captain Salt in Oz,* (1936) and *The
Yellow Knight of Oz,* (1930) were their favorites, in that
order. Miss Thompson's own choices were *Ojo in Oz,*
(1933) *Speedy in Oz,* (1934) and *Captain Salt in Oz.*

Edward Eager, writing in the *Horn Book* magazine,
argued that Miss Thompson brought vigor back into the

Oz series which it had lost in Baum's last work. "In her earlier books," he wrote, "she shows a fine ear for pun, a real feeling for nonsense, and in lieu of style, a contagious zest and pace that sweep the reader beyond criticism."

Snow, a faithful disciple who created two books in the long series before his premature death, caught the atmosphere, imagination and style of his master with uncanny success in such a book as *The Magical Mimics in Oz.*

But good or bad, the sequels to Baum's Oz books and the policy of continuing the series by various writers have undoubtedly cast a shadow on his posthumous reputation. Librarians and historians of children's books dislike serials, and while the former have shown little warmth toward these most popular children's books of the century, the latter have generally ignored *The Wizard of Oz* and the other Oz titles. As Martin Gardner wrote: "Baum's *Wonderful Wizard of Oz* has long been the nation's best known, best loved fairy tale, but you will look in vain for any recognition of this fact in recent histories of children's books." Wanda Pringle, in a term paper on library science, written at the University of Illinois, explains this paradox in part: "Librarians have adopted the view that serials running to more than four volumes are unsafe . . . because children become so used to the author's style and vocabulary in reading a long series that they no longer want to exert the mental effort needed to try some other author. . . . Each book should open new doors to the child's imagination and bring him new visions of unconquered worlds instead of the same old ones." She adds that librarians also feel that serials tend to "repetition of the same pattern with wilder and wilder events being added to the framework to give an appearance of variety. The Oz books are unquestionably guilty of this."

In 1957, Ralph Ulveling, director of the Detroit library system, ruffled the composure of the literally millions of Oz enthusiasts by asserting at a librarians' conference in Lansing, Michigan, that the Oz books "have a cowardly approach to life," are guilty of negativism, and that "there is nothing uplifting or elevating about the Baum series," which he compared unfavorably to the Grimm and Andersen fairy tales and to more recent children's books. Instead of discarding *The Wizard of Oz,* however, as the public library did in 1956 in Washington, D.C., the Detroit library keeps its copies in the stacks of the general collection, where they may be called for. But the book is no longer on the shelves in the children's room.

This is, of course, an extreme position. Baum does not lack for defenders among the librarians. Norma Rathbun, chief of children's work in the Milwaukee library system, said of *The Wizard of Oz:* "As for me, I like it. So do the children. They demand it. They've worn out about 135 copies in the last eight years; they're rapidly wearing out the 50 we have left, and we have about 25 more on order. That's a terrific showing for a book more than fifty years old. The fact is that *The Wizard of Oz* is a natural part of a child's reading heritage."

"We have *The Wizard of Oz* on our shelves and we regard it as a landmark among children's books," said Miss Catherine Adams, supervisor of children's books for the Chicago Public Library.

Nearly two thousand persons attending the June, 1959, American Library Association Convention in Washington, D.C., were asked informally their opinion about the desirability of the Oz books as children's reading. In the light of previously well publicized criticism, the warm regard expressed by the convention delegates and visitors toward Baum's work was heartening. Most quotable of the comments was that of a delegate who said that "as mother, teacher and librarian I heartily approve of the Oz books for my own children and for my pupils."

Recent developments have made it clear that *The Wizard of Oz* is only one of the bones of contention in a battle of the books between those who favor newly written works that keep up with the pace of American life, as a committee of public school teachers in Philadelphia phrased it, and those who cherish the lasting values of the classics of childhood. For *Treasure Island* and *Silas Marner,* too, are in disfavor. Their race is run, according to the modernists; the time has come to toss them on the bonfire with the Oz books. Skirmishes in the battle are common. At a library convention in Miami, Florida, in February, 1959, the state librarian verbally swept most of the children's favorites of yesteryear from the shelves of libraries in her state and provoked a controversy that arrayed even the governor against her. Governor LeRoy Collins gently chided the librarian by suggesting that the "judgment of what is good and bad should rest with the great body of people who read the books, rather than with those who feel they are in a special position to judge."

Some years previously—in 1924—Grace C. Williams, children's librarian of the State Teachers' College at San Jose, California, wrote: "We have a peculiar scale for measuring values. Why should a doll of wood be better than one of tin? On almost every reading list you will find *Pinocchio* given as a good book for children. It is. In few

lists will you find *The Wizard of Oz*. One is the story of a
doll made of wood, an Italian doll. The story is told by
an Italian for Italian children. The other is the story of a
doll made of tin, known as the Tin Woodman, an American doll. The story is told by an American, for American
children. Yet we approve of one and bar the other. . . .
Why, pray tell me, shouldn't we have both tales?"

Editorial writers and columnists must have been
brought up on the Oz books, for they have risen to their
defense against recent criticism. For example, the judgment of the *Chicago Daily News* was: "We have no doubt
that L. Frank Baum's Oz books will live as long as children have the capacity to dream." John Sherman in the
Minneapolis Sunday Tribune hailed Baum as a creator
who "ranks on a level with those who have contributed
unique characters to fairy tale fiction, characters who
won't be dislodged from the world of the imagination by
librarian's edicts."

When Clifton Fadiman listed his choice of the fifty best
children's books in 1958 and omitted *The Wizard of Oz*,
Herman Kenny of Lake Linden, Michigan, wrote a letter
to the *Chicago Tribune's* Magazine of Books, which had
printed the list, commenting that *Alice in Wonderland* is
excellent, but that all the children he has ever known
preferred *The Wizard of Oz*.

And Dr. Wagenknecht, who had called attention to
Baum's work as long ago as 1929, in a newspaper article
published at the Christmas season of 1958, testified to the
lasting influence of the Oz books on him: "When I was
six years old, I read *The Wizard of Oz*. . . . Not only did
this work in itself tremendously stimulate my imagination
but it caused me then and there to make up my mind that

when I grew up I, too, should become a writer." Dr. Wagenknecht, Professor of English at Boston University, is only one of a number including Roland Baughman, Columbia University librarian; Dr. Russel B. Nye, of Michigan State University, and C. Beecher Hogan, lecturer in English at Yale University, who have testified to the academic respectability of Oz and its creator. Allied with them are such familiar writing personalities as James Thurber, Phyllis McGinley, Philip Wylie, Anthony Boucher, and the late Dylan Thomas.

Continuing sales of Baum's masterpiece and of his many other titles in the Oz series, with nearly a dozen publishers competing for the market with editions of *The Wizard of Oz*, are the soundest evidence of their robust youthfulness. Even the second-hand book sellers testify that no children's books are so frequently called for or so quickly turned over as the Oz books, while children's books of more recent date languish on the shelves and end up in the pulp mill. But the most touching tribute to the continuing power of these books is the average of four letters a week addressed in childish hands to L. Frank Baum, which come to the Reilly and Lee Company, forty years after the author's death. Such testimony speaks for itself.

Baum is even by way of becoming a literary cult, like Conan Doyle, whose memory is kept green by the Baker Street Irregulars. In like manner there exists an International Wizard of Oz Club which has a small magazine, *The Baum Bugle,* to knit the threads of common interest in a fabric of usefulness to its members. Particularly prophetic of this enduring interest in the many chronicles of Oz was an editorial in the *New York Times* of May 11,

1919. It caught the feeling of loyalty that would make Baum's work timeless when it said:

L. Frank Baum is dead, and the children, if they knew it, would mourn. The endless procession of "Oz" books, coming out just before Christmas, is to cease. *The Wizard of Oz, Queen Zixi of Ix, Dorothy and the Wizard in Oz, John Dough and the Cherub,* there will never be any more of them, and the children have suffered a loss they do not know. Years from now, though the children cannot clamor for the newest Oz book, the crowding generations will plead for the old ones.

And so, indeed, they do. Frank Baum was writing more truly than he knew when he described the Oz people as Immortals.